Bizarre
Thailand

Bizarre Thailand

TALES of CRIME, SEX and BLACK MAGIC

by JIM ALGIE

Marshall Cavendish
Editions

Cover design by OpalWorks Pte Ltd

All photographs provided by Jim Algie

Published by Marshall Cavendish Editions
An imprint of Marshall Cavendish International
1 New Industrial Road, Singapore 536196

Other Marshall Cavendish Offices

Marshall Cavendish International. PO Box 65829, London EC1P 1NY, UK • Marshall Cavendish Corporation. 99 White Plains Road, Tarrytown NY 10591-9001, USA • Marshall Cavendish International (Thailand) Co Ltd. 253 Asoke, 12th Flr, Sukhumvit 21 Road, Klongtoey Nua, Wattana, Bangkok 10110, Thailand • Marshall Cavendish (Malaysia) Sdn Bhd, Times Subang, Lot 46, Subang Hi-Tech Industrial Park, Batu Tiga, 40000 Shah Alam, Selangor Darul Ehsan, Malaysia.

Marshall Cavendish is a trademark of Times Publishing Limited

National Library Board Singapore Cataloguing in Publication Data
Algie, Jim, 1962-
Bizarre Thailand : tales of crime, sex and black magic / Jim Algie. – Singapore:
Marshall Cavendish Editions, c2010.
p. cm.
ISBN-13 : 978-981-4302-81-4 (pbk.)

1. Thailand – Social conditions. 2. Thailand – Miscellanea.
I. Title.

DS563.5
959.3 -- dc22   OCN654690266

Printed in Singapore by KWF Printing Pte Ltd

To my mom, Patricia,
and my brother, Richard,
for putting up with me for so long.

Contents

Introduction: Into the Thai Twilight Zone

Where else in the world could a womanising black magician become a political advisor and chat-show celebrity, or the abbot of a Buddhist temple try to construct a pagoda out of water buffalo skulls? Where else would a town be overrun with sacred tortoises that mate in the streets, or the preserved corpse of a serial-slaying cannibal be on permanent exhibition in the most macabre of museums?

Where else but in bizarre Thailand? A Twilight Zone where nothing is what it seems.

In 1994, I started writing a series of columns and feature stories for local newspapers and magazines that led to contributions to a wealth of international publications such as the *National Geographic Traveler* and *International Herald Tribune*, regional papers like the *Japan Times* and *Sydney Morning Herald,* as well as guidebooks for major publishers in the United States and London, focusing primarily on the dark and exotic side of Thailand and detours off the well-rutted and over-glutted travel map of hotspots. The inklings of a few other stories came from the pages of *Farang Untamed Travel* magazine, co-founded by Cameron Cooper, Bobby McBlain and myself in 2001.

There are hundreds of books—and tens of thousands of stories, websites and blogs—devoted to the 'palm-fringed beaches' and 'majestic mountains' and 'delightful gastronomy' of the kingdom. This is not one of them. Beyond those obvious attributes, the country has many other enchantments and enticements that can be enjoyed without bowing to the tyranny of the politically correct, or snorkelling in a cesspool of vulgarities.

Starting off the collection with a bang is the 'Crime Scenes' section. Few people know life and death 'Behind the Bars of the Bangkok Hiltons' like the country's last executioner. Trading in his electric guitar for a machine-gun, former rock musician Chavoret Jaruboon sent 55 men and women to the crematorium during his 18 years on the firing line. Interviews with convicted drug traffickers and prison authorities provide an overview of crime and capital punishment in Thailand.

Only in the sea-straddling resort of Pattaya are you likely to hear stories of a middle-aged Scandinavian man running amok in a shopping mall, throwing bottles of acid in the faces of local office ladies, because he had been spurned and sucked dry of his life savings by a bargirl. In 'Pattaya: The Vegas of Vice?', retirees on Viagra rub shoulders with Russian gangsters and 10,000 marchers calling for an end to violence against women as they parade down Beach Road, beside scores of streetwalkers in the country's most bipolar city.

For chills and blood spills, readers can ride shotgun with Bangkok's rescue workers and corpse collectors. In 'Museums of the Macabre: See Uey the Chinese Cannibal', the wretched life and unspeakable crimes of the forensic museum's mascot—who is also the country's most infamous serial killer—are autopsied.

'From Ayuthaya to Bangkok: A Bizarre Expat Odyssey' looks at an astonishing spectrum of expatriates who have come here over the past five centuries: pirates and samurai, writers and filmmakers, maverick entrepreneurs and mass murderers. Apart from that famous Thai tolerance of other cultures and nationalities, why do they keep coming here? The answers are as varied, and as eclectic, as the characters themselves. Also detailed are a few of the defining moments from expatriate history. Many will know about the building of the 'Death Railway' constructed by Allied POWs and Asian slave labourers at the behest of the barbarous Japanese Imperial Army. Few, I suspect, will be familiar with the most moving memoir of that tragedy, *The Railway Man* by Eric Lomax, which tracks the strange, five-decade-long relationship that develops between the Scottish POW and a member of the Japanese secret police he longs to maim and murder.

In the middle of 2010, the carnage on the streets of Bangkok during a series of showdowns between the military and the red-shirted protestors exposed more than a few fault lines running through Thai society and its long-standing love and loathing for the army. Those incidents are flashpoints in 'Weekend Warriors: Military Tourism in Thailand', where the presence of so many troops and bases has created what may very well be a tourist phenomenon unique to Thailand: undergoing military training at real army bases scattered across the country. Despite finding it a challenge to arrange and endure, I did my basic training with the paratroopers from the Royal Thai Airborne in Lop Buri province.

The overblown genre of what I normally deride as 'Bangkok dicklit' has mostly been neutered from 'The Sex Files' section. The only organisation I've kept tabs on from that overexposed scene is

Empower, one of the few NGOs in the region that promotes sex work as a viable form of employment for women. That said, they have been lobbying the Thai government for some two decades to get sex workers the same rights enjoyed by other members of the service industry, and they routinely deal with the Thai police in trying to get justice for women victimised by sadistic clients. Over the last 10 years, they have implemented an incredible array of projects—a radio station featuring bargirls as DJs, setting up a miniature go-go bar at an international conference on AIDS and, more recently, setting up the only bar in the country (possibly in the world) run by and for sex workers.

Cross-cultural relationships are already weird enough without the presence of love charms, sex potions and phallic amulets. Yet they all play a part in the world's oldest obsession as it's practised in Thailand. Stories like 'Erecting a Tribute to a Fertility Goddess' look at how the mystical flirts and fornicates with love.

Profiles are travel stories, too. For the country's architectural giant, Sumet Jumsai, his lifeline weaves through World War II, when the Japanese occupied Bangkok, to his schooldays in Paris and England, and his designs for groundbreaking buildings that resemble a robot, a ship and a Picasso-like Cubist structure, as well as a number of character-forming encounters with everyone from filmmaker Roman Polanksi to Nelson Mandela.

In any profile, it's incumbent upon the author to locate the circumstances that have shaped the subjects' personalities and pushed them in certain directions. The so-called 'Angel of Bang Kwang Central Prison' could only have come from the shrink-wrapped suburbs of Australia, as part of a generation that fled to Asia and found refuge in philanthropy.

Other forces also delineate characters and shape reputations. The growing worldwide interest in the work of Thailand's first lady of forensics, Dr. Porntip Rojanasunan, owes a lot to the ballistic success of TV shows like *CSI* and the bestselling, bare-bones thrillers of Patricia Cornwall and Kathy Reichs. At first glance, Kathy and Porntip may seem to have little in common except for middle age and gruesome CVs. Dig a little deeper and the two women are case studies in similar pathologies and how they deal with mass fatalities in the most pragmatic of ways.

A dual profile of the 'Scorpion Queen' and the 'Centipede King'—the country's most infamous freaks since the original Siamese twins became the 'Eighth Wonder of the World'— spotlights the reappearance of the sideshow in popular culture.

In any agrarian society like Thailand, where rice remains the largest export, rural folks develop a kinship with wildlife and their beasts of burden that take on the fraternity of family. Inevitably and invariably, wildlife features tend to focus on the roles these creatures play in ecosystems and food chains. Rarely discussed, but equally important, is the cultural and spiritual significance of these creatures. All across Southeast Asia, the water buffalo has bred songs, festivals, religious rites, beauty contests, and in the case of Thailand, the most unlikely cinema star. As the creature lumbers towards obsolescence, all these mainstays of rural culture are also en route to extinction.

Elsewhere in the 'Creature Features' section are stopovers at the world's first and only monkey hospital, a town overrun with tortoises that are deemed sacred and treated like pets, as well as a trip to a Siamese fighting fish gambling den where gangsters, gamblers and a businessman with degrees in philosophy and computer science wager bets in a millennium-ancient tradition.

Chulalongkorn University is Thailand's oldest and most venerable institution of higher learning. Consistently ranked in the top 20 of all Asian universities for its research facilities and international programs, the institution has produced a lot of influential people over the course of a century. In the Faculty of Science, however, freshman students are advised not to use the front stairway in the White Building (the faculty's oldest structure), because corpses once used for studying medicine were previously buried there. In the Faculty of Political Science, the main icon which students and staff pray to is the Black Tiger God. Freshmen students should not have their photos taken with the statue of the 'Serpent King' (*Phaya Nak*) from Buddhist lore in the Faculty of Art, for fear they may not graduate. Conversely, graduating students are urged to come to this auspicious place to get their photos taken.

These strange beliefs and superstitions are not secrets whispered among the students and faculty. No, they are all included in an official history book on the university that I edited for them in 2010.

Students of the supernatural can do a minor in this vast and ancient subject with the stories in the last section. During the grisly Vegetarian Festival in Phuket, spirit mediums—allegedly possessed by the nine Emperor Gods of Taoism and other deities—skewer their faces with hacksaws, chains, swordfish and cymbal stands, in shows of penance and piety. Meanwhile, what must be the world's only radio show to feature callers reciting tales of the paranormal also takes listeners out on ghost-hunting expeditions, and they have set up their own pub with a gallery devoted to ghostly images sent in by their fans. The crew's most terrifying encounter came after a visit to the shrine of Thailand's most legendary ghost, Nang Nak—a woman who died in childbirth some 150 years ago, yet whose vengeful and loving spirit has haunted more than 20 feature film productions.

On the Buddhist Wheel of the Law, where life, death and rebirth spin in endless cycles, the book comes full circle, from the cradle to the crematorium, with 'Funeral Rites: The Thai Way of Death'.

A few of the characters are repeated in different stories. All are introduced chronologically. Although one running character needs to be briefly introduced here. Anchana, my former partner, who came along on research trips for earlier drafts of about seven or eight of these stories, also played the roles of cultural advisor, translator par excellence and clown princess. Born on a sugarcane farm in the northern province of Kamphaeng Phet, in a house with no electricity, running water or a proper bathroom, Anchana (which means 'The Winner' in Thai) put herself through university, majoring in English and tourism, by working as a waitress and a nurse's assistant in an emergency room in Bangkok, eventually earning a master's degree in marketing from a university in Australia. Her witticisms and saucy remarks about everything from local men to Cambodian women, her personal encounters with ghosts and favourite country songs about water buffalo add insights, comic relief and a distinctly Thai female slant to a few of these stories. Without her contributions, the stories in which she appears would have been impossible to cover with any degree of depth.

Whenever a writer is approaching such sensationalistic subject matter, they can only go in one of two directions: the senseless shock value and moral indignation of tabloid journalism and TV, or trying to look at the subjects and the subject matter with a bit more balance and empathy. Aside from the occasional headless motorcyclist, I have tried to navigate the latter route.

A lot of the new material has never been published before. Many of the older stories have been revised, rethought, restructured and continuously updated over the years, just as many of the people profiled like Dr. Porntip and the 'Scorpion Queen' I have met and interviewed a number of times over the past decade.

Filed under Directory of the Bizarre, the listings in the back of the book are intended as pathfinders and other mines of information. Many of the destinations and museums are easy enough to visit. Some tours of duty, such as military training at Thai army bases, can be very difficult to organise and should not be undertaken lightly.

In any event, I will not be held responsible for anyone who goes in search of a 'love potion' made by an occultist melting the flesh of a corpse's chin.

Jim Algie

July 2010

CRIME
SCENES

Behind the Bars of the Bangkok Hiltons

For Chavoret Jaruboon, the hardest part of being on the execution team at the country's biggest maximum-security jail was walking into the death-row cell to tell the prisoner that he was about to be executed. "Whatever crimes the person had committed, they were still heroes to their families," said the former chief executioner of Bang Kwang Central Prison. "The inmates had time to write a letter to their family, and have a last cigarette and a meal, but they usually didn't feel like eating. They were also given the chance to see a Buddhist monk for a final blessing."

Blindfolded, and with chains around their ankles, the condemned man or woman would be escorted by guards into the death chamber. There, their hands were tied together with the sacred white thread that monks use to bless devotees and to ward off evil, so they could clutch three unopened lotus blossoms, three joss-sticks and a small orange candle, as if they were going to pray at a Buddhist temple. While Chavoret waited behind the gun, the guards would then tie the inmate to a wooden cross with his hands above his head, and put a white screen between him and the machine-gun, which was bolted to the floor and pointed at his back. Finally, a doctor put a target on the screen where the prisoner's heart was, so the executioner could take aim and fire.

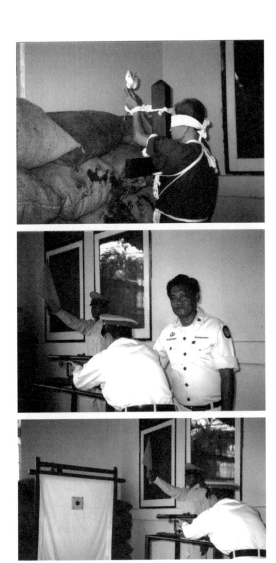

These tableaux of execution scenes, including the original machine-gun used to execute inmates at Bang Kwang Central Prison, are on permanent exhibit at the Corrections Museum. Also pictured is Chavoret Jaruboon, the last executioner.

That was how the death penalty was carried out after the government outlawed beheading in 1932, and before Thailand switched to lethal injection in late 2003.

Chavoret recalled the condemned men and women being led in to the chamber. "I heard it all—crying, begging and cursing. But some of them just walked in without a word. They were ready to die."

Until being diagnosed with cancer in 2010, these were the kind of tales that the former rock 'n' roll musician recounted for rapt audiences at Thai universities and remand centres for juvenile delinquents, which he also included in his 2007 autobiography, *The Last Executioner*.

Until recently, Chavoret also volunteered as a tour guide at the Corrections Museum once a month. The museum is on the grounds of Romanee Lart Park, not far from the Golden Mount and Khaosan Road in Bangkok. On display are knives and syringes made by former inmates, along with implements of torture once used in Siamese jails. On the ground floor, there's a huge rattan ball—like the ones used in *takraw,* the Asian version of volleyball—with sharp nails protruding from the inside. Curled up inside the ball is a mannequin of a prisoner. To punish the inmates or amuse themselves, the authorities would let an elephant kick the ball around. After it got bored, the tusker would often trample the bloody ball and squash the prisoner. This type of torture (and others like it) was outlawed by King Rama V at the end of the 19th century.

Filled with flowerbeds, shrubs, joggers and school kids, the park was once the site of Bangkok's most draconian jail, as evidenced by the vacant row of jail cells on the north side and the guard towers that stand like stone sentinels. Built by the French at the end of the 19th century, most of the Maha Chai penitentiary was demolished in the 1980s. Some of the inmates were transferred to Bang Kwang Central Prison, such as convicted heroin trafficker-turned-author Warren Fellows who did 'hard time' in both penal facilities, and wrote an autobiography about his experiences titled *The Damage Done: 12 Years Of Hell In A Thai Prison.*

To punish certain convicts, he wrote, they were locked in a 'dark room' for 23 hours and 55 minutes a day. These hellholes were so cramped there was not even enough room for all of them to lie down, so they had to take turns sleeping. Left there for months at a time, he and his fellow inmates caught cockroaches and mashed them up with a little fish sauce to supplement their meagre ration of one bowl of gruel per day. During one such punishment stay, the author recalled hearing a scratching noise that went on for hours. It turned out to be a Thai inmate sharpening a nail so that he could attack another prisoner. Screams bounced off the walls as he stabbed his victim again and again, but the guards did not remove the corpse until the next day.

In his autobiography, which remains a perennial bestseller on the backpacker trail in Southeast Asia, the sadism of the prison guards goes far beyond anything in the book and film that raised the bar for the foreign-jails-are-hell genre—*Midnight Express*. In one particularly nauseating episode, Fellows (who was first imprisoned at Maha Chai in the late 1970s) wrote how a guard forced a bunch of the convicts to stand in a septic tank, chin deep in excrement for many hours, because they'd been playing a dice game in their cell.

The popularity of his book has had some positive effects, such as the banning of the 'dark rooms'. The prison's former director Pittaya Sanghanakin took great pains to announce some of these improvements at what must have been the most bizarre anniversary celebration ever held at any correctional facility. In 2002, Bang Kwang Central Prison—located just outside Bangkok in Nonthaburi province—celebrated its 72nd anniversary (an auspicious occasion given the 12-year cycles and 12 different animals in Chinese astrology). The Corrections Department set up a stage across from Bang Kwang for Thai bands, retinues of sexy female dancers, comedians and beauty pageant contestants. Commenting on the festivities, Pittaya said, "The people around here have supported us, so we wanted to do something in return for them." Up and down the roads near the jail, scarecrows wearing the prison's blue uniform, straw hats and happy faces had been tied to power poles. "Since the inmates are not allowed out of their cells," Pittaya said, "we thought that they could enjoy the festivities through these effigies."

For many of the foreign inmates watching the events unfold on closed-circuit television, the celebration was a kind of torture. One of them, who asked to remain anonymous, said, "What's there to celebrate? Seventy-two years of injustice?"

For many of the locals visiting the two-day party, the biggest lure was the display of archaic torture instruments, complete with life-size mannequins, on loan from the Corrections Museum. These included the original machine-gun used at Bang Kwang, a tableau of two machete-wielding executioners dressed in red outfits about to lop the head off a blindfolded prisoner, and a mannequin whose arms and legs were locked in a pillory so splinters could be hammered under the nails of his hands and feet. Watching families, beauty queens and rich matriarchs walking their poodles past these exhibits was a crash course in the country's bizarre contrasts.

Perhaps these exhibits were intended to show how much more humane the prison system has become. Aside from some of the improvements, such as introducing bachelor's degree correspondence courses (with instructors coming into the jail to oversee the final exams), the director said the biggest problem facing the Thai penal system was overcrowding—to the point where cells at Bang Kwang intended for four people actually hold twenty. In the early 1990s, there were 90,000 prisoners doing time in Thailand. Now there are three times that many (around 70 per cent on drug-related charges). The Corrections Department has been trying to decrease these numbers, he said, by arranging early releases for the elderly and those serving less than 30 years.

Only a few days after the jail's anniversary, however, Amnesty International filed a report titled 'Widespread Abuses in the Administration of Justice' in Thailand, accusing warders of severely violating prisoners' basic rights, and using torture as punishment for minor infractions. The report cited an incident in May 2001 where a Thai inmate named Sinchai Salee was punched, kicked and smacked with batons by several guards until he lost consciousness and eventually died. Earlier, the 30-something Sinchai had got into an argument with a guard because he wanted to nail a water bottle to the wall of his cell. Amnesty reported that many of these punishments were doled out by 'trusties'—other inmates who receive special privileges from the warders in return for keeping, and sometimes disturbing, the peace. The report also noted that, in direct contravention of Thai law, the men on Bang Kwang's death-row have to clank around with heavy leg irons on 24 hours a day. These shackles are welded together.

When the Corrections Department admitted for the first time ever that some of these abuses were true, the story made front-page news in Thailand. Siva Saengmanee, the Correction Department's director-general at the time, said they had received numerous complaints about warders ruling over their charges with iron fists and guards extorting money from prisoners or demanding sexual favours from visiting wives and daughters.

"It is the responsibility of prison officials to turn convicts into valuable members of society, not ruin their morale by handing out unauthorised punishments," Siva said during a press conference.

In *The Last Executioner*, Chavoret blamed the persistent problem of corruption in the prison system on the poor pay the guards bring home—a rookie only makes about 7,000 baht a month—and pointed out that some guards have been punished and wound up in prison. A case in point is Prayuth Sanun. To supplement his meagre wage, he began working as a bouncer in a bar, where he fell in with a gang of drug-dealers. Nabbed with 700,000 methamphetamine pills, an M16 and a load of cash, the former guard has now languished on death row for nearly a decade.

Although he has never downplayed the corruption of some guards, Chavoret said there have been some genuine moments of levity and compassion prior to executions. One example he cited was of a Thai woman who had been arrested 12 different times for trafficking in narcotics before finally getting the death sentence. When the female guards escorting her to the chamber—that bore a sign in Thai euphemistically referring to it as the 'room to end all suffering'—could not control her, a male guard stepped in to hold her hand, asking if he could be her last boyfriend. That made her laugh and she kissed him on the cheek. Arm in arm, the guard escorted her on a blind date with death.

The former executioner often resorted to Buddhist teachings to soothe the infuriated men sentenced to death. In the case of the serial rapist Sane Oongaew, that showed remarkable restraint on his part. Sane and several cohorts raped and strangled a ten-year-old girl to death in Samut Prakarn province back in 1971. The autopsy report revealed that she was covered with bruises and abrasions, her hymen had been shredded, semen clogged her vagina and clay had been stuffed down her throat all the way to the larynx. Sane's cohorts confessed, but he steadfastly denied any complicity in the sex crime and homicide. When the superintendent read out the execution order to him, Sane screamed, "I didn't fucking do it! I don't know a goddamn thing about it. I will haunt you all for the rest of your lives. Let me see the face of the detective in charge! Where's the son of a bitch?"

Chavoret walked over to remind him of the Buddhist teaching about thinking positive thoughts before you die so as to be reborn in a better place. "Just think of it as bad karma coming back to you for what you have done. If you are positive when you 'go' you will end up in a better place, so empty your mind of anger and negativity." That calmed him down a little. For a last will and testament Sane wrote a letter to his father, repeating the Buddhist tenet that the only certainties in life are birth, ageing, pain and death, while reminding him to visit his brother Narat who had confessed to his role in the rape and murder.

"Dear Dad,

"I just want to say goodbye to you. I hope you won't be too sad. Just think of it as a natural occurrence. We're bound to be born, age, be hurt and die anyway. Please look after my wife and don't let her struggle. Tell her not to take another husband. Don't bury my body, keep it for three years. Don't forget, dad, to visit Narat as often as you can."

Much of the violence in Thai jails, the former executioner said, is the result of chronic under-funding. The daily food budget is still less than one US dollar per day. Without money coming in from relatives and friends for inmates to buy food in the prison shops (usually run by gangsters continuing their lives of crimes from the other side) and medical supplies, inmates are prey to starvation and opportunistic illnesses. They also end up doing odd jobs for other inmates—sexual services included—to make ends meet.

For many of the 700-plus foreign convicts incarcerated in Bang Kwang, the country's largest maximum-security penitentiary (population: 7,000), the worst part of prison life is the boredom.

Visits from tourists are reprieves from that tedium. Partly because of the popularity of Warren Fellows' memoir, Bang Kwang has become a strange stopover for travellers.

Garth Hattan, the former rock drummer and convicted heroin trafficker who served eight years there, said the inmates refer to some of the visitors as 'banana tourists' "because they make us feel like monkeys in a cage. Some women even asked me to take off my shirt for them, or they say shit like, 'How could you have been so stupid?' Some of them have also asked me to where to score drugs or how to set up deals."

The magazine columns Garth wrote are crammed with similar tales and bytes of humour rare in the prison genre. One guard, trying to suck up to a former security chief Garth described as the 'evil love child of Pol Pot and Imelda Marcos', discovered a stash of what looked like marijuana in Garth's locker. The guards rolled up 'bombers' to test the weed, which turned out to be green tea.

Many of the inmates, particularly the poor Asians, have to work inside the technically illegal sweatshops or do laundry and perform sexual favours for the other inmates. "You may assume that being indigenous to Thailand, *kathoeys* (ladyboys) would be the sole purveyors of the prison sex trade, but you'd be amazed to see what levels some ostensibly normal guys have plunged to just to get a little extra chicken with their rice. It's as if walking through these gates, no matter how turbo-hetero they claim to be, gives them a license to—poof!—turn into 'Bang Kwang Barbie' (Malibu Barbie's twisted Siamese sister)," wrote the Californian in another column.

The prison authorities knew that Garth's then-fiancée, Susan Aldous (also known as 'The Angel of Bang Kwang'), was smuggling his columns out to be published in our magazine, but they didn't mind because he included enough cautionary anecdotes about mixing high times with lowlifes to deglamourise prison life and the backpacker chic of doing drugs in Thailand.

"There's a message in here somewhere and it's not just targeted at you hell-man adventure cowboys, and you ennui-plagued, insouciant heiresses-in-waiting who are out to shock the world—maybe your parents—by taking the fateful walk from the conventional wild side into something you feel exudes a truly radical allure—like an impulsive jaunt into narco-trafficking, for instance.

"There's no glamour here, no promise of success, no proverbial pot of gold to pick up on the other side, just a sweaty inanimate existence riddled with the futile dreams of what could've been, mingled with the aching regret of having let so many good people down—especially yourself. Enjoy your travels, and never put yourself in a position that would jeopardise your freedom to do so."

In recent years, the number of 'banana tourists' and backpackers has declined, said Susan. "The prison authorities have made it more difficult to visit inmates so you don't see so many of the Khaosan Road types, or the messages on notice boards in guesthouses about visiting prisoners. If you want to visit an inmate now you have to dress up a little and act like a friend or relative."

Transfer agreements between many Western countries, and more recently with Nigeria, have ensured that there are less black and white men in the jail. "The atmosphere at Bang Kwang has changed in recent years," noted Susan, "because of all the transfer agreements, but there's a lot more inmates from Laos, Vietnam and Hong Kong who tend to blend in and are forgotten. Their governments don't care and they don't get much attention."

Until a few years ago, African men made up the overwhelming majority of foreign prisoners. When I visited a 25-year-old Nigerian inmate, who had been sentenced to 50 years for serving as a heroin courier, or 'mule', he told me, "Compared to life in Nigeria, this prison isn't so bad. Some of the crime syndicates we work for make a special deal with our families, so if we get caught the syndicates give our families about 20 dollars per month for the time we serve in jail. In Nigeria that's not a bad income. At least I can feel like I'm still taking care of my wife and three children."

Beautifully landscaped with flowers and hedges, the visiting area demonstrates the Thai penchant for painting the happiest of faces on the grimmest of backdrops. Recently, the authorities have also put in plexi-glass and telephones, which, if the connections were better, would make it easier to talk to a prisoner. It's an improvement from the old days of having to yell through a pair of wire fences separating a four-metre gulley in the midst of ten other yelling matches. During one such visit, Garth shouted, "This place is still hell, but it's nowhere near as bad as it was when Warren Fellows was here. A few of the older dudes and guards remember him as being a terrible junkie."

Garth and Warren are not the only ones who have turned headlines into bylines. A glut of prison memoirs has emerged from Thailand, such as Susan Gregory's *Forget You Had a Daughter*, Debbie Singh's *You'll Never Walk Alone* (her brother received ten years in jail for fencing a check worth a thousand dollars) and a few forgettable films like *Brokedown Palace*—principally shot in the Philippines with Claire Danes and Kate Beckinsdale as the leads—in addition to an Australian mini-series for TV called *The Bangkok Hilton* featuring a young Nicole Kidman.

All of these shows and books play excruciating variations on the Thai-jails-are-hell theme. The only book to break out of that creative cellblock is David McMillan's *Escape*. Believed to be the only Westerner to ever successfully escape from the 'Bangkok Hilton' (a nickname give to many Thai jails, but in this case Khlong Prem), McMillan (a pseudonym) comes across as a pathological criminal and unrepentant drug dealer who, nonetheless, pulled off a death-defying escape that required as much cunning as courage a decade before the book came out in 2007. After sawing through the bars of his cell window, he used a piece of wood and straps to abseil down the wall. He bridged an internal moat with a ladder he'd made out of bamboo and picture frames, which also allowed him to scale an electrified fence. By dawn he was creeping across an outer wall, using an umbrella to shield his face from the guards up in the watchtowers. If he had been spotted, chances are he would've met the same fate as the four Thai inmates who commandeered a garbage truck inside Khlong Prem Prison in 2000. As they tried to ram their way through the front gates, the guards shot all four of them.

Richard Barrow, the British expat who runs the largest collective of English-language websites on Thailand, posted a map of the escape route on the Paknam Web Network. In an interview he did with the author, MacMillan told him, "Every element of good fortune became essential: the existence of an army-boot factory for the rope; the paper factory for the long bamboo poles—even the umbrella factory, as I'm sure I would have been spotted by the tower guards without that umbrella shielding my pale face."

Using a fake passport, MacMillan fled the country after serving three years in Khlong Prem. Having done ten years in an Australian jail and other stints in prisons across Asia, he said, "I've been in worse prisons [than Bangkok]. By that I mean terrifying. There was two months in solitary in Pakistan when I was fed only watery beans poured through the bars with a piece of roof guttering, for the solitary door was never opened."

The book that may blow these all away is slated for release in late 2010. *A Secret History of the Bangkok Hilton* is a collaboration between Pornchai Sereemongkonpol and Chavoret Jaruboon. Pornchai has dug deep into the pits of the prison's history to excavate more than a few buried skeletons, as well as provide an overview of the Thai judiciary and the beheading ritual, and personal letters from death row convicts. Now that Chavoret has retired from the prison and has terminal cancer, the book is kind of a last will and testament for him. Of all the characters that have populated Bang Kwang over the last eight decades, he remains one of the most colourful and contradictory.

Growing up in the Bangkok neighbourhood of Sri Yan, the son of a Buddhist father and Muslim mother, as a boy Chavoret had to walk past a brothel that doubled as an opium den on his way to a Catholic school. Learning English from his father's collection of albums by Frank Sinatra and Hank Williams, he played guitar in a series of rock 'n' roll cover bands that entertained the GIs all over Thailand. True to his self-deprecating wit, he said, "I was never that handsome or talented and I needed a steady job with a government pension to support my family." His musical talents were more noteworthy than that. Some of the journalists or relatives of prisoners coming to Bang Kwang would be treated to his soulful versions of sob songs by Hank Williams or upbeat rockers by Elvis, sung in a rich baritone as Chavoret finessed the fretboard of an acoustic guitar he always kept in his office.

Ironically, the man who executed 55 inmates over 19 years has also been hailed as a prison reformer. Susan—the 'Angel and She-devil of Bang Kwang'—recounted, "If it wasn't for Chavoret helping me with the paperwork and dealing with all the bureaucracy, I wouldn't have been able to do half of what I've done here. You'd think the inmates here would hate him, but he's very well-liked and respected."

On one occasion, Susan was visiting a group of older Thai inmates serving life sentences—many of them hadn't had a visitor in years—and she went over and hugged a man covered in sores. "Out of the corner of my eye, I saw Chavoret shed a few tears. He's a bit more of a softie than he lets on," she said, "and I think he's dealt with the guilt of his old job by drinking a lot."

Pornchai, his co-author, drew a different bead on this complex character. "He's not really a man given to introspection. So I don't think he dwells too much on his old job. But I have been pleasantly surprised by the way he's handled his cancer diagnosis. He's still in good spirits and sometimes he invites me out for a steak dinner."

While we were sharing drinks and dinner with Chavoret one night in a restaurant overlooking a pond filled with water lilies, his wife of 30 years joined us at the table. Tew said, "At home he won't even kill ants or caterpillars. He has a good heart and we never talk about the prison at home."

Chavoret took a banknote out of his wallet and handed it to her. Everyone at the table laughed. "We're always joking around like this," he said. "That's what keeps our marriage fresh and the friendship has kept us together for this long." Later on, he insisted on paying the tab for everyone at the table.

In his early years at the prison, some of the misfires he witnessed in the 'room to end all suffering' would have sent more sensitive souls on a one-way trip to the madhouse. Such was the case with Ginggaew Lorsoongnern, a nanny who kidnapped the son of her wealthy employers. When the ransom money did not materialise, her two male accomplices stabbed and buried the boy while he was still alive. To ward off any threats of a haunting, the killers (just like the guards in the death chamber) put flowers, incense and a candle in the boy's hands before tying them with the scared white thread monks use to repel evil.

Ginggaew did not participate in the murder, but she was sentenced to death in early 1979, along with her two accomplices. The young woman struggled all the way into the death chamber and kept struggling as they tied her to the cross. The executioner fired ten bullets into her back and the doctor pronounced her dead. But as they brought one of her accomplices into the room, Chavoret and the guards heard her scream in the tiny morgue. Not only that, Ginggaew was trying to stand up. Pandemonium ensued. One of the escorts rolled her over and pressed down on her back to accelerate the bleeding and help her die," wrote Chavoret. "Another escort, a real hard man, tried to strangle her to finish her off but I swept his arms away in disgust."

Even after they executed one of her accomplices, the doctor found that the woman was still breathing. He ordered the guards to tie her back on the cross and this time they used the full quota of 15 bullets to ensure she was dead.

That was not the end of it. Pin, her other male accomplice, was still breathing after the first round of 13 bullets and had to have ten more shots.

Chavoret and the rest of the guards were all struck by the fact that Pin and Ginggaew had suffered much the same fate as the little boy they had stabbed and buried alive. It was karma, they decided. The boy had choked to death on dirt. The man and woman had choked to death on blood.

After a decade of helping the prison authorities by serving as an escort or one of the men who tied the inmate to the cross, Chavoret received an official order to become the chief executioner in 1984, a job he did not want and only took to earn more money to support his wife and three children.

Before pulling the trigger, he would pray to a powerful spirit for absolution, explaining that he was not killing the person out of malice, he was just doing his duty. "I had no power in the judicial process. After the police, the witnesses and the judge all had their say, I was just the final link in the chain."

Afterwards, he would go out drinking with his fellow prison officers in order to ward off the guilt and the haunting sensation that the dead person's spirit was shadowing him. He was paid 2,000 baht for each execution, money which he religiously donated to a Buddhist temple to make some merit for himself and the condemned men and women. The temple's abbot was stunned to find out that one of his most regular donors was a man who had broken the first precept of not killing any life forms time and time again. When Chavoret asked him who should shoulder the blame for these executions, the abbot responded by repeating the Buddhist belief in the interconnectedness of life. "It's everyone's fault: society, the government, the laypeople, the criminals, television, poverty, hopelessness, desperation, anger, greed—everything and everyone is at fault."

In person and in his book, Chavoret has detailed the many improvements at Bang Kwang. Paramount among them is a new breed of guards, who must now have a university or college degree, unlike the old days when a fair number of the guards had no more than six or seven years of basic education. The new recruits have brought with them a bevy of new projects, from boxing matches and vocational programmes to more correspondence courses and workshops.

The medical facilities have also gotten better. When Susan first began undertaking projects there in the mid-1990s, the ramshackle 'hospital' had no mattresses or wheelchairs, no dental care or even aspirins, and the medical budget per year was less than US$3,000 dollars for 7,000 prisoners. "If you got sent to the hospital back then, it was assumed you would never get out again. Many inmates died on a metal frame covered with bare boards, but the mattresses we put in are still there and the conditions are much more hygienic now, and they've got a proper doctor and dentist. If their families and the embassies push, the prisoners can get prescriptions filled and even anti-viral drugs for HIV and AIDS. The conditions still aren't great, but they're much better than before," said the altruist, adding that conditions have also improved in many of the homes for orphans and the elderly and disabled where she has worked. "Thailand has made incredible progress in the last 30 years."

For all the pros, however, there all still plenty of cons. For one, the legal system is as corrupt and haphazard as ever. In many surveys of Southeast Asian countries, only Burma and Indonesia consistently rank lower than Thailand for corruption in the judiciary system.

"If you sentenced me to an indefinite sentence, even in a five-star hotel with congenial company," said Susan, "it would still be hell. But the kind of indefinite sentences they give out here are completely arbitrary and the punishment rarely fits the crime. The police force is corrupt, the evidence is tainted, the judges rotate, there's no juries, or background checks or extenuating circumstances that look into poverty and ignorance. What can you say about a justice system where a 75-year-old man who accidentally killed a friend in a drunken argument gets sentenced to 104 years and six months in jail, while a real murderer gets out after a few years because he's got the right contacts?"

Drug dealers continuing their lives of crime from behind bars and substance abuse are two other plagues that continue to poison the populace of Thai prisons. As former inmates and heroin-traffickers Garth Hattan and Warren Fellow have said, it is a tragic irony that the drugs which landed them (and many others) in jail, or on death row, are widely available to inmates at inflated prices.

The current director-general of the Corrections Department, Chartchai Suthiklom, held a press conference in 2010 to announce that they have installed mobile phone signal jammers in jails in Ratchaburi and Nakhon Ratchasima provinces to stem the flow of drugs. He said that guards have found mobile phones hidden in hollowed-out books, thrown over prison walls and wrapped in condoms found in prisoners' sphincters after court appearances. With a phone, the drug dealers can set up deals from behind bars and have the money transferred into their bank accounts by relatives. The dealers also vie for cuts of the lucrative prison market, where drugs sell for up to five times the street price. Of the 210,000 convicts incarcerated in Thailand, the director-general estimated that around half are addicted to drugs, primarily methamphetamines.

For human rights advocates, however, abolishing capital punishment is at the top of their agenda. That seemed like a probability after Thailand switched to lethal injection at the end of 2003. Earlier, former director Pittaya and a task force had visited

Texas—which has more inmates on death row than any other state— to observe an execution. The former director of Bang Kwang said, "A muscle relaxant and sedative is given to the convict shortly before they inject him with the lethal dose so he's already asleep and doesn't have any convulsions. It's a much more humane form of capital punishment and only takes about four minutes in total."

After three convicts were executed in late 2003, the courts were still handing down death sentences (mostly for trafficking in methamphetamines), but there were no more executions until 2009, when two middle-aged men Thai were executed by lethal injections. In the media blitz that followed, some inmates have alleged that prisoners are paying 'life insurance' to authorities, anywhere from 1,000 to 5,000 baht per month, so that their names do not come up next on the list.

Although Chavoret believes that capital punishment has not caused the crime rate to decrease, he insisted that it's still necessary in Thailand, citing the example of one of the two Thai women he executed.

"She had a long history of previous offences. She killed an infant and packed its body full of heroin—the same technique some American GIs used to use with their dead comrades to export the drug into America—and then she tried to carry the dead child across the border to Malaysia. What can we do with people like this?" he asked rhetorically.

He had a point. What did the parents of the child who was used as a drug courier's 'doll' think was just punishment? What about the family members of the ten-year-old girl raped multiple times by three different men, or the boy who was buried alive and choked to death on dirt? Would they not feel justified in wanting to see the killers of their children and siblings receive the maximum possible punishment for those unspeakable crimes?

In theory, the reasons for abolishing the death penalty are clear enough. In reality, the issue is stained with too much blood and clouded by too many warring emotions impossible to codify in the heartless terms of legalese.

Asked if he was happy to see death sentences being executed with needles instead of firearms, Chavoret said, "Sure, I'm happy about it. It's more humane and I've never liked guns and never had one at home. Besides, I'm going to go down as the last executioner in Thai history." He cracked a grin and laughed.

True to the festive Thai spirit, the change to lethal injection occasioned another party at Bang Kwang Central Prison, not dissimilar to the 72nd anniversary celebrations held the previous year. For the TV cameras, celebrity pop stars jammed on-stage, ladyboy dance troupes kicked up their heels and smiling prisoners waved flags, as a group of monks sprinkled holy water on the machine-gun to 'purify' it. They then released more than 300 balloons to symbolise the spirits of all the condemned men and women who had lost their lives in the 'room to end all suffering'. By all appearances, it was another jolly and ritualised occasion in the land of contradictions where the justice of karma, not jurisprudence, overwrites the letter of the law.

Pattaya: The Vegas of Vice?

With golf courses and scuba-diving, go-karts and shooting ranges, cheap hotels and bars with Happy Hours from 10am to 10pm and working girls on tap 24/7, Pattaya is a young man's wet dream come true.

As diverse as the city and its denizens are—from a motorcycle club of Harley riders who do charity work for underprivileged kids, to a mosque and sizable Islamic community beside a Catholic church—its reputation is best summarised by the popular T-shirt slogan: 'Good Guy Goes to Heaven, Bad Guy Goes to Pattaya'.

The city's name is practically a synonym for 'debauchery' and a mere mention pricks up ears, causing either smirks of approval or scowls of disdain. The Vegas-like excesses of late-night carousing and serial womanising have inspired a local twist on an often-quoted line from Martin Scorsese's film *Casino*: 'What happens in Pattaya stays in Pattaya.'

As a hotbed of vice, or so the legend goes, 'Fun City' has racked up substantial media coverage on both local and international fronts for harbouring foreign criminals and sexual deviants. Within the same week in mid-July 2010, the police arrested a former cop from Belgium wanted for impersonating one of the embassy's staff, and a Finnish man who changed his nationality to Swedish after he was caught bringing kilos of cocaine into Thailand. He later swindled a Swedish real estate company out of almost 1.5 million dollars before being nabbed in Pattaya when he returned to see his Thai wife.

These men were small fry compared to Mikhail Pletnev, the Russian pianist and conductor arrested for allegedly raping a 14-year-old boy. After arriving at the Pattaya provincial court on 19 July, the 53-year-old read a prepared statement, "I have always stated that I will assist the police in every way I can with their enquiries into the allegations that have been made against me. I say again these allegations are not true. I also state, contrary to media reports, that during the police search of my home nothing connected with the allegations—no photographs or other visual material—was found in the computer." The highly regarded virtuoso also denied running a music school in Thailand or ever being a full-time resident. For the last decade, Pletnev said he had only ever stayed in the country for a week or two a time. If convicted, he faces up to 14 years in prison and a 40,000 baht fine.

To ferret out foreign criminals on the lam in Pattaya, the police opened a branch office of the Transnational Crime Data Center (TNCDC) off Jomtien Soi 5 in August 2010. Cooperating with Interpol, the FBI and the US Drug Enforcement Administration, as well as that of EU countries and Australia, the office's sign outside the building lists the top crimes in order: 'International Terrorism, Identity Fraud, Arms Smugging (sic), People Smugging (sic) or Legal Labour, Money Laundering, Drug Trafficking.'

At the press conference to open the centre, Police Superintendent

Colonel Athiwit announced, "Information technology is used to expedite the identification and capture of fugitives. The TNCDC gives us the technological support and databases we need to catch criminals who have become more sophisticated in hiding their identities."

Considering these preventive measures and the numerous crime stories, surely Pattaya must be one of the most dangerous cities in Southeast Asia? Not so, say the expats. Gavin, a young Brit whom I spoke to—who, along with his Thai wife, co-runs the New Hope Massage and Fish Spa over on Soi 13, where patrons sit outside with their legs immersed in a glass tank as dozens of fish nibble on the dead skin—said, "I think the danger element is overrated in Pattaya. Anywhere can be dangerous if you're looking for trouble."

His claim is echoed by Christopher Moore, the Canadian novelist and Bangkok expat, who has spent a lot of time in the city over the years, especially when researching his 2004 thriller *Pattaya 24/7*. "I don't find it very threatening, but like most things in life, the level of threat correlates to the risks you're taking. You can take those kinds of risks in Bangkok or Des Moines, Iowa. Pattaya is no more dangerous than any mid-sized American city." During his research, however, he discovered that the amount of smuggling along the coast is prodigious. "It's impossible to police a coastline that long. It's like the border between Mexico and the United States."

According to Chris, a lot of the crime in Pattaya is foreigner against foreigner, mostly in the form of bar room brawls, football hooligans on a rampage, or territorial disputes over a bargirl. Serving as a breakwater against outbursts of violence, and to cut down on unscrupulous locals preying on visitors, are the Foreign Tourist Police Assistants (FTPA). Every night, from 9pm to 3am, they cluster around a white van at the top of Walking Street. Clad in black SWAT-esque uniforms, some of them carry handcuffs, batons and pepper spray. In person, they look intimidating. In reality, they're benign. Much of their work involves helping tourists find their hotels, settling disputes over bar bills and pouring drunks into pick-up truck taxis.

At night, the FTPA patrol Walking Street, which is the lay of the land for Vegas-like razzle-dazzle—go-go bars, discos, ritzy seafood restaurants and Elvis and The Beatles impersonators. The FTPA works hand in hand with the Tourist Police, although they are not allowed to conduct investigations. Like any local, they can make citizen's arrests. That rarely happens. Made up of ex-cops, ex-soldiers and businessmen, the unit is well respected by locals. They are a friendly and benevolent bunch that would probably rescue your kitten from a tree. The former leader, Howard Miller, was appointed as the Honorary British Consul in August 2010. One of the city's most successful expat entrepreneurs, Howard also runs *Pattaya One News*, a cable TV show and website.

The Thai Police Volunteers who work out of the cop shop near Soi 8 on Beach Road had nothing but praise for the FTPA. These volunteers are not allowed to make official statements to the press, but speaking on condition of anonymity, one of the almost 400-member force commented, "The problem a lot of tourists face is that the regular police don't speak much English, so the FTPA is practically a translation service that saves us a lot of time and trouble."

In front of the station, next to the strip of beer bars with hostesses calling out "Hello, welcome", the cops and volunteers enjoy taking billiard breaks on an open-air table. The volunteer said the biggest crime nuisance in the city has nothing to do with foreign mobsters or international criminals on the run, but juvenile delinquents. "This province [Chon Buri] has the highest rate of juvenile crime in the country. Many of the rural couples that come here to work end up working in bars at night and the children don't have much supervision or money. So they run amok and get into trouble. Mostly they form gangs and attack each other."

From time to time this youthful angst and desperation boils over into homicide. Two Russian women on a package tour to Pattaya were shot to death on Jomtien Beach in 2007 by a Thai youth. In mid-2010, drive-by shootings ricocheted across the crime pages. A hostess at one of the beer bars off Second Road was shot in the leg by a pair of motorcyclists speeding past. The majority of crimes committed by juvenile delinquents are petty: snatch-and-run robberies, thieving motorcycles and picking pockets. For most locals, tourists and expats, these incidents happen off the radar.

In 'Fun City', it's the whiff of sex not gunpowder that clouds the air and senses. In and around South Pattaya, taxis whiz past bearing signs for the Lolita's Pattaya Gentlemen's Lounge. This lounge specialises in fellatio, and their slogan reads, 'Our girls will blow you away'. A 'love hotel' has an opaque window with a half-naked female figure next to a sign that reads 'Thai Chicks Rock' and, above that, 'Welcome to the Good Life'. The Windmill

Club advertises its 'wares' in local papers with ads showing dancers that promise 'Pussy Without Attitude'. Along Soi 6 is a series of bars-cum-bordellos with hostesses dressed in everything from schoolgirl outfits to flight-attendant garb, standing or sitting outside neon-splashed venues with telltale names such as 'Sex in the City', 'Lick' and 'The Hole in One Bar'.

In an age of sensationalism where the world's oldest obsession is used to sell almost everything, no one can accuse these establishments of false advertising or hyberbole. In Pattaya, you get what you come and pay for.

This degree of constant titillation has given rise to a number of gossip and advice columns in the local press. *Night March* (recently renamed *Night Walker*) is a regular rundown of the sexier local bars in *Pattaya Today*, in which the author refers to the women as 'damsels' or 'chrome pole molesters'. Beers are 'liver wasters', and the dialogue revolves around 'tumescence'.

The presence of so many foreign men getting involved with bargirls (mostly immigrants from poor farming communities in the northeast) has spawned a lot of friction, heartburn and Agony Aunt columns in the local English press. Oi, of the *Pattaya Times*, happily dispels the delusions of Western men looking for soul mates and true romance in the city with younger women. "You know Jeremy, even though you've been here sometime, I really don't think you understand Thai people or their culture. Life is very hard here which you have seen. It's not really all about, 'I love you!'. Ordinary people don't have time for heart and romance, there's not much romance in the village when your kids are crying and hungry and you have nothing to give them. It's really more about taking care and providing. We're not a romantic race like Western people, we're more realistic. If a woman stays with you it's because you provide for her and her family and she loves you. She doesn't have to tell you every five minutes like in the movies. I'm not saying it's right or this is how it should be. I'm just saying that's the way it is. For a man to write to women half his age and expect true love without the finances to support them both in a decent lifestyle is just totally unrealistic. One day you will pass on and she will be old already and now alone with no one to provide for her. Did you ever consider that?"

Toss in a few of these misunderstandings, add alcohol and frustration to the mix and it's a Molotov cocktail that goes off now and then, like when an ageing Scandinavian man ran amok in the Royal Garden Plaza, throwing acid in the faces of any Thai women he saw, because a young bargirl had spurned his affections and drained his bank account back in 2007. That's an extreme take on a familiar tale in Pattaya and Bangkok, where the bookshelves in local shops are filled with similar tales of foreign men penning their self-published memoirs of being conned by duplicitous women.

Such stories have given the city its reputation, but many long-term expats think the sordid tales are exaggerated. "Pattaya is an easy target. It's a scapegoat for anything Thais or expats or tourists want to pin on it, for sexual diseases, or drinking too much, or anything negative," said an American English professor who goes by the nickname 'Scooter'.

A 12-year resident of Pattaya and a film buff fond of quoting Nietzsche, he said, "I've never had a problem on Walking Street or any of the bars on Soi 6. One night a friend lost in his wallet on Soi 6 and went back thinking they'd stolen it, but he got it back with all the money intact. I've never heard of anyone getting ripped off or mugged. Of course it could happen if you're drunk out of your mind at 4am and staggering around."

As much as people try to paint the city in black and white terms, or denigrate it as some Asian Babylon, Pattaya and its floating populace of visitors, migrant sex workers and expats is far too colourful for these monochromatic stereotypes. One of the biggest events of 2010 was the 'Say No to Violence Against Women' parade on Pattaya Beach. Led by Thai aristocrats and dignitaries, with students representing each major school and a UN Goodwill Ambassador, the procession drew 10,000 marchers to the same strip of Beach Road peopled day and night with streetwalkers sitting on benches and the spiky tail of a life-size dinosaur in front of a mall. Even some of the pickup truck taxis with racy ads also sport stickers for a UNIFEM campaign to stop violence against women.

The most bipolar city in Thailand—and possibly Southeast Asia, or maybe the entire world—has an upside, too. Head over to Jomtien Beach and it's a different planet, with five-star hotels, families, groups of screaming teenagers being pulled through the water on 'banana boats' and Thais having seafood picnics. According to the Tourism Authority of Thailand, the Russians, Chinese and South Koreans lead the tourist pack. Of these vacationers, the Russians are the most obvious. There are entire streets filled with signs in Russian, restaurants replete with specialties from the Ukraine and Uzbekistan and hotels booked solid with package tourists from the motherland off the lanes near Jomtien Beach, with the Pattaya Park Beach Resort and its 170-metre-high Tower Jump in the background. Over on Walking Street, there are nightclubs with karaoke in Russian and a go-go bar named Galaxy staffed by Eastern European women.

When I spoke to a couple of university professors in their 40s from Moscow, they explained the city's free-and-easy appeal for the survivors of communist blight and repression. "Under the communist system, it was difficult to get travel passes to go anywhere and even if you could, nobody had any money to travel. Everything, I remember, was grey and polluted. There were always scarcities of basic things. Even today, Moscow is more crowded and jammed with traffic than Bangkok. So we come here and it's all very beautiful, exotic and tropical," said Vladislav, an aeronautics professor and former weightlifter with the Soviet Olympics squad.

With a refreshing brusqueness, he added, "What is this early closing time in the rest of Thailand? We don't need government babysitters treating us like children—it's bullshit! Pattaya is much more progressive and liberal than the rest of the country and we Russians enjoy all the entertainment and restaurant options. My wife she enjoys the shopping. Sometimes she gets drunk and likes to get onstage and dance with the girls…" He exchanged a knowing smirk with his wife, Sonia.

Sonia, a professor of anthropology with a lobster-red tan,

nodded. "Do you know how cold it gets and how long the winter lasts in Russia? Many characteristics of any people are informed by the weather. That is why Eastern Europeans and Russians sometimes seem like cold people and why we need so much vodka to warm up." She smiled. "Thais have a tropical personality which is much warmer, so we come here and feel much more warm, too. These days, everyone talks so much about freedom and free trade and free speech, but as abstract concepts. Freedom is also a destination and we Russians feel that, to use a communist expression, Pattaya is a liberated zone."

The city's freewheeling nature that she complimented has never been curbed. The Social Order Policy implemented by the government in 2001, stipulating that bars must shut by 1am, never caught on in Pattaya. These establishments still stay open until 3 or 4am or later. The nationwide no-smoking policy in bars and clubs fizzled out in Pattaya within days. During the aftermath of the May 2010 protests, when a curfew was imposed in Bangkok for weeks, the nightspots of 'Fun City' shut down for just one night.

But here's the rub. On the surface, Pattaya seems like a free and easy-going place. Delve a little deeper and you get stonewalled. The FTPV will not speak to anyone without the express consent of the Tourist Police. Any questions put to the honorary consul have to be vetted by the British Embassy. None of the crime reporters from any of the local dailies returned my calls or requests for interviews. What appears to be an open city is rigidly controlled by vested interests. As an example, many locals said the brothels on Soi 6 are only allowed to open from 1pm to 1am because the cops call the shots.

Simultaneously open and closed, this tension defines the city and provides much of its fascination. It also sanctions the most heinous kinds of hearsay. "Did you know that half of Pattaya is run by the Russian mafia?" "That Thai guy was set up as a scapegoat for the murder of those two Russian women on the beach. It wasn't a robbery gone wrong; the two women still had their cell phones and all their valuables on them. Russian mobsters killed them." "The world's biggest arms dealer, the 'Merchant of Death', who was arrested in Bangkok but got off on a technicality before they could extradite him to America, used Pattaya as his base of operations."

These tales are all shots in the dark, impossible to confirm or deny. As Scooter said, "A lot of these stories are rumours that come from expats talking, but I've never seen anything to confirm them. The theory is the average Russian wouldn't make enough money to come here for a big holiday, so people assume that they must be gangsters or former communist officials who made a killing, or corrupt business people."

For gangster-spotting, *Pattaya 24/7* (one of the most explosive and richly characterised 'shells' in Christopher Moore's series of books) is insightful. The story's Thai 'godfather' has a penchant for flaunting his ill-gotten gains in the form of expensive cars, watches and clothes. Some of the bearish Eastern European men strutting down Walking Street with the penultimate 'fashion accessory' for any mobster on their arms—a statuesque blond—adhere to the same ostentatious dress code. This is not unusual in the criminal underworld, the novelist explained. "It's true of gangsters all over the world. It doesn't matter whether they're Hell's Angels in Toronto, the Russians, or the Italian mafia in Chicago, New York or Philadelphia, or drug barons in Latin America. These are not terribly complex people. They want to flaunt their status, power and influence. Most of them don't even think of themselves as godfathers or criminals. In their own eyes, they're businessmen... businessmen doing good things for the community."

In the funhouse mirror that is 'Fun City', appearances are distorted and deceiving. The Harley-riding bikers, whose nightlife haunt is the Tahitian Queen Rock 'n' Roll Bar on Beach Road, are not the outlaw motorcycle gang they resemble. Dressed in their leathers and jeans, and rumbling down the roads astride their 'hogs', the members of the Jesters Motorcycle Club are actually good Samaritans who pride themselves on working for underprivileged children and other charities. Their biggest event of the year is travelling en masse to Phuket for the annual 'Bike Week' held every April, when motorcyclists from all over Southeast Asia gear up for rallies, revelry, tattoo contests, a Miss Phuket Bike Week pageant, and—yes, doing good deeds for the community.

Opened in 1978, the Tahitian Queen is the oldest bar in the city. Run by former GIs, it has not changed much in the last three decades. There are no 'naughty' shows, the dancers do not strip, the décor is gilded Vegas kitsch and the medleys of vintage rock—from the Doors and the Stones to KISS and Jimi Hendrix—echo the soundtrack of the Vietnam-era film *Apocalypse Now*, famously described by filmmaker Frances Ford Coppola as 'the first rock 'n' roll war'.

Until the late 1960s, Pattaya was a comatose fishing village. During the Vietnam War, it became an enclave for GIs on "R 'n' R", catering to the soldiers with all the down-home comforts of America such as go-go bars and Western-style clubs with Thai musicians (most notably the former executioner Chavoret Jaruboon) playing covers of rock-solid standards.

Much of the city was planned and built by American engineers. That explains why the lanes along Beach Road are arranged in numerical order and why the city's grid-like and wide roads make it one of the country's most well-planned and easy-to-navigate destinations. By the time the war ended in 1975, around 700,000 GIs were descending on Pattaya every year. Many traded in their army fatigues for shorts and flip-flops, married local women and set up travel-oriented businesses and nightspots.

Over time, the American influence has waned. It's most prominent every year during the joint naval exercises called 'Cobra Gold', when the warships of the United States, Thailand and, in 2010, Korea, formed an armada of Marine Corps might. "You used to see all the American warships in Pattaya Bay," said Scooter. "But in recent years they've docked at Sattahip, the Thai navy base. Maybe in the past the sailors were rowdier when they came into town, but they're pretty well behaved now. The Shore Patrol checks up on them. The Marines also get involved with some charity projects like building houses for the less fortunate."

With 'pillars-of-the-community' gangsters, good Samaritan bikers, massive campaigns to stop violence against women, well-behaved sailors and quite possibly the only group of foreign police volunteers in Southeast Asia... what is Pattaya coming to? This might be the most philanthropy-minded citizenry in the entire country, but few of those stories will ever make it beyond the city limits. As Michael Moore discovered during the making of his documentary *Bowling for Columbine*, the murder rate had actually decreased in many large American cities. At the same time, TV coverage of murders had increased by more than 700 per cent. Good news means bad ratings. Hence, the majority of do-gooders will continue to get cropped out of Pattaya's big picture so the media can blow up mug shots portraying the minority of scoundrels such as Jeff Savage. The video of Savage threatening to loot and torch CentralWorld in Bangkok during the 2010 protests went 'viral' on the Internet. The British citizen and Pattaya resident was given a 45-day sentence after pleading guilty to violating the Emergency Decree. Since he had already spent some time in jail, Savage was released from custody pending deportation. Upon hearing the judge's verdict, he burst into tears. "It's a miracle, I am surprised, and there is justice in Thailand. I want justice for all—the dead, red shirts and even yellow shirts," he told the press.

Lest anyone finger certain nationalities as the chief troublemakers in the city, Christopher Moore said with a dry chuckle, "No countries have a monopoly on producing morons and hooligans."

As the influx of different ethnicities changes the complexion of the city, the crime syndicates are drawing fresh blood from different sources, such as the Middle East. An Iranian couple caught with 67 million baht worth of crystal methamphetamine, or 'Ice', at

Suvarnabhumi International Airport in Bangkok in July 2010 were bound for Pattaya. The police said it marked the first time the drug had ever been seized in liquid form. Increasingly popular for smuggling, the drug is liquefied and soaked up with towels. Even though it loses some of its potency, the narcotic can be smuggled in far greater quantities that are more difficult to detect.

'Ice' may be the club drug of choice for many in Pattaya, but it faces some 'stiff' competition from Viagra, which dominates the local drug news—with multiple variations on that double entendre and the inevitable tabloid headlines: *'Police Come Down Hard on Seller of Knockoff Viagra'*. The more hardcore chill-seekers combine Ice with Viagra. The combination can be fatal. Every year, a few foreign men die of heart attacks in Pattaya from a double dose of meth and sex.

In spite of all the improvements and developments spawned by an increasingly polyglot populace, Pattaya will continue to be pilloried as a place where old lechers come to prey on younger women. Like the rest of this bipolar community, these guys are not always what they seem to be either. Take Bill Evans for example. A mechanic specialising in farm equipment, he spent the first 60 years of his life in rural Ohio raising a family and running his own business. When his wife died and his daughters went off to university in a different state, he retired with no intention of spending his twilight years in the frigid weather that aggravated his arthritis. "Cold enough to freeze the balls off a brass monkey," he said.

Why did he choose Pattaya?

"This town has got it all. There's so much goin' on with

international marathons and cricket matches and music festivals and bowling leagues, I don't think it's even possible to get bored here. I always wanted to learn about boating and scuba-diving and that's what I've done here. People call it Vegas, but for me it's been more of a Fountain of Youth. I see that a lot here with some of the older guys. It's a new lease on life. Back in the States, I was just another old fart collecting a pension. Sure, there's a few bad apples in the bunch out here, but most of 'em are pretty decent folks."

Bill bought himself an ocean-view condo and married Oi, a 44-year-old former go-go dancer. Oi, or 'Sugarcane', said, "I like men 40 and up because they are more stable and honest. Young men want to be butterflies. They go from lady to lady."

Did she feel exploited by working the bars in Pattaya for more than a decade?

"No, I felt worse working in a factory!"

After being diagnosed with terminal cancer in 2008, Bill set up a trust fund for his wife and her daughter. In some of the final emails he sent out to people on his list, he pondered his mortality. "For places to die, this is one of the best. Not too sure what's waiting for me on the other side. Only thing I'm sure of is that I hope Sugarcane will be there too, with that all-forgiving smile of hers, a glass of beer in her hand, and I hope it looks just like Pattaya. Sometimes good guys can to go heaven and Fun City, too."

Museum of the Macabre:
See Uey the Chinese Cannibal

Many Thai children who grew up in the 1960s received the same warning from their parents—"Don't stay out after dark or the ghost of See Uey will eat you."

The cannibal-turned-supernatural legend and movie villain was, in reality, a poor Chinese man who went on a killing spree around Bangkok and some of the nearby provinces. He had a taste for children. No one is certain, but it's believed that he murdered and ate anywhere from five to eight children. Speculation also ran rife that his omnivorous 'diet' may have included some adults that he was never charged with. Caught in the act of burning one of the corpses by the young boy's father, See Uey Sae Ung was finally arrested in 1958. His confessions traumatised Thailand, giving birth to a bogeyman who still haunts the nation's psyche. After stabbing the children in the throat, See Uey told the police, he then slit open their chests and ate their hearts and livers.

A Hainanese immigrant who toiled as a coolie, rickshaw-puller and vegetable farmer after arriving in Thailand, the country's most legendary serial slayer was a former soldier, fighting against the Japanese invaders on the Chinese island during World War II. Some believe that his bloodlust was stoked on the battlefields of Hainan province. Said Professor Somchai Pholeamke, the former head of

Siriraj Hospital's Forensics Department, "His military commanders told the troops to eat the livers of the enemy soldiers to take on their strength and power." Many of the Thai movies about See Uey use the battlefield as the focal point of his motivations. A scene in one such film shows the young soldier, famished and alone, after all his comrades-in-arms had been slaughtered, with nothing to eat but human carrion.

Eating livers is a ghastly rite often associated with black magic in Southeast Asia. Over the centuries it has been practised during times of warfare to dehumanise the enemy and feed on their strength. Just

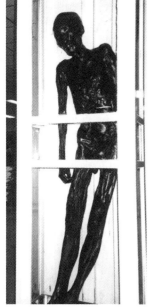

as the samurais believe that a man's courage resides in his guts (which is why the ritual suicide of *seppukko* consists of disembowelment with a sword), the troops of the ancient Khmer empire and the more recent Khmer Rouge ate the livers of their enemies to increase their strength and stamina.

See Uey's cadaver, waxed with the preservative formalin, is the most popular exhibit at the Songkran Niyomsane Forensic Medicine Museum on the grounds of Siriraj Hospital—the country's oldest medical facility—in Bangkok. The

The preserved corpse of Thailand's most infamous cannibal on display at the Songkran Niyomsane Forensic Medicine Museum in Bangkok.

cannibal's cockroach-brown corpse stands slumped in an upright glass casket off to one side of the room. The empty eye sockets, as well as the bullet holes left by the executioner's machine-gun, have been filled in with white paraffin. Beside his final resting case are several others occupied by killer rapists and murderers also sentenced to death.

Of the two actual skeletons in the museum, the one in a glass case belongs to the former chairman of the hospital's forensics department, Songkran Niyomsane, who founded the museum in 1965. "He was a true man of forensics," said Somchai with a chuckle. "He wanted the students to be able to be able to study him after he died."

Elsewhere in this academic bone-yard are Exhibits A through Z of murder weapons (knives, pliers, ropes, a hammer and a screwdriver) as well as bullets extracted from the dead during autopsies. More macabre still are the glass jars in which human foetuses, plucked from the womb after the mothers had perished, swim in formaldehyde. One jar houses a two-month-old victim of hydrocephalus with a grotesquely swollen head that makes him look like an alien's offspring. As a testament to Buddhist compassion, many Thai visitors leave dolls, candies and toys for the spirits of these kids.

Near the preserved cadavers of the mass murderers is a glass case full of skulls with bullet holes in their foreheads. There is no signage in either English or Thai to explain this display. Somboon Thamtakerngkit, the division chief of the hospital's Forensic Pathology Department, said there is a modus operandi to the morbidity. "King Rama VIII, the eldest brother of our present king, was shot in the forehead back in 1946," she said. "Not much was known about entrance and exit wounds caused by gunshots then, so they used the skulls of these unclaimed bodies for tests." The results of these early shots at forensics proved that claims of suicide were skullduggery. Riddled with question marks, the case remains Thailand's most contentious murder mystery.

But the real gallery of grotesque is the collection of autopsy photos lining the walls. They portray, in livid reds and bruising blues, exactly what an exploding grenade does to a torso, how a broken beer bottle can tear out a throat, a train sever a head, or a knife shred a woman's genitals. As repulsive as most of these images are, the doctors who work with the dead learn invaluable lessons from them to help the living. The autopsies and photos,

For early shots at forensic science, the skulls were blasted from point-blank range in attempt to solve the country's longest-running murder mystery.

Somboon noted, also assist the doctors, the police and judges to bring the perpetrators of these murders most foul to justice.

The museum doubles as an ad-hoc classroom for students boning up on forensics and anatomy. They refer to the skeletons and cadavers as *ajaan yai* ('headmasters') and *wai* them—a prayer-like gesture that is local sign language for respect and gratitude.

Professor Somchai pointed to a glass box containing the cadaver of a killer rapist. "The museum also might teach the students something else. If you commit a big crime you could end up like this," he added with a wry smile.

The Songkran Niyomsane Forensic Medicine Museum has no age restrictions. Some visitors are but schoolchildren on the eve of adolescence. Should they be allowed to witness such horrors? That is debatable. Perhaps what both the young and the old need to see are the horrendous effects of violence: not the slow-motion cinematic ballet of gunfire and falling bodies, but the ugly anatomy of real death.

In 2007, the terror trove was renovated and linked with five other facilities under the banner 'Siriraj Medical Museum 6'. For a miniscule entry fee, visitors can drink in a sobering six-pack of mortality checks and loathsome diseases.

The Ellis Pathological Museum is devoted to the pioneering work of Professor A.G. Ellis, an American who stayed in Thailand with the assistance of the Rockefeller Foundation from 1919 to 1921, and again from 1923 to 1928. He was the first pathologist in the country. Touring this museum of organs infected with cancer, hearts deadened by strokes and livers pickled with alcohol could very well make you never want to drink, smoke or eat another cholesterol-heavy cheeseburger ever again.

The squeamish and the anally retentive will have an especially foul time in the Parasitology Museum. Every worst fear and phobia any traveller ever had about the intestinal horrors lurking in Asia has been graphically outlined and exhibited: roundworms, pinworms, hookworms, whipworms and tapeworms. Idolaters of Stephen King and the medical thrillers of Robin Cook may relish opening this can of parasitic worms, but most visitors give it a miss.

Of the six facilities, it is the Forensic Medical Museum that draws the biggest crowds and, of all the exhibits, See Uey's upright casket generates the greatest number of glares and gazes. Older Thais who grew up with admonitions from their parents that are straight out of a monstrous fairy tale are hypnotised by the cannibal. Younger Thais who have seen the movies and TV shows are baffled by his tiny size. Many of the travellers and expats look stupefied by this medieval exhibition of killers on public display. After all, the crimes of the serial lady-killer Ted Bundy and the cannibalistic necrophiliac Jeffrey Dahmer were much more heinous than See Uey's, but no one ever put their corpses on display.

For all the movie frames and column inches he has racked up, See Uey remains an enigma. The only information about him in the museum is a newspaper clipping in Thai, taped to the side of his final resting case, reiterating the few known facts about him—his upbringing on Hainan, his days as a soldier, his alleged body count and his execution in 1958—along with a black-and-white mug shot in which the rodent-faced man is baring his teeth. But it's difficult to read the expression on his face. Was he mugging for the crime photographers and living up to his reputation? Is this the glower of an extraordinarily angry and embittered man? Or does he look more like a cornered rat, baring his teeth and snarling out of fear?

To answer those questions, I spent a lot of time in Chinatown, over the course of many years, writing all sorts of features and guidebook entries about the history of the area and the exodus from China that brought in tide after tide of immigrants during World War II and after the country fell to the communists in 1949. An elderly woman who sold vegetables in the 'Old Market' (little changed in the past century) told me, "There's a Thai expression about 'travelling with a pot and a mat' to describe any trip taken on the cheap. But it actually came from the fact that those were the only two things that most of us Chinese immigrants brought to Thailand. Even thinking about that journey by boat makes me seasick: stuck in a cargo hold that stank of shit and vomit and piss for months, roaches and rats everywhere." She shuddered in disgust.

"It was bad enough coming to all these foreign lands where people hated us, but our own people preyed on us too. My brothers and sisters never made it to Thailand. They were on another boat, but the sailors knew we'd be travelling with all our valuables. Once the boats were at sea, some of these pirates would rob people and throw them overboard to drown or get eaten by sharks. That's what happened to my siblings," she confided, tears glittering in her eyes.

As a 'boat person', See Uey would have shared some of those experiences.

Wen Liang, another immigrant from Hainan and a retired police officer on active duty at the time See Uey was on the loose, spoke of the xenophobia directed at the Chinese wherever they washed up after the exodus—Thailand, Malaysia, Indonesia, the United States. "There are many Thai slang terms for us. Because we were seen as 'reds' they sometimes called us 'pussy blood Chinks'. Since the communists wanted to destroy religion and the temples we were also referred to as 'the Chinks who killed the temples'. That one I still hear quite often, but some of the older expressions like 'rickshaw Chinks' and 'human animals' that were used to describe our status as the lowliest manual labourers, aren't really used anymore, except by a few older people."

As a coolie and vegetable farmer, See Uey would have also been a punching bag for many of the same jabs and swipes.

Like many people interviewed for this story, the retired cop expressed skepticism that the cannibal killed and ate as many children as he was charged with. "Let me put it this way. It would not have been difficult to pin some other unsolved murders on a poor, illiterate 'human animal'. He did confess to killing some of the children, but it's possible he may have targeted some adults, too. We found a few other corpses that had been cannibalised in Bangkok around that time, but he was never charged with those crimes or confessed to them." Slowly and solemnly, the ex-cop nodded. "We detectives are forever examining motives. Some of my colleagues in the police force interviewed him after he was arrested and they did not think he was insane. I have often wondered if his anger was not a more generalised rage against the world, mixed with a kind of sorrow that came from knowing he would never see his homeland again. Many Chinese immigrants of the time could probably identify with those misgivings."

In the forensic museum, Professor Somchai had also addressed the quandary of whether See Uey was insane at the time of his homicidal binge. He pointed to a long scar on the cadaver's forehead. "Here you can see the incision. After he was executed, they did an autopsy to see if See Uey's brain was normal, and it was. But of course it was impossible to really assess his state of mind during the period leading up to his arrest."

No matter what anyone might say to humanise this enigmatic killer, refugee, coolie and soldier, he will remain an inhuman monster—frequently compared by younger Thais to Jack the Ripper, Hannibal Lecter and Jeffrey Dahmer—while drawing crowds bound to be disappointed by the fact that his tiny shell does not live up to the monstrous legend created by cinematic hype and xenophobic overkill.

Feeding on all these different quotes and anecdotes, facts and fictions, features and guidebook entries— and after a lengthy period of indigestion—I combined a bunch of them, adding a few of my own embellishments and allusions to Franz Kafka's *The Metamorphosis*, for a novella that was long-listed for the Bram Stoker Award in 2008 (which you can read at www.bizarrethailand.com).

A Night in the Lives of
Corpse Collectors

6:30pm. In the main Bangkok office of Poh Teck Tung Foundation on Bamrung Muang Road.

A volunteer for the famous charity foundation that wheels out the ambulances and morgue-mobiles of Bangkok is flipping through a photo album of crime-scene shots and accidents. He stops at a photograph of a motorcycle lying on its side. "We found a helmet down the road from here and I went to pick it up... the driver's head was still inside the helmet." A grin curls his lips. It's either that Thai penchant for making light of the darkest situations, or this guy's had a few too many nightmares about headless motorcyclists.

7:12pm. In the videographer's pick-up truck.

Poh Teck Tung pulls in millions of baht in donations every year. Started as a tribute to a Chinese monk who lived 900 years ago, the foundation (which means 'Goodness, Merit and Remembrance') was officially founded in 1937. Donating to the organisation is good karma, says the videographer, who asked not to be named as we weave through Friday night traffic, because they help to rush the injured to the hospital and take the dead to the morgue. They also arrange coffins and funerals for the poor. If nobody claims the body, they bury the remains at their cemetery in Samut Prakan province.

Every few years, dozens of volunteers help to unearth and burn the bones of thousands of corpses in a mass cremation ceremony.

The foundation's rescue work on the blood-slicked streets of Bangkok has been documented by National Geographic TV, the BBC and CNN. When the latter network attempted to follow them around one night, their van crashed and Poh Teck Tung had to come to their rescue, the videographer says with a smug grin. It's an apt warning for the kind of driving these speed demons do. When saving a life is a matter of minutes, speed is of the essence.

A call comes in on the radio, he guns the gas and we're off, bulleting down the road like a getaway car. The speedometer needle, glowing green, creeps up... *40, 55, 80, 100*. He's too busy passing cars to talk now. And we have no idea what the emergency is.

Snapshot memories whizz by like the cars and lights. In 1997, I interviewed photographer Philip Blenkinsop about his grisly collection of black-and-white photos, *The Cars That Ate Bangkok*. Many were taken when he travelled around with Poh Teck Tung for a few weeks. The book is a horror-monger's gallery of bodies lying in the street, surrounded by chalk-line skeletons and rivulets of blood and close-ups of pulped faces. The cover shows a bloody hand hanging from the bonnet of a car, making it look as if the person has been eaten alive by what Philip refers to in the text as a 'petrol-powered beast'.

In reference to this image, the Australian photographer—who went on to win the World Press Photo Award and many others—told me, "An old woman was crossing the highway outside Bangkok when she was cut in half by a car, which was abandoned by the side of the road after the driver fled the scene. Her hand was left on the bonnet. It was unbelievably depressing."

His experiences with them had driven home the fact—and the fear—that road accidents are the leading cause of death in Thailand: an average of two people die on the roads every hour. It has one of the highest rates of traffic fatalities in the world. More tourists and expats die or are injured in road accidents than by any other means.

"It was crazy, driving at 160 kilometres an hour on a Friday night, trying to beat other body-snatchers to the cadaver. Thais won't get out of the way for an ambulance, but they will for Poh Teck Tung, so we'd often get to the accident before the police. One night I was in the back of the van with three dead bodies rolling up against me every time it turned. We'd picked up one of them from a hospital and he'd already been dead for a few days. The stench was terrible," he said.

Near a footbridge on a busy road out in some industrial suburb of Bangkok, we pull over behind a fleet of Poh Teck Tung rescue vehicles. Staff members are running towards the bridge, jogging up the stairs. A policemen stringing yellow crime-scene tape across the top of the stairs lets us pass. Then we see the body: young, male, Thai, on his back. The glare of orange streets lights lends the scene a hellish tint.

Whether he was shot in the forehead or hit with something heavy like a crescent wrench, nobody's sure. For once, there's none of that Thai cheeriness. The mood is sombre, voices drowned out by the drone and din of traffic. Speculation runs rife that it might be a drug-related killing, or possibly a mugging—common on footbridges—

gone violently wrong. The dead man, in his faded T-shirt and rubber flip-flops, may have lost his life... for a few hundred baht?

A few members of Poh Teck Tung kneel down beside the corpse, pointing at the fatal wound, while a crime photographer from the police propaganda magazine, *191* (the emergency line in Thailand), takes some blood money snaps. A few of the cops standing by look lost in troubled thoughts. *Who's going to have to tell his family?*

11:02 pm. Ram Intra Road.
A dozen volunteers from the foundation, half of them female, are sitting around beside a mini-mart and petrol station, near one of the most accident-prone roads in Bangkok. Anchana is relating some of her experiences as a nurse's assistant in a Bangkok Emergency Room, which encourages them to relate the grisly details of their work.

One volunteer shows off a prominent tattoo of the foundation's emblem on his forearm. Another man, Kitti Cheounarom, says he's been volunteering for ten years now while waiting on a lengthy list for a position among the 200 paid workers.

One night, he says, they received a call from a guy who'd been taking a piss in someone's backyard and smelled the stench of decomposition. Members of Poh Teck Tung dug up the backyard and found some bones. A minute later, an elderly woman opened the back door and yelled at them, "What the hell are you doing? I buried my dog out there a few weeks ago!"

Kitti and the crew double over with laughter. In a high-pressure job like this, black humour is the best safety valve.

2:58am. Poh Teck Tung Hospital on Bamrung Muang Road.

We've been waiting here for hours now. The videographer is asleep in the front seat, Anchana has gone home, and a French photojournalist and I are sitting on the curb beside the pick-up truck, chatting about Thailand's other main group of volunteer rescue workers, the Ruamkatanyu Foundation. Their main office is on the corner of Surawong and Rama IV Road, right beside Wat Hua Lamphong.

I tell Remy how Anchana and I donated a few hundred baht to the lady at the counter and received two pieces of paper to write our names on. In another room were stacks of empty coffins. Following the other donors, we glued the pink slips to one of them. Connected to the office is a Chinese-style shrine. Here, we lit sticks of incense for deities such as the Tiger God, then burnt the other pieces of paper with our names on them to make merit for the dead. Within the span of ten minutes, there were about 15 people performing the same ritual.

One of the ladies in the office gave us a brochure about the foundation, witten in both Thai and English. Among the old photos of train wrecks and visitors from the royal family is a brief history of the foundation. During World War II, a teenager named Somkieat Somsakulrungruang was aghast at the sight of all the dead bodies and the walking wounded he saw around the Tha Tien Pier, close to the Grand Palace and the Temple of the Emerald Buddha. Allied bombers had shelled the area again and again. Somkieat, whose leg was severely lacerated by a bomb fragment, helped to collect the corpses.

Those physical and psychological wounds may have scarred him for life, but they also opened him up to the suffering of others. Years later, when he was running a small shop in the Bangkok slum of Khlong Toey, Somkieat allowed his poor customers to pay on credit. One of these labourers told him he could not afford the 80 baht to buy a coffin for his cousin. Somkieat agreed to pay for the coffin and to sponsor a religious ceremony for the deceased. With the help of his wife, Rattana, and Dr. Roj Chotirungruang, Somkieat formed the Ruamkatanyu Foundation in 1970, to not only pick up the dead and tend to the dying, but also train fire-fighters and rescue divers.

Across the country, they now have 3,000 staff and volunteers, as well as 40 rescue vehicles. True to Somkieat's original mission, they still provide free coffins and cremation services. The needy and the grieving can contact the branch office at Wat Hualamphong, which is open 24 hours a day throughout the week.

All of a sudden, a voice crackles over the radio and the videographer, who's been sleeping in the front seat, bolts upright, revs the ignition, and beckons for me and the photographer to jump in. Within ten minutes, we're entering the military barracks near the Samsen Railway Station.

Hundreds of soldiers and their families live in these concrete cinder blocks. There are no balconies, only long open-air hallways. Up on the fifth floor, standing on a ledge, is a soldier dressed in shorts and a T-shirt. A policeman standing about five metres to his left—we can only see his head and cap—is trying to talk him down. Surrounding us are a dozen ambulances from different hospitals and other charity foundations and at least 40 or 50 staff, volunteers and curious bystanders. Everyone's getting cramps in their necks and taking shallow breaths as we stand around like a pack of hyenas waiting for him to jump.

In the local press, it's no secret that battle-lines have been drawn up between rival foundations and they've even carved up parts of the city like street gangs. But if they're charity groups, why are they scrapping over cadavers?

"That's a really hazy, sketchy topic," Philip Blenkinsop told me. "The nice way to put it is that people know how many bodies the foundations bring in, so to make more merit they'll donate more money to them. But I've also heard that some foundations have deals with hospitals to bring accident victims in and that even if there's a hospital nearby they'll take them to one five kilometres away."

In this regard, they are certainly no worse than the doctors at some Thai hospitals who refuse to treat badly injured patients if they do not have the cash or credit cards to pay for the treatment.

Defending the much-maligned 'body snatchers' (as they're occasionally called), Philip said that he has seen members of Poh Teck Tung save lives. "They also took really good care of me out there."

As we watch the policeman talking to the soldier on the ledge, I hear a few bystanders asking what his room number is so in the case that he dies, they can use the digits to choose lottery tickets. It's the same superstitious deal with the license plates of accident victims.

Not until I taste the coppery flavour of my own blood do I realise that I've been gnawing on my bottom lip for the last few minutes and my neck is aching from staring up at the ledge. For some much-needed comic relief, a male medic from one of the other charity foundations begins chatting me up. I ask him, "Who's the soldier up there? Do you know what's happened to him?"

"He's just a psycho. Do you want to go for a cocktail after?"

There's something about the way he said 'cocktail' that made it sound like the most frightful of double-entendres.

Just then, with a whoosh of air-brakes, a fire truck pulls in. Excellent, finally some action. The firemen inflate a huge yellow bag and place it directly under the soldier. Our muscle tension slackens. Interest wavers. People look away, talk, light cigarettes. Soon the policeman coaxes the soldier off the ledge. He's handcuffed, brought downstairs and put into a police truck. I'm not sure why he's getting arrested. Perhaps it has something to with the Buddhist belief about suicide being worse than murder.

In a way, everyone looks relieved.

In another perverse way, we're all disappointed.

One of the crime photographers complains, with the dark humour that is a necessary evil in this line of work, "If he would've jumped I could've gotten paid 1,000 baht for the photo. I guess I won't be going out drinking this weekend." A few of the other photographers laugh as they put away their cameras.

I'm exhausted and exasperated, too. It's late and I don't have a suitably gory climax for my story. On the other hand, at least the medic with the cocktail shaker has melted into the night.

4:07am. Driving back to their office with the videographer and Remy. That first murder scene of the night is still tattooed in my memory.

The young man lying there on his back. The wound on his forehead. The cheap flip-flops. The hellfire orange of the street lights above the footbridge.

Who was he? Who murdered him? Will there even be an investigation into his death? Will any relatives claim his body?

The staff and volunteers of Poh Teck Tung live with these agonising questions every night. I tell the videographer that the best thing about most jobs is that you can go home and forget about them. He smiles sadly and says that's not the case with his work.

"We've saved a lot of people but the cases that haunt you are all the dead souls. One night we got called to the scene of a school bus crash a few hours outside Bangkok... absolutely horrific. Body parts were scattered everywhere and these kids were only nine or ten.

"When I was walking around the bus, this little girl who I thought was dead stood up and came staggering towards me. For a few seconds I thought I was actually seeing a ghost. But she only took about six or seven steps before blood began pouring out of her mouth and down the front of her school uniform. Then she fell straight on her face. By the time I checked her pulse, she was already dead."

Headlights flicker across the videographer's face. A face rutted and potholed. A face that's seen too many murders, catastrophes and the drinking binges that provide some short-term amnesia. He looks a decade older than his 50 years. "That accident happened almost a decade ago, but it still gives me nightmares sometimes. It's still so fresh in my mind that it could have happened tonight."

MISADVENTURE
TRAVELS

From Ayuthaya to Bangkok:
A Bizarre Expat Odyssey

When Jerry Hopkins—the man who wrote the book on rock biographies with tomes on Elvis, Jim Morrison and Jimi Hendrix—moved to Bangkok in 1993 in search of a "high-energy city with a damn interesting expat community", he walked into Nana Plaza—wall-to-wall and floor-to-floor with go-go bars—for a drink on his first night. Then he struck up a conversation with the man at the next table, who turned out to be the Oscar-winning screenwriter who had, in the 1970s, blueprinted the still-exploding genre of 'disaster movies' with scripts for *The Towering Inferno* and *The Poseidon Adventure*, as well as found acting jobs for his martial arts instructor, a then-obscure actor named Bruce Lee.

"When he told me his name, I said, 'You're Stirling Silliphant? No shit?' He said, 'That's not the usual reaction I get, but never mind.'"

Many of the expats Jerry profiled and later included in a book called *Bangkok Babylon*, he met in bars. They form a cast of colourful and eccentric expat characters—a CIA operative who moonlights as a movie fixer, the world's foremost expert on the Asian elephant who spent years living in the Thai jungle with them, and a classical pianist who ended up as the most hunted pedophile in the world.

Ever since the days of Ayuthaya, when the Siamese city surrounded by a natural moat of three rivers outshone Paris and London (earning the nickname the 'Venice of the Far East'), the country has welcomed countless adventurers, merchants, artists, traders, libertines, criminals and financial prospectors. In the National Discovery Museum Institute in Bangkok, multimedia exhibits document the influence of the West and Far East on Siam during its golden heydays of Ayuthaya (1350–1767). The Dutch, British, Indians, French, Vietnamese, Portuguese, Chinese and Japanese are all depicted in stereotypical fashion, along with their contributions to this grand port city: the Europeans brought firearms, alcohol and luxury goods, the Chinese packed tea leaves and ceramics, while the Indians stitched up the trade in textiles. An exhibit notes, 'The Siamese state designated an area of settlement within the city for each of the major peoples. Here they could form communities and live according to their own customs.'

That openness and tolerance has rarely changed. Nor has Siam's welcome mat ever been rolled up except for those periods when it was trampled by invaders like the Burmese and Japanese, or pulled out from under the feet of foreigners by rabble-rousing nationalists, such as after the economic crash of 1997 when Western materialism was denigrated by ads showing neckties as nooses and corkscrews as murder weapons. A favourite Thai joke of the time was, 'What does IMF [the International Monetary Fund] stand for? I am fucked.'

Even today, the sizable expat community—numbering

anywhere from 250,000 to 300,000—has retained a certain autonomy to live as they please. And the maverick entrepreneurs first drawn to the kingdom's shores some four centuries ago continue to come in search of business and hedonism. Take Kevin Noah Windfield, for example. A finance broker on Wall Street, Kevin was sent to Thailand in the early 1990s by a firm anxious to capitalise on the country's double-digit fiscal growth that inspired a *Newsweek* cover story entitled 'Thailand's Economic Miracle'. After coming to the country on and off for more than five years, the native of New York and New Jersey became 'semi-permanently based here' in 1999, before being confronted with the classic expat conundrum—*should I stay or go*? Because he did not graduate from an Ivy League school and does not have a bankable surname, Kevin realised he was battering his head against a low career ceiling on Wall Street. "Better to be a big fish in a small pond here than a little fish in a big pond back home," he reckoned.

If he had stayed in the States, the casino-like odds against him ever owning a small business would have been dicey at best. Nor would he have had the chance to travel through India, Australia, Indonesia and Cambodia, meet two American presidents in Bangkok (George W. Bush greeted him with, "Hey, big guy.") and have a five-star lunch with the former CEO of General Motors, Rick Wagoner. "I asked him if he could bring affordable Hummers to Thailand. He laughed and offered to sell me the entire company," said Kevin, still looking a little awestruck by his encounter with the man who was at the wheel when GM crashed and burned in what amounted to the largest corporate bankruptcy in American history.

In starting his own business, the Manhattan Asset Management Co Ltd, Kevin took advantage of the long-standing relationship between America and Siam. In 1833, the two countries signed the Treaty of Commerce and Amity. It was the first treaty the US signed with an Asian power, further opening Siam to Western influences, after the kingdom had previously inked treaties with the Portuguese in 1511, the Spanish in 1598, the Dutch in 1604 and the English in 1826, once the final shots of the first Anglo-Burmese war were fired.

Signed in 1966, the Treaty of Amity and Economic Relations allows Americans the opportunity to own certain kinds of businesses outright. That treaty was signed in the midst of a burgeoning American military presence as four big military bases were constructed by the Americans in northeast Thailand during the 1960s, when the Westernisation of modern-day Thailand began in earnest. (Until this point, the Thai slang term for 'trendy' was based on the English word 'postcard', pronounced *bosacar*, because most of what was known about the outside world came from the mailbox.)

The composer and symphony conductor Somtow Suchartikul (better known in the West as the horror and sci-fi novelist S. P. Somtow) grew up on Sukhumvit Soi 24 in the 1960s when the area was still awash with rice fields. "Our greatest cultural influences then were American. The TV channels at the time showed programs like *Leave it to Beaver* and *The Twilight Zone*," he said. At the time, Thai gangsters like the notorious Daeng Bailey (nicknamed after the soft drink he loved) sported Elvis-emulating coifs and hung around American-looking bars, dancing to rock 'n' roll with Thai women in beehive hairdos. (American rock culture of the 1950s is also featured in an exhibit at the National Discovery Museum Institute, nicknamed the Museum of Siam.)

Somtow, who first rose to infamy in the 1970s by combining the strains of Western symphonies with Thai classical music—a local taxi driver once chased him down the street for daring to create such a cacophonous racket—is a mascot for how the nation has always flavored the ingredients of other cultures with distinctively and piquantly Thai spices. A short video in the Museum of Siam illustrates how the street sweets known as *foy thong*—golden strands made from the yolk of duck eggs and coconut—are of Portuguese descent. So is chilli for that matter. The museum's exhibition on the quintessence of 'Thainess' has a *tuk-tuk*. Actually, these 'flatulent' vehicles are a Japanese invention given a Thai spin; the *pad thai* noodles were brought to Thailand by Vietnamese vendors in the 1920s; the parliamentary system is British; the royal barges and classical dances came from the Khmer; and the injustice system is hopelessly mired in Third World venality.

From time to time, these expat contributions and influences—particularly the American variety—have been scorned and shunned by Thai thinkers and politicians. Thailand's leading architect, Sumet Jumsai, who designed the Robot Building on

Sathorn Road and *The Nation* structures on the edge of Bangkok, lived in France and studied architecture at Cambridge, before returning to his homeland in 1967. "There were American military bases in Thailand for bombing Vietnam, so I was very angry when I first came back. But I could only write articles in English so I suppose our generals—dictators—must've thought, 'Oh, he's quite harmless', because nobody reads English here."

"That was the first big boom period in Thailand and the red-light districts in Patpong and Pattaya got started because of all the American GIs. It was much more negative than positive, but we've only adopted the negative side of America here. I know the good side of America more than most Thai people because I've been there... America is a wonderful concept."

Yet, American involvement in foreign countries has always been a double-edged bowie knife. Thank the CIA for helping to get the first big office tower in Bangkok off the ground. Built in 1969, the Chockchai International Building (near the Emporium on Sukhumvit Road) was equipped with the most efficient communications system at that time in the whole country, perhaps even in all of Southeast Asia. The 24-floor structure laid down the template for the construction boom to come, with the first air-conditioning system, an elevator and internal phones. Once again, Thai ingenuity rose to the fore as architect Rangsarn Torsuwan designed the building so it could withstand the tropical heat.

The surge of expats and tourists resulted in the formation of the Tourist Organisation of Thailand in 1960 (now the Tourism

Authority of Thailand). That year, the country notched up 81,000 arrivals. By the early 1970s, those figures had risen tenfold. The proliferation of sex and drug tours gave Bangkok its sleazy image, which still persists, and the budding popularity of homegrown marijuana (colloquially known as 'Thai stick' or 'Buddha stick' in the West) yielded the only Thai word ever loaned to the English language: *bong*. Byron Bales, a former Marine-turned-insurance investigator and private detective recalled landing at Don Muang International Airport in Bangkok "when there was still a dirt runway in the '60s and I could carry my gun on the plane. Many of the cases I worked in the '60s and '70s were about young Westerners overdosing on drugs in Thailand."

Tourists, drug dealers and opportunists make for a perverse threesome. Among the new arrivals following the wealth of the traveller's trail was the notorious serial killer Charles Sobhraj. Living off Silom Road in Bangkok, the Vietnamese-Indian's hunting ground encompassed the upscale hotels in the area, where he sold gems for exorbitant sums and cajoled tourists into staying with him for months on end, ensuring their compliance by drugging and poisoning them. After two white women in bathing suits were found strangled on the beach in Pattaya, the perpetrator was dubbed the 'Bikini Killer' by the local press. But Sobhraj, who allegedly paid the Thai police a US$15,000 bribe and fled the country, continued to kill backpackers and steal their identities, before being apprehended in India while attempting to drug a whole busload of French tourists.

The presence of all those American troops sowing their wild oats on Thai soil also gave rise to a second coming of the mixed-marriage phenomenon, not seen since the days of Ayuthaya. Some Thais denigrated these local women as *mia chao* ('rented wives'), but, in their own unwitting way, the GIs and their partners were psychosexual pioneers. As the northeast became a breeding ground for both love and war, the number of mixed couples, and their offspring, grew exponentially.

Those unions are still spiking. A 2008 study by the National Economic and Social Development Board (NESDB) revealed that there were almost 30,000 women in the northeast married to foreigners. Most, but certainly not all, of the men are of retirement age. According to the NESDB, the foreign Romeos have pumped some 14 billion baht into local coffers and created around 650,000 jobs.

Across the 19 provinces of Isaan, there are now enclaves of foreigners, invariably nicknamed 'Soi Farang' (a road of 'white foreigners'). Unofficial estimates state that the number of *farang*-Thai households across the region may number 100,000, or about three per cent of the married populace. Many of these expats have been reduced to a stereotype, based on a morality tale, and retold as a dirty joke. In this case, one size does not fit all. Steve, a young Brit in his early 30s, who has his own IT business he runs from the Northeast, is hardly a caricature of the obese and lecherous, *homo erectus* species known as the 'sexpat'. Married to a local woman with whom he has two children, Steve (who did not want to give his surname), said he prefers the friendly, pastoral and easy-going life in the Thai hinterlands, to the dreary city and sullen people he left behind in London.

Still, the clichés about men like him do rankle. "Many people think that our girlfriends or wives are only with us because of the money, but Western women are incredibly materialistic these days. In places like Singapore or Hong Kong you've got what Chinese women call the four Cs—'cash, credit cards, a condo and car'—which they look for in male partners. So materialism is a facet of relationships everywhere and the fact is, many foreign husbands treat their wives a lot better than some Thai men do, and there's far fewer incidents of domestic violence," said Steve, a former falconer who once taught fencing in Korea.

Read the memoirs and chronicles of the merchants and expatriates from centuries ago and those references to 'beautiful, languorous women' persist, as does the fascination with a land where elephants are part of an extended family, where spirits haunt banana trees and a hedonistic populace alternates between gentility and extreme bursts of violence. As author Jerry Hopkins said, "The beautiful women are both the cheese and the trap, but if you stay long enough you find plenty of other things to think and write about."

Jerry, whose first rock biography on Elvis was suggested to him by his drinking buddy Jim Morrison of The Doors (who subsequently became the subject of his number-one bestseller *No One Here Gets Out Alive*), also lived with a local transsexual streetwalker in Hawaii. This is a man with almost superhuman tolerance levels for debauchery and strangeness. Out of all the stories he compiled for his non-fiction collection *Thailand Confidential*, the weirdest tale, he said, came from watching a sex-change operation in Bangkok. "I don't know anyone who's done that." The operation took place when a friend of his ex came to town for an operation that has become so globally renowned that Thai Customs and Immigrations has considered adding a box for 'Gender Reassignment Surgery' to the list of reasons for visit. In *Venus Envy*, he wrote, "Dr. Preecha then turned his attention to the penis, skinning and removing most of the interior and leaving the hollow flap of skin still attached to the body. The end and open side were then sewn to form a kind of sleeve, which then was pushed into the vaginal cavity, an act that gives this procedure its medical name 'penile inversion'."

Around the time Jerry arrived, the English-language press began to flourish with a number of new magazines and a third English daily. For many of us aspiring writers and editors, the *Thailand Times* was a journalism school. It would not be hyperbole to call this the worst and most preposterous English daily that has ever existed anywhere. During the paper's reign of errors from 1993 to 1998, one of the most famous was the front-page gaffe showing a photo from the gruesome Easter celebrations in the Philippines of a stand-in for a Roman centurion staring up at a surrogate Christ who is crucified on a wooden cross. The photo caption reads: 'Prime Minister Chuan Leekpai chats with Foreign Minister Prasong Soonsiri during a break at parliament.' The actual photo of the Thai politicians had the caption from the Philippines.

Because the majority of the Thai layout artists did not speak much English, these kinds of errors were common. On the features page I edited, they somehow managed to put the cover of a book written by the Pope upside down. No one mentioned the error. Even the head honchos and the staff did not read the paper. As far as I remember the only complaint we ever received was from a high-ranking minister in the government of Laos, who was in Bangkok for an economic forum. He was irate that the paper had referred to his government—this was a joke between two sub-editors that was supposed to be edited out—as the 'Lao People's Undemocratic Republic'.

Because our deadlines were so early, we often missed important late-breaking stories. Although the masthead referred to the paper as the 'Voice of the New Generation', most of the staffers referred to it as 'Yesterday's News Tomorrow'.

Where else would a major English daily like this be allowed to exist? (As it turned out, the company needed one English-language publication in its portfolio to get listed on the Dow Jones Stock Exchange.)

The *Thailand Times*' most trenchant wit-in-residence, Cameron Cooper, came up with headlines that even a British or American tabloid would have found in bad taste. After John Wayne Bobbitt's battered wife famously castrated him, and they reattached his penis only it did not function properly, Cameron titled the story, 'John Wayne's Six Gun Only a Pee Shooter'. After country star Tammy Wynette (best known for the single 'Stand By Your Man') was hospitalised with bowel cancer, Cameron entitled that story, 'Tammy Stands By Her Pan'. And as if that wasn't enough, when Jack Lord, the star of the TV detective series *Hawaii Five-O*—whose tagline was 'Book 'em Dano'—passed away and was cremated, the incorrigible Canadian headlined that snippet, 'Cook 'em Dano'.

Riddled with mistakes and laced with obscenities, this only-ever-in-Thailand publication gave many of us the opportunity to report on the repercussions of the boom-in-progress, as the first Cineplex and the first Tower Records opened in 1994, as 500 new cars and 1,000 motorcycles came on the streets of Bangkok every day, as the city resembled a gigantic construction site with the worst air pollution in the world, and as the second invasion of British bands first came to Bangkok with gigs by Suede, the Manic Street Preachers and Radiohead.

All the groups played in a hall above the MBK shopping mall. When the crowd began leaping up and down to Radiohead, the entire roof of the mall began buckling so shoppers fled for their lives. I was there to review the gig, but the crowd surged backwards when Radiohead started, knocking my pen and notebook out of my hand only ten seconds into the show. But in Thailand, a country where motorcyclists make mudguards out of tree branches and people put plastic bags on their heads during the rainy season, you have to learn how to improvise and discard any formalities that don't harmonise with the merriment of the moment. I yelled in the ear of a fellow staffer, Pradip, to remember more or less what songs they played in more or less what order, and then we leaped into the dancing melee of what was one of the weirdest crowds I've ever seen at a gig. Many of the kids were wearing Sid Vicious T-shirts and dog collars. Some had used food dye to colour their hair and combed them into Mohawks. A few of the college kids were still wearing their uniforms. And almost everyone on the dance floor was pogoing up and down like it was a punk rock gig in London in 1977—except they were all smiling and laughing. The clothes and the safety pins didn't matter, the constant bombardment of Western culture and music videos didn't matter, even the anguished music of Radiohead didn't really matter: it was still a distinctly Thai event. Five centuries of Western and Asian imperialism had done almost nothing to tarnish those smiley facades.

Through another bizarre series of circumstances that only seem to happen in Bangkok, I ended up ferrying two members of the group back to their hotel room in a three-wheeled taxi known as a *tuk-tuk*. Singer Thom Yorke said, "That was the happiest crowd we've ever played to." Guitarist Ed O'Brien chimed in with, "When we played 'Creep' it was like being in a massive karaoke bar. Who smiles to a song like that?"

Both Thom and Ed were impressed by the fact we could drink in the backseat of this glorified golf cart and that the driver, upon learning they were from England, wanted to know what their favourite football teams were. Once or twice Thom smiled. He made a few jokes with the driver and he actually laughed too. Yes, Thom Yorke, often referred to as 'that miserable bastard from Radiohead', had caught a Bangkok joy buzz. Instead of going back to their hotel room, Ed and Thom decided they wanted to see some of the city's historic sites and monuments. Neither of them was interested in the nightlife or girly bars. "We've been to Amsterdam, mate." So we spent the next few hours cruising past Democracy Monument, the Grand Palace and Parliament Buildings, while they gave me an exclusive backseat interview and we carried on drinking for a few hours. When I dropped them back at their hotel, Thom said, "This is a brilliant city. You're lucky to live here."

But our quest to find the British Club that night had gone awry. The club's lineage is an expat history lesson in itself. Begun more than a century ago, it was based on Victorian coffee houses, where women were forbidden to enter, said Warwick Newton, one of the members of the elected general committee. "It's only been about 20 years since women were allowed to drink here and granted full membership rights."

During World War II, the club was commandeered by the Japanese military, which destroyed many of the archives and vintage photos. "I've heard stories, perhaps apocryphal," Warwick said, "that expats and some of the club's members were also arrested and interred in dreadful Bangkok prisons, where the Thais treated these prisoners much better than the Japanese did."

The British Club reopened in 1946. Located off Silom Road, the venue's original, colonial-style buildings and fixtures are still intact. Approximately 60 per cent of the 1,000 members hail from Commonwealth countries (Britain, Australia, New Zealand and Canada), who must compose the majority. But if you look at any of the photos from their events or sports tournaments, you will see a multi-nationality contingent of Indians, Europeans, Thais and other Asians. They even have a bagpipe band. "We try not to discriminate, and drinking ability will make you a strong candidate for membership in the British Club," said Warwick with a laugh.

Warwick is one of those life-long expats you meet in Thailand, who worked in footwear manufacturing for companies such as Nike, where he was posted to Vietnam, India and Eastern Europe, but finally returned to Thailand for the people and the climate (those meat-locker winters in the Czech Republic still give him chills), as well as the Jekyll and Hyde life of dividing his time between a house he owns in the rural Northeast ("It's a bolt-hole really."), and the metropolitan madhouse of Bangkok.

As subdued and old guard as the British Club can be, its annual events take on a distinctly Thai slant. At a recent Guy Fawkes Night, the burning of the effigy, the fireworks and the food were most British, but the entertainment was supplied by a troupe of young Thai dancers and sword-fighters, musicians and acrobats from a Bangkok orphanage, performing against a diorama of a London skyline punctured by Big Ben and edged with fairy lights. None of the English people on hand stiffened their upper lips about the lack of traditional British entertainment on tap. As Ben Hopkins, the Birmingham-born editor of *Traversing the Orient* magazine, said, "Sure beats Morris dancers. No sane English person can enjoy them."

Among the expatriates of Thailand, the British are vastly

outnumbered by the Japanese, who remain the largest demographic. Around 46,000 nationals are registered with the Japanese embassy in Bangkok, but unofficial estimates put the total at twice that. During the Ayuthaya era, the Siamese court prized the Japanese, and the samurais in particular, for their military expertise. By fighting alongside the Siamese, Yamada Nagasama, the head of the few-thousand strong Japanese colony, rose through the ranks to become the governor of Nakhon Si Thammarat, which the one-time pirate and deerskin trader administered with the help of 300 samurai. A statue in Ayuthaya's Japanese Village, which demarcates the old settlement, shows Yamada dressed as a Siamese soldier.

The Japanese also committed the gravest slaughter of expatriates and Thais in the 20th century with the building of the 'Death Railway' from Kanchanaburi to Burma. Working by hand, Allied POWs and conscripted labourers (many of them Thai) carved a railway line out of malarial jungles, tunnelling through rock and working by torchlight, which gave 'Hellfire Pass' its name. Officially, around 16,000 POWs and 90,000 Asians perished, but the unofficial numbers are much higher.

By far the most moving chronicle of that tragedy I've ever read is *The Railway Man* by Eric Lomax. A signals officer in the British army, Lomax was brought before the Japanese secret police in Kanchanaburi after being caught with a concealed map and radio. The tortures he suffered were so traumatic that he could not even begin writing about them until the early 1990s. Of all his captors and tormentors, he came to despise the young interpreter Nagase

Takashi most of all. The interpreter never touched him, but for decades he would hear echoes of that cold, inhuman voice, "Lomax you will be killed", spawning vengeful fantasies of beating the interpreter with the same pickaxes and pipes the secret police had used on him, then caging him under the boiling sun for days on end while red ants feasted on his flesh, like the Japanese had also done to the railway engineer.

While writing his memoir the Scotsman received an 'extraordinarily beautiful' and contrite letter from Nagase, asking to meet him on the fabled 'Bridge Over the River Kwai'. Unbeknownst to him, Nagase, equally tormented by guilt, had helped the Allied War Commission identity the graves of some 13,000 POWs buried in the shadows of the railway over the course of seven weeks after the war ended. Nagase then became a vehement anti-war campaigner, speaking out against not only the Japanese Imperial Army but the emperor as well. Using his own money, he built war memorials in different parts of Thailand and a 'Buddhist Peace Temple' near the River Kwai. Beginning in 1976, Nagase organised a series of reunions between former POWs and members of the Japanese army on the bridge that symbolised all they had fought and died for. Towards the end of his memoir, in a scene fraught with high-wire tension, Lomax recalled their emotional reunion on the River Kwai Bridge in 1993, almost five decades after they'd last seen each other, under very different circumstances. Unexpectedly, it was the Scotsman who had to console the weeping and profusely apologetic Nagase. In what must be the most unlikely ending to any chronicle of war, guaranteed to melt the hardest of hearts, Lomax and his wife accepted an invitation to visit the former English professor in Japan, where the two men finally buried the hatchet and forged an enduring friendship.

Part of Japan's post-war reparations involved the setting up of the Japan International Cooperation Agency (JICA). From Mongolia to Madagascar, the agency has put that famous Japanese technical wizardry to work, with various transport and infrastructure projects getting off the drawing board in Thailand. They also financed the building, and oversaw the construction of the Japanese Village in Ayuthaya in 2005. Working with their office in Bangkok for nine years, Eri Nigasaki first came to Thailand as a teenaged backpacker, which has become a rite of passage for many young Japanese. Speaking about the roots she has put down in her transplanted homeland, Eri said, "It's an easier way of life with less stress. You can talk about everything here. It's not so closed as Japan. And you don't have to wake up at 5am and then work until you catch the last train home." She grinned. "Sometimes I like to stay out late drinking with my friends and get up late, but I couldn't do that in Japan."

Living in Thailand has been a bonanza of strange opportunities for her, from playing a traditional Irish drum in a Celtic band doing regular shows in Bangkok to being a cover girl on a local travel magazine, and showing up on the first date with her current boyfriend covered in blood and flecks of glass glistening in her hair. "The taxi driver was too busy talking to me so he didn't see the car in front of us. I wasn't wearing a seatbelt and my head crashed into the windshield. But another taxi driver let me get in his cab. I didn't want to be impolite so I thought I should go to the pub and apologise to Peter for being late before I went to the hospital." She smiled and cringed simultaneously. "Thai people are so kind. The driver let me bleed all over his taxi."

Bangkok's notorious edginess, softened by Thai politeness, is a running motif when expats start trading their most bizarre stories. Ellen Boonstra, a former IT professional in Holland who later worked as a business analyst in Tokyo, before gravitating towards magazine journalism in Bangkok and then becoming a consultant in Thailand for Garde (one of the top Japanese interior design firms), recalled the bloodless coup of 2006, "All the TV channels went off the air before a message flashed up on the blank screens, which my Thai friends translated as, 'We have taken control of the city. Apologies for the inconvenience.' It was really sweet of them to apologise like that. Then a group of generals with royalist armbands appeared on the screen to say they'd ousted the prime minister and seized power."

Having never seen a tank before, her mother wanted to go to Government House the next day. Ellen followed the day after that, astonished by the fact that she could have her photos taken with the soldiers and even climb on a tank to hold the gun turret. "It was almost a tourist attraction kind of thing, with soldiers handing out bottles of water," said Ellen, who is part of an 8,000-strong Dutch community in Bangkok.

But tourists and expats also thronged Government House in

2008 when it was squatted for several months by yellow-shirted protestors, and two years later when the red shirts occupied the glitzy area of Bangkok known as Ratchaprasong. Some of the foreigners came for a vicarious thrill, some came to express solidarity with the protestors, and a loathsome few used it as an excuse for acts of malignant violence and vandalism. That also hasn't changed since the golden heydays of Ayuthaya, as free and easy Thailand provides expatriates with endless opportunities to reinvent themselves. Like Jim Thompson, the CIA spook turned silk trader who disappeared in the Cameron Highlands in 1967, or Charles Sobhraj who sunk into crime and depravity, or even the famously powerful and wealthy Bill Heinecke—the son of a war correspondent in Bangkok—who rose above the mainstream and became a captain of industry and Thai citizen after building a business empire in retail, hospitality and fast food, which has seen him valued at US$400 million.

And the expatriates still keep coming. While I was talking to author Jerry Hopkins outside the Old Dutch Restaurant at the end of Soi Cowboy, he pointed at the pharmacy across the street. "They shot some of the scenes from *Bangkok Dangerous* there. That's where Nicholas Cage's girlfriend worked in the movie. I watched them shooting 'cause my friend Jim Newport was working on the set." (A set designer in Hollywood, Jim recast himself as a vampire novelist in Bangkok.) "Some of the old CIA spook bars on Patpong are still there like the Madrid and the Crown Royal, but the older ones are dead now."

Did Jerry think that the expat community has gotten more conservative and less colourful in Thailand?

"No, the other week I met the guy who came up with the infamous 'Twinkie defense'. He's been living in Bangkok on and off for quite a few years."

Jerry was referring to the trial of Dan White, a Vietnam vet, cop and firefighter elected to the San Francisco Board of Supervisors. In 1978, White shot and killed San Francisco Mayor George Moscone and his fellow supervisor, Harvey Milk, America's first openly gay politician and the subject of the biopic *Milk* (played by Sean Penn). But White only received five years in jail for manslaughter, partly because of the half-baked defense insisting that his diet of sugar-saturated Twinkies was a symptom of depression.

It was 10pm on a Friday night. Most 75-year-olds would be at home dozing in their easy chairs or talking to their cats. Not Jerry. Not in Bangkok. He was off to see a group I'd never heard of called Peter Driscoll and the Cruisers at a bar on Silom Soi 4. "You have to see Pete. He played the working class pubs of England for 40 years. The band's great and he's got an Aussie bass-player. It's pure rockabilly!"

Just when the jaded and calloused old hands of Bangkok think they've seen, heard, groped and grasped it all—the city is now a rotating bandstand for an unsung rockabilly singer that opened shows for gods of the genre like Eddie Cochrane and Gene Vincent; and a winter retreat for a lawyer whose ingenius defence has become one of the most often-repeated legal slang terms of the last three decades.

In the suite dedicated to Graham Greene (*The Quiet American*) in the Oriental Hotel, there is a framed letter he wrote. "Almost anything may happen and one may meet almost anybody, from a mere author to an international crook on his way elsewhere." Greene was writing about the Bangkok hotel, but he may as well have been penning a diary entry for any expat who ever resided in ancient Ayuthaya or modern-day Thailand.

Weekend Warriors:
Military Tourism in Thailand

During the 2010 protests on the streets of Bangkok when thousands of red-shirted demonstrators squatted in the ritzy area of Rachaprasong, gaggles of travellers and tour groups shepherded by Thai guides descended on the danger zone, walking past barricades of tyres spiked with bamboo spears and brambles of razor wire, through checkpoints where their bags were searched for firearms, and into an atmosphere that almost resembled a temple fair. Vendors hawked sunglasses, T-shirts and red, heart-shaped clappers. Noodle stalls served up bowls of soup. On the stage, in between leaders delivering diatribes attacking the government as a 'dictatorship' and, in displays of schoolyard bravado mocking the prime minister's virility and sexual preferences, the crowds danced, cheered and grinned to the tune of the heartsick love songs that have long dominated the Thai pop charts.

None of the tourists could have missed the glaring disparity between the haves and the have-nots, reflected by the sight of hundreds of rural folks camped out beneath signs for designer brands in the soon-to-be-torched-and-gutted CentralWorld, where few of them could ever have afforded to shop. Many visitors also spotted a familiar figure walking through the crowd. Clad in army fatigues, the rogue general nicknamed 'Seh Daeng' was besieged by admirers. Group after group of Thais wanted their photos taken with the soldier who had defied army orders to become the red shirts' security chief—a man who frequently boasted about how many communists he had killed in the 1970s; a man whose plan to oust the yellow-shirted protestors from government house in 2008 involved dropping snakes on them from helicopters.

But the general-gone-AWOL did not command such respect from the downtrodden for these dubious deeds and plans. Many of the protestors I interviewed expressed variations on a similar theme: at last someone in power had come over to their side; at last someone with military and political clout was treating them with respect and consideration. To be fair, the yellow shirts and the urbanites of Bangkok charged that the protestors were being paid by former prime minister Thaksin Shinawatra and used as pawns to checkmate the government on a political chessboard.

In person, it was difficult to dislike the charismatic and congenial soldier. Seh Daeng smiled and shook my hand. Patiently and politely, he answered all of the questions I fired off in Thai. And he was equally considerate to a troupe of travellers who wanted their photos taken with him. Watching the crowds surrounding him, a young Englishwoman said, "This guy is like a rock star." She had a point. Where else in the world would a soldier command the kind of adulation usually reserved for rock and film stars?

Only a week later Seh Daeng was shot in the head by a still-unidentified sniper. He succumbed to his injuries a few days after. The mourning and celebrations that greeted his death were reminders of Thailand's long-standing love and loathing for the military, paired with respect for men, women and children in all kinds of uniforms. That's easy to see. Scan any street in the kingdom for the schoolgirls, boy scouts, bank tellers, bureaucrats, college students, soldiers and sailors, all in their neat and crisp uniforms. Watch the security guards in the gated residences of the rich as they give military-style salutes to the BMW-driving tycoons. Try and navigate the serpentine minefields of political, economic and judicial power that are tangled up in the red tape and remnants of military might. Work in any big Thai company where a militaristic structure of top-down rule ensures a chain of command that keeps the rank-and-file in a state of unquestioning subservience. Flip through any newspaper and the names of the main players in the theatre of politics, such as General Chavalit Yongchaiyudh and Major General Chamlong Srimuang, reveal a military pedigree. Even the most fundamental of Thai gestures, the *wai* (sign language for hello, goodbye and thanks), made up of palms clasped together and head bowed, reveals different degrees of deference to those of higher social rankings.

As a kind of buffer zone in the 1960s and '70s against the spread of communism in neighbouring countries, the presence of so many GIs and military bases on Thai soil caused seismic upheavals in the country's cultural and political landscapes. As an aftershock, Thailand served as a double for Vietnam and Cambodia in many Western movies. The first glimpses most Westerners would ever have of the kingdom came from films like *The Deer Hunter*, with its infamous set piece of Russian roulette. At the

River Kwai Floatel in Kanchanaburi province, where that scene was shot, you can still see the framed signatures of Robert De Niro and Christopher Walken, while Patpong Road in Bangkok stood in for Saigon's red-light zone. Because there was a military curfew in Bangkok, the producers had to get the approval of the army to shoot on Patpong, where many of the bars had lock-ins after 1am, with patrons crashing out on the chairs and floors.

Joe Cummings, the author of the original *Lonely Planet Thailand* guide, worked as an extra on *The Deer Hunter*, not long after arriving in Thailand to witness a massive burning of books with red covers on the front lawn of King Mongkut's Institute of Technology in Bangkok. Directed by Michael Cimino and starring Walken, De Niro and Meryl Streep, the film won five Oscars in 1978, including Best Picture. Joe played one of the ten Marines who had to guard the gates of the American embassy in Saigon, which was actually a Catholic school in Bangkok. "In the costumers and props department we were issued full combat gear, including flak vests and M-16s. The props were real, although the rifle was missing the firing pin," he said, adding that a Thai extra—who was a soldier in the 10,000-strong People's Liberation Army of Thailand—tried to buy the machine-gun from him.

"For that scene four of us were stationed along the top of the embassy's fence, standing on the rooftops of Jeeps. Cimino instructed us not to let any of the Thai extras, who were portraying Vietnamese trying to hitch a ride out of Saigon on US army helicopters, over the fence no matter what they did. Madness ensued take after take. I was knocked off the Jeep twice, and the soldier extra standing alongside me had his wrist skewered all the way through on one of the spikes at the tip of the wrought iron fence. They stopped that take and carried him away. A friend who was on the ground during that scene got punched in the face by Cimino, who was trying to rile him up for the scene."

De Niro was in all of those scenes and Joe couldn't believe how he "stayed in character all the time, even during the breaks when we Marine extras stayed in character by staying stoned and having fun." In Patpong, he also got to have a bowl of noodles with Christopher Walken, who won the Best Supporting Actor for his performance. In person, Joe said, Walken projected the same aura of menace he usually does on movie screens.

Most of another Oscar winner, *The Killing Fields* (1984), was also filmed in different parts of Thailand, including the most agonisingly suspenseful part when the Sofitel in Hua Hin—a vision of pan-colonial splendour—stood in for the French embassy in Phnom Penh, where the real-life photographer Sam Rockoff (played by John Malkovich) tries to forge a passport photo for the Cambodian journalist Dith Pran, so he can flee the city which has fallen to the barbarous Khmer Rouge. Still later, Oliver Stone would shoot parts of a film called *Heaven and Earth*, based on the memoirs of a Vietnamese woman who survived the war, on the tourist-drenched isle of Phuket, where *Good Morning Vietnam* (starring Robin Williams) was also filmed.

The upshot of this interest, and the presence of so many

military bases across the country, was that in the late 1990s the Tourism Authority of Thailand began what may well be the world's only campaign to promote military tourism, with a team of Thai authors penning a lengthy book on the subject and myself writing an English-language chapter for a brochure on adventure travel. At the Cavalry Center in Saraburi province, visitors can drive a rattletrap of a tank salvaged from the scrap yards of World War I. At the Chulachomklao Royal Military Academy, which has polished the CVs and credentials of many of the nation's top brass, and is located only a few hours outside Bangkok in Nakhon Nayok province, travellers can hit the shooting range, play golf, go mountain biking and pursue a little "R 'n' R" with the soldiers. The more intrepid weekend warriors, ready to work their way through the rigmarole of bureaucracy and organise a tour group, can experience the full arsenal of a serviceman's life at bases scattered around the country.

Our three days and two nights of very basic training began at the army base in Lop Buri, which is the second biggest one in Thailand. Thirty-five new recruits (men, women and teenagers) from all over Asia and the West, wearing khaki vests and black baseball caps emblazoned with the winged logo of the Royal Thai Airborne, gathered in a clearing for a brief demonstration on how to catch poisonous snakes. Spinal cords slithered and women gasped as a Thai officer showed us how to trap a writhing cobra by putting his boot down on the serpents' head. Then he picked it up by the tail. Although the snake-handling lecture was in Thai,

Sergeant Paitoon was on hand to provide the Westerners with a running translation in English.

As we hiked down a dirt road nearby, flanked by palm trees, we saw a ten metre-high jumble of rocks off to our left. Suddenly, there was a loud explosion and the soldiers in our platoon started yelling. Were we under attack? Everyone looked up to see two Thai soldiers standing on top of the rocks. Yelling and grunting, with a rope tied around his waist, one of them leapt, bounced and abseiled down the rock face.

After this demonstration, another soldier handed out ropes and showed how us to tie them around our waists and attach them to a clip on our belts. Wearing gloves and motorcycle helmets, we then practised walking backwards, our ropes tied around the trunks of trees. After that some of us were ready to cliff-walk and abseil. If becoming a soldier means learning to conquer your fears and trust the men in your unit completely, this was a great way to learn the ropes. While rock climbing is a potentially dangerous thrill sport, the Thai troops took such good care of us that nobody suffered anything worse than a few scraped knees, heart palpitations and some heady doses of adrenaline.

Those conscripts who didn't feel like participating in any of the activities did not have to fret, because there weren't any nasty drill sergeants spitting bullet-point orders.

After a ten-minute ride across a nearby lake in a big, rubber dinghy, we hiked through the jungle to a shooting range. There, one of the soldiers with a red beret and black shades showed us how to load, aim and fire an M-16. Each of us was then given five bullets and a pair of earplugs. While we loaded our guns, the soldiers knelt down beside us to give shooting tips and to ensure that no latent psychopaths were allowed to go ballistic.

Shooting an M-16 is a powerful kick. As Terry, a young Aussie backpacker said, "It feels a bit like playing God. You can see what Mao meant when he said, 'Power comes from the barrel of a gun'."

At the same time, it was frightening to realise how gunning someone down on the battlefield could be so easy and so impersonal. The paper target we were shooting at—meant to look like an enemy soldier—was about 20 metres away. I was reminded of a US Marine telling me in Bangkok how he'd shot two people crossing a river in El Salvador, "It wasn't like killin' real people, man. Sad to say, but it felt like target practise."

Nonetheless, I don't think the Marines will be recruiting me any time soon; all of my shots went wide of the target.

In marked contrast, the young Thai woman beside me, who smiled each time she squeezed the trigger, could probably freelance as a hit-woman for the Yakuza; each of her bullets pierced the paper heart of the enemy soldier.

As night cloaked the sky in indigo and staged a shadow play in the jungle, our unit sat on chairs in a clearing, watching another sergeant from the Airborne Division of the Royal Thai Army show us what kind of leaves are edible and which plants contain water. He then had us take turns drinking water from a particular kind of vine I didn't recognise. While they grilled feral pigs and rice inside a piece of bamboo on a makeshift barbecue, the soldiers demonstrated how to broil fish when you're nowhere near an oven. Inside a square metal tin they stood three fish upright in a circle. Another soldier then put the top on it and wrapped burlap sacks around the whole tin, before setting the sacks on fire. Ten minutes later, when the sacks were blackened rags, he removed the lid like a magician and—presto!—the fish were perfectly broiled.

For our open-air feast that night, we sat cross-legged on mats, in the usual Thai style, and ate a huge communal meal of barbecued pork, broiled fish, rice, and the spicy soup laden with lemon grass called *tom yum goong*. For dessert, there were slices of sweet mango and guava.

But it wasn't time for bed yet. Instead, we were marched over to another pavilion where an informal 'cultural show' was about to get underway. From the speakers blasted Thai country tunes with trebly melodies, rhythmic backbeats, wailing vocals (that sounded as if the singer was being given a root canal without the benefit of anaesthesia) and a bamboo flute solo: mournful music for such a happy-go-lucky people, suggesting that some of those lip-service grins in the so-called 'Land of Smiles' are bypassing the heart. In typical Thai festival style, the music was cranked up to the point where it was distorting, but none of the locals seemed to mind.

Some of the soldiers and their wives got up to do traditional dances. Soon, they had most of the crowd on their feet and dancing around in a circle—the traditional *ramwong*. Since Thai society and culture are so regimental, none of the conscripts in our platoon (including the only two foreigners, myself and Terry) were allowed to go MIA.

But the real soldiers joined in too. A few of them got on-stage to play a party game. An announcer called out the Thai names of different fruits: rambutan, papaya, banana and mango. In response, one of the soldiers had to do certain movements like shaking his hips or wiggling his butt. Given the Thais' racy sense of humour, it wasn't too surprising that the troopers had to do pelvic thrusts to the tune of '*gluay, gluay*' (the Thai word for banana, which is quite similar to the one for a man's closest friend, anatomically speaking). All the locals were in hysterics.

With our leg muscles begging for sleep, we then headed off on a one-kilometre moonlight hike through the jungle. But I couldn't complain too much, because I had two Thai women, both journalists in their late 20s, clinging to each of my arms, not because they were scared of snakes or spiders. No, they were terrified of encountering some malicious jungle spirits.

After bedding down for the night in two-person tents, the members of the Royal Thai Airborne tried to wake us up the next morning at 6am. After they called Terry and I three times and we still refused to budge, one of them, laughing gleefully, collapsed the pup tent on us.

The highlight of Day Two was a three-hour trek through some lush jungle in a wildlife sanctuary. We marched along the trunk of a huge uprooted tree, crossed streams on slippery stepping stones, waded through knee-deep water in a cave, climbed up ropes beside gushing waterfalls, and soldiered on to a well-earned break beside a big lake with turquoise water so clean the military men drank from it with cupped palms.

Considering the fact that some of these paratroopers are highly decorated veterans who fought alongside the Australians and Americans in Vietnam, it was surprising that they were so boyish and friendly. One of the older guys kept swinging past us on vines while laughing and shouting, "I am Tarzan!"

In a way, their friendliness was very much in the tradition of the Thai military. During World War I, Thailand sent several thousand troops to Europe to bolster the Allied forces. Although their bravery on the battlefield was legendary, so was their compassion. After Germany was defeated, the Thais, along with many other Allied troops, were sent to Germany to help round up soldiers who hadn't yet surrendered. Several groups of renegades said they would only give themselves up to the Thais because they treated their prisoners much more humanely than the troops from other countries did.

The Allies were similarly impressed by King Rama VI, who attended the Royal Military College in Sandhurst, England, and who also founded the national paramilitary group known as the Wild Tiger Corps in 1911, partly to protect the throne from the growing power of the military. That was a prescient move. Only a year later, the military tried to overthrow him in what was effectively the first coup in Thai history. But the soldier elected by lottery to assassinate him confessed and the coup was put down before a single shot was fired. For a short time Rama VI, a prolific playwright and the first person to translate Shakespeare into Thai, served as a lieutenant in a British infantry regiment. During World War I, he volunteered to fight with the Allies, but was refused on the grounds that it was too dangerous. A framed telegram on the wall of the museum devoted to Rama VI in Bangkok shows how King George V bestowed upon him the rank of Honourary General of the British Army. In 1925, the king's deathbed wish was to have a full military-style funeral procession. The wish was granted just a few days after his only child was born.

On our second night of basic training, a local professor, who taught the soldiers about astronomy and meteorology, set up a telescope in the clearing beside our tents. It was a perfect, cloud-free night for stargazing, the forest and clearing tinted silver by a mother-of-pearl moon. Afterwards, we 'liquidated' bottles of sugarcane rum while reprising the bragging rites common to all servicemen: complaining of bruises and scrapes, and boasting of targets hit and accidents missed, like a bunch of overgrown boys playing 'war games'. Much hilarity ensued. Alcohol—that great leveller of social rankings—washed away the usual divisions of Thai society and allowed Terry and I the chance to banter more freely with them. As it goes on any multi-day odyssey like rafting, diving or trekking, the intensity of the shared experience made for some intense camaraderie.

Everyone was glad the paratroopers had effectively court marshalled a local ex-soldier on the tour, who had beer for breakfast and the bleary eyes and sour disposition of a veteran alcoholic. He had picked up on a silly Thai joke I had made to a couple of the real soldiers as we watched the women preparing dinner. Since few of the paratroopers spoke much English, and Terry's local lexicon extended to about four words, I was charged with the task of playing interpreter, quipping that Terry and I were 'too lazy to cook but not too lazy to eat'. The ex-soldier overheard this remark and began repeating 'lazy foreigners' again and again, until a fight broke out between the two of us on the green army bus taking us to the wildlife sanctuary. As far as fights went it was nothing to write to Manny Pacquiao about, but let that serve as a cautionary anecdote about some of the 'weekend warriors' you may meet on any of these tours of duty.

The scariest part of the weekend was the jump from an 11 metre-high parachute tower. Even the high-flying members of the Royal Thai Airborne go to pray at a nearby shrine to Ganesha, the elephant-headed god of the Hindu faith, before they do a jump.

After paying our respects to the deity, we listened to a lecture and watched some demonstrations on how to put on the parachute, and how to jump, keeping your elbows by your hips and your forearms straight out in front of you. Having a natural fear of heights, pain, paralysis and death, I had some seventh and eighth thoughts about doing the jump, but I wasn't going to let a 12-year-old Singaporean girl make me look like a total wimp now, was I?

So I scaled the wooden tower, with the straps of the parachute grabbing at my thighs, and waited for my turn. Five cables were strung from the top of the tower, each one arcing hundreds of metres to the ground in the distance. This meant that five rookie 'parachutists' could jump at a time, one after the other. A Thai soldier connected the cable to my vest. After an excruciating wait, I was next in line. One of the supervising soldiers tapped me on the back and yelled, "Go!" With my stomach doing somersaults, I leapt, keeping my eyes on the distant trees. After freefalling for what seemed like an eternity, the cable snapped tight and my head whiplashed back and forth. Grinning at the distant mountains, I flew down the line.

In the afternoon we did a brief reconnaissance mission of the Military Museum in Lop Buri. Then there was a special ceremony, in which a high-ranking officer pinned badges bearing the insignia of the Royal Thai Airborne to our shirts. It's a thrilling, but not easy to organise way of 'earning your stripes'—made easier if you're going out with a bigger Thai group. Even if you don't have to face down any suicide-bombers or clean any latrines, you still have to combat your fears and test your mettle, discipline and teamwork skills to the maximum: invaluable lessons for travellers or anyone on the frontlines of business.

* * *

From the highest mountain passes of the north to the lowest roads of the far south, warring militias have made inroads in Thailand. Up in the Golden Triangle—the crossroads where the borders of Laos, Thailand and China converge—some of the roads were paved (quite literally) by the CIA and sealed with drug money, according to *The Politics of Heroin* in Southeast Asia by Alfred W. McCoy and Cathleen B. Read, written when they were graduate students at Yale University in 1972. Remnants of the Chinese nationalist forces known as the Kuoumintang (KMT), which fled to the jungles of Burma after Mao Zedong's communist party swept to power in 1949, then relocated to the Shan States of Burma, where they received CIA support to launch failed military operations into China and boost opium production. From 1950 to 1962, the authors estimate that opium production grew by a thousand per cent. Even after the KMT was ousted by the Burmese military, they set up base camps in northern Thailand where they continued running mule caravans into Burma with the help of the CIA and the Thai military. For the next 20 years, the KMT battled left-wing insurgents in Thailand. In a statement he made to many journalists, General Tuan Shi-wen of the KMT said, "We have to continue to fight the evil of communism, and to fight you must have an army, and an army must have guns, and to buy guns you must have money. In these mountains, the only money is opium."

After an amnesty was declared, the soldiers of what has been called the 'Lost Army' changed from growing opium to planting oolong tea. The town of Mae Salong where their descendants still live is an outpost of China, with Mandarin the dominant language and Yunnan-style pork a speciality in local restaurants. The popular Mae Salong Resort was built on the grounds of a former training camp for KMT soldiers.

Another small town in that area, Toed Thai, has a small museum devoted to Khun Sa, the opium warlord and mandarin of heroin who supplanted the KMT as the biggest cultivator of poppies in the Golden Triangle, who lived on and off again in northern Thailand.

Many of the roads built in the mountainous northeastern

provinces of Loei and Petchabun were constructed by the Thai military to attack outposts of the People's Liberation Army of Thailand. Joe Cummings, the *Lonely Planet* author, said, "The military would do roadwork during the day and the reds would come down from the mountains at night and destroy the equipment again." Many of the insurgents were students from Bangkok protesting against a military regime. They fled to the jungles after the military-backed crackdown and bloodbath at Thammasat University in 1976. The most famous photo from the massacre shows a student who had been lynched and set on fire by a right-wing paramilitary group. As he hung from a tamarind tree in the green oval of Sanam Luang, an older man was about to smash him over the head with a folding chair.

Around 8,000 left-wing insurgents came out of hiding in 1982 when they were granted a general amnesty by the government. Touring those tortuous roads of the northeast with a Thai guide in tow, or listening to the older folks spin stories of those days, illuminates some dark corners of Thai history.

In the early 1980s, many of the guerrillas hiding out in the southern provinces also laid down their arms. Dick Chandler, one of the country's oldest adventure-travel entrepreneurs, visited a cave in Khao Sok National Park, "where there were tables, chairs, blackboards and a whole classroom" in 1985, after setting up a company called Lost Horizons and establishing Our Jungle House. None of those caves are on their regular trekking itineraries, but they will do tailor-made packages for military historians, said Dick, who also spent a weekend doing military training with the troops and travellers at the Chulachomklao Royal Military Academy in Nakhon Nayok province. "It was really fun, especially the shooting range."

Holed up in caves and jungle lairs in the far south, around the town of Betong, the last holdouts of the People's Liberation Army of Thailand did not lay down their arms until 1989. Now and again travellers return with tales of visiting those outposts and lairs, with older guides providing local, colour commentary on the left-wing's last stand in Thailand.

During the 'Black May' crisis of 1992, which took place almost 18 years before the bloodshed of 2010, the soldiers' shooting of protestors on the streets of Bangkok was precipitated by the military toppling the elected government of General Chatchai Choonhawan, after accusing his administration of being 'unusually wealthy', and installing its own party the National Peacekeeping Council in place. Yet another charismatic rogue in a long line of martial leaders, the Harley-riding Chatchai's favourite slogan was 'Turning the battlefields of Indochina into marketplaces.'

With military tourism, the late statesman's words have proven prophetic. In northern Laos, the caves where the left-wing Pathet Lao once lived have become tourist attractions, with guides telling visitors about the direct hit from an American bomber that killed several hundred people at once and how the ghosts of their cries still echo through these subterranean chambers. In Vietnam, the military museums and the tunnels of Cu Chi, where the Viet Cong once lived, are flashpoints on travel itineraries. And in Cambodia, the

Tuol Sleng Genocide Museum and the Killing Fields, near a military shooting range, are perennial hits with travellers. Some people think it's an urban legend on the backpacker trail that, for a sum of about US$100, you can kill a goat with a rocket-propelled grenade (RPG), or an AK-47, on the shooting range used by Cambodian soldiers on the outskirts of Phnom Penh. That's not a myth. It's true. A young American traveller sent me the photos and the story, which we published in *Farang Untamed Travel* magazine. The images show him killing a goat with an RPG before posing for photos, naked except for a strategically placed army helmet with two local prostitutes serving as his 'cheerleaders' and 'handmaidens'. (I wonder what PETA, People for the Ethical Treatment of Animals, would make of that?) For the Khmer troops it was no big ordeal; they would have killed the goat anyway. Afterwards, they carted it off to serve as sustenance for the soldiers.

None of the tours of duty in Thailand are that extreme, but the military still ranks right up there with the most powerful echelons of Thai society. Much of the tug-of-war between the red shirts and the government in 2010 was over who would control the annual military reshuffle in September. Signs of the army's fiscal and political might are everywhere—broadcast by the military-owned Channel 3 and bankrolled by the wealth of bank branches across the country. Once known as the Thai Military Bank, the name has been shortened to the more innocuous TMB. Nevertheless, the two dots above the M have always struck me as strange. Do they look more like bullet holes or eyes?

Double Lives:
Searching for the Siamese Twins

Because of their brotherly bond made flesh, and their astonishing, perfectly synchronised acrobatics, the original Siamese twins Chang and Eng were billed as the 'Eighth Wonder of the World' when, at the age of 18, they arrived in New York in 1829. For the next decade, they performed for packed houses all over America and Europe in circuses and on freak-show bills with other human oddities, such as the 'Amazing Wolf Children of Australia'. Chang and Eng were twice managed by the infamous showman P.T. Barnum ("There's a sucker born every minute."), Herman Melville scorned them as a monstrous metaphor for conflicting passions which reside within the same body in *Moby Dick*; and they put on private spectacles for Queen Victoria and Russia's Czar Nicholas II.

Although they shared no internal organs, and were often derided as a fraud, the brothers were actually joined below their breastbones by a ligament about eight-centimetres long and four wide. Otherwise, they both had normal limbs and were healthy. Through their performances—walking on their hands was a showstopper—the twins were already wealthy before they turned 30, and they tried to retire to a family and farming life in the American south, soon to be torn asunder by the Civil War.

Over the last decade, their dramatic history has been the

inspiration for a pair of much-lauded literary novels—*Chang and Eng* by Darin Strauss and *God's Fool* by Mark Slouka—along with a Singaporean musical helmed by Thai expatriate Ekachai Uekrongtham, who also directed and co-wrote the 2003 film *Beautiful Boxer* about the transsexual *muay thai* fighter Nong Toom.

As a result, the steady trickle of foreign and Thai visitors to the twins' hometown, in the eponymous capital of Samut Songkhram, has become more torrential. Still, Siam's most famous citizens are not mentioned in any of the major guidebooks to the kingdom and even the promotional literature of the Tourism Authority of Thailand for the province includes nothing about them.

Fascinated by their legacy, and these sins of omission, Anchana and I went in search of relics from Chang and Eng's past. Much of the twins' early life is still a matter of conjecture. Both the musical and the two novels are accurate, however, in documenting their birth in a floating riverside home, 70 kilometres southwest of Bangkok, during the rainy season of 1811. If the old bamboo-and-thatch floating homes have long since been replaced by a Caltex oil refinery and some fish sauce factories, traces of the maritime life Chang and Eng once led (their father was a fisherman) are still high water marks in the country's smallest province. Head down the roads beside the Mae Khlong River near their birthplace to see fishing trawlers on the water and boatyards along the banks. Workmen—pounding, polishing and patching— cling to ten metre-high scaffolds of bamboo hanging from the sides of trawlers. And the stench of rotten fish will make you squint.

A few kilometres north, past tiger-prawn farms, salt flats and ornate temples, is Don Hoy Lot, where the river's mouth kisses the Gulf of Thailand. Here, the banks are crowded with enormous wooden restaurants up on stilts. And the seafood is as famous as the crab-eating macaques that scamper across the mudflats around dusk in search of their staple diet.

As conjoined children of mixed Siamese-Chinese parentage, Chang and Eng were jeered at and taunted endlessly by their peers. Worse, much worse, was how they came to be blamed by superstitious Siamese for causing a cholera epidemic which killed 30,000 people and left the river clogged with corpses. In the Singaporean production, *Chang and Eng: The Musical*, a song titled 'Living Curse' details their frightful ordeal at the hands of a potential lynch mob.

But what sustained the twins in their most despairing hours? In the opinion of Ken Low, the musical's composer from Malaysia, it was the unconditional love of their mother. This motif has played well in Asia: the musical is the longest-running theatrical work in Singaporean history, was well received in Bangkok, and also became the first English-language musical ever staged in China towards the end of the millennium, where the composer told me, "We were treated like rock stars."

Today, every Thai person knows who the Siamese twins are. But most would not recognise the names Chang and Eng. In Thai, the twins are known as '*In Jan*'. It's an auspicious name, meaning 'Earth Moon'. But it does lead to the common misconception that they were one entity. Not so. The brothers had very different demeanours: Chang was gregarious and playful, whereas Eng tended to be more withdrawn and studious.

In Thai history books, children learn that the brothers were the favourite performers at King Rama II's court. Renowned as a patron of the arts and comedy troupes, the monarch often had them perform at the Grand Palace in Bangkok. It has been speculated that his patronage saved them from the wrath of superstitious villagers. Like the twins, King Rama II was also born in Samut Songkhram, where a park featuring a museum of the monarch's personal effects, a garden with 100 different kinds of plants mentioned in Thai literature, and an open-air stage for annual performances of masked dramas on Thai Artist's Day, February 24, is named after him in the provincial capital.

As adolescents, Chang and Eng helped provide for their hard-luck family by raising ducks and selling their eggs. Bigger than chicken eggs, and with a darker yolk, duck eggs are a crucial ingredient in the piquant seafood salad called *yum*, in rice porridge, and, when mixed with coconut milk and sugar, in many Thai desserts. The brothers would also have known how to make one of the province's specialties—'thousand-year-old eggs'. To preserve them, the duck eggs are boiled in salty water and left for a week to soak. They are then wrapped in rice husks and earth and packed away in a box for up to a year. Even today, local fishermen take a good supply of them on long journeys for protein.

Along one of the province's many canals, we stayed in an old-fashioned Siamese-style house with a verandah overlooking the water. The roofless shower outside in the garden was overhung by the cannonball-sized fruits of a pomelo tree. This was one of the 'home-stays' run by local families in the Amphawa District. Along with appetising local meals, Moo Baan Song Thai also offered boat tours of a floating market, fruit orchards, Wat Amphawan Chetiyaram where King Rama II's ashes are interred, and a nocturnal outing to watch fireflies.

Even without booking a tour all we had to do was sit on the verandah and watch a portal into the past open before our eyes. In the early morning, with birds gossiping and fish splashing, monks in saffron robes paddled down the canal, just as they have done for centuries. The Buddhist faithful congregated on rickety piers to put plastic bags of food in the monks' alms bowls. A short time later, a wizened old woman in a conical hat paddled by to serve us steaming bowls of noodles right on the waterfront. Because the canals and weatherworn buildings of wood have been so well preserved, the Amphawa District won a UNESCO prize for Cultural Conservation. Those enticements, and a 'floating market' in the early evening (yet to be watered down by mass-market tourism), have made the capital a favourite escape for weekend parolees from the concrete prison and workaday world of Bangkok.

After breakfast, I asked Anchana if she'd ever learned about the twins from Thai history books. She said she had, but did not know much about their later lives. I explained how they married sisters in North Carolina, adopted the surname of Bunker, and sired 21 children.

Anchana looked quizzical. So I told her about Darin Strauss' novel, *Chang and Eng*, and a middle chapter entitled 'The Mysteries of the Bridal Bed' that details how the twins lost their virginity. After their wedding in 1843, the conjoined brothers agreed that when one of their wives was in bed with them, the other brother would go into a trance and try to be 'mindless'.

When he was sleeping with his wife, Sarah, for the first time, Eng thought, "I felt my wife had become a strange part of me, not integrated fully—but not fully only because this new part of me was experiencing its own pleasure. In my hand, her hand, trembling and weak, her fingers hooked around mine—and the only way to describe what I experienced is as a new-sprung void in my chest, sucking out a solitary life's worth of loneliness and wanting now to be filled with something new."

Anchana's next question was whether their children were normal. To find out, we visited the museum dedicated to them, four kilometres from the centre of Samut Songkhram city. Outside the museum stands a statue of the twins alongside a full-scale replica of their floating home. Even though it was early on a Friday afternoon, this sporadically open and frequently shut museum was closed, necessitating a flurry of increasingly angry phone calls from Anchana to local authorities in order to get them to open it for us. No wonder so many Thais fear the flare-gun tempers of the Southerners. But her persistence paid off; they came down and opened it for us.

This was the most pitiful museum I have ever seen. Even Hitler's final bunker must've been a cheerier place. Half of the old posters and photos were propped up against concrete pillars and the bare concrete floor was salted and peppered with bird droppings. Whatever its shortcomings—and they are legion—the gallery of fading images provided some touching glimpses into the twins' personal and professional lives: their wives, their children, their one-time manager P.T. Barnum, and a few of their old circus posters. Most of their kids looked normal and healthy. The portrait of their two lovely daughters—Eng's Kate, who looked Asian, and Chang's Nannie, who looked American—was particularly heartrending when I read the caption detailing how both daughters died of tuberculosis at the age of 27. The true sideshow connoisseur will not want to miss the promotional photos for their final, disastrous tour in 1866 after the Civil War had devastated their farm in North Carolina and their slaves were freed. By that stage, the twins were already in their 50s, their star had dimmed, and Chang, once the gregarious wisecracker of the duo, had become a gloomy alcoholic. Eng, a lifelong teetotaler, was repulsed by his brother's habit, partly because the alcohol had a physical effect on him, too. Doubly defeated, their performances became erratic and they made little money.

The officials assured us that thanks to a recent visit by some of the twins' distant relatives, who had promised additional funding, the museum would be undergoing extensive renovations. I hope that's true. As it stands now, the local prejudice against the twins, and the superstitions surrounding them, have barely changed in almost two centuries.

***

For many visitors to the province, the highlight is an evening ride via long-tail boat to see the nesting grounds of fireflies. Motoring along the dark canals, a fan of light from the boat illuminated long-abandoned houses on stilts and bats swooping across the water. In places the foliage was so thick, it blocked out the sky and moon. This trip into the swampy heart of Siamese darkness was suddenly lit up as the mangrove trees growing out of the muddy banks blinked on and off with thousands of fireflies making quicksilver flashes.

On the way back to our canal-side hideaway, I imagined the two young twins watching the fireflies beam their SOS of loneliness some two centuries before us, as I explained to Anchana the ending to Darin Strauss' novel. In spite of all the bad blood between them caused by Chang's alcoholism and Eng's embitterment, twinned with their mutual poverty, when Eng woke up in the middle of a cold January night to find his brother dead beside him, the final act of his life was one of reconciliation. It was witnessed only by his wife Sarah:

"He twists away from her—he draws his brother closer to him. Eng takes his twin into his arms: This is the image Sarah keeps of her husband for the rest of her life. Eng dies."

Although Strauss has used poetic license to recreate their final hours, it is true that the brothers died within hours of each other. An engraving on the side of the twins' statue outside the museum in Samut Songkhram shows that even in death they could not escape the morbid voyeurism that turned their lives into a lifelong sideshow: Their corpses were sent to a hospital in Philadelphia for an autopsy and the doctors made a plaster cast from them. But the connecting ligament, which helped to bring them from a floating hovel to the court of King Rama II, from being the 'Eighth Wonder of the World' to family men and farmers, was never severed.

The original Siamese twins are buried in a double coffin in North Carolina.

Country 'n' Eastern:
Home on the Dude Ranch

In some of the earliest photos of my brother and I in the family album, we're dressed up in cowboy outfits and sitting on a rocking horse; in another shot we're posing in the backyard with our friends, wearing cowboy hats and brandishing cap guns that look like Colt .45s. As children growing up on the Canadian prairies, we wanted to be outlaws like Billy the Kid and Butch Cassidy. After school, we played 'Cowboys and Indians' and calibrated our fantasies by watching re-runs of old TV shows like *Gunsmoke* and *Bonanza*; we learned to swagger and talk tough like Clint Eastwood and John Wayne in the old Westerns ("Vamoose, ya doggone varmints!"), and gave ourselves nicknames like 'Tex' and 'Hoss'. To practise our roping skills, we tried to throw a lasso made out of a belt around the neck of our mom's Pekingese. But the miniscule yap-dog wasn't much of a surrogate for a Texas longhorn steer.

During the summer holidays, our most memorable times were spent riding horses in the mountains of Jasper, and watching cowboys wrestle steers and race chuck-wagons at the world's most famous rodeo, the Calgary Stampede. But we never got to rob any stagecoaches or fight off a horde of whooping, circling and scalping Apaches. And the only real Indians we ever saw were panhandling winos fleeing lives of deprivation on squalid reservations.

Little did I realise that my childhood aspirations would not come halfway true for another few decades until I visited the Pensuk Great Western Resort in northeast Thailand.

A LIVING GHOST TOWN

The main streets in the resort's town of High Hill could be the set for an old 'horse opera'. There's a sheriff's office and a jail, a gunsmith and the Deadrock Bull Saloon, a blacksmith and a barber. Between the bank and Lydia Pinkham's Vegetable Compound is a fading sign: 'Deputy Wanted: Looking For A Few Good Men To Help Out The Law. Must Be Good With A Gun And A Good Horseman'.

All of the tumbledown buildings, made of wood and bricks, looked authentically weather-beaten. Hidden speakers played a hit parade of 1970s' country chestnuts like Waylon Jennings' '*Mamas Don't Let Your Babies Grow Up to Be Cowboys*' and Charlie Daniels' '*The Devil Went Down To Texas*'. As photographer Jason Lang and his girlfriend, coupled with Anchana and I, sauntered down the street towards the enormous corral for the first time, Jason said, "It all looks so real you expect some cowboy to run out on the balcony, get shot, and fall down into the street." Then the Californian yelled, "Yee haw! Yip, yip, yip, yip!"

Many of the resort's rooms are actually inside High Hill's buildings. Behind the horseshoe-studded façade of the blacksmith shop, our room had a plaster mock-up of an antelope's head on the wall, beside cut-outs of pine trees that framed the TV set. An old rifle was mounted on the bricks above the electric fireplace.

Glaring down at us from over the mirror was the bust of an Indian warrior with a feather headdress. Instead of leaving sweets on the pillows, the maid had left us a pair of cowboy-style neckerchiefs.

The owner of the resort, Yuttana Pensuk, modelled the buildings and signs on a real 19th-century ghost town in Nevada named Calico. When construction began in the mid-1990s, he said, with a cowboy-hat grin, "All the local people thought I was crazy."

At first it was only intended as a weekend dude ranch for him and his friends, but little by little, they added air-conditioned teepees, shooting ranges for rifles and archery, a karaoke room, a swimming pool, a tram that resembles an old steam train and a 'Cowboys and Indians' theme show on Saturday nights. Now it's a 25-horse town with 70 full-time employees and 30 part-timers, and the resort can accommodate up to 300 guests.

The owner's obsession with the Wild West began around the same time as mine did, but under much scarier circumstances. His father was a Thai soldier during the Vietnam War, and his kinfolk all lived together on a big military base in the northeastern province of Udon Thani, where he was stationed. Yuttana recalled how, every ten minutes, an American fighter plane would shriek down the runway on its way to drop a payload of bombs on Vietnam, Laos and Cambodia. In their down time, the American bomber crews watched lots of Westerns.

And so did Yuttana—who can be seen every weekend at the resort, walking around in a black hat and complete cowboy duds, a holster with a fake six-shooter strapped to his thigh.

Much of the resort's appeal to middle-class and well-heeled Thais (who make up about 90 per cent of the visitors) and other Asians (mostly from Hong Kong, Singapore, Taiwan and Japan) comes from Hollywood films and old TV shows. In Thailand, the allure of cowboy folklore and the dozens of Western-themed bars with water buffalo skulls and wagon wheels, also stems from the fact that the kingdom is, like the Wild West, an agrarian society rife with outlaws (read: gangsters and hit men). As the owner's wife—nicknamed Ping Pong—said, "Thai people don't have heroes like Americans do, but you see the old films, and wow, cowboys are cool."

When she said 'heroes' what she was really referring to were 'heroes' from rural farming areas, like the cowboys in the American Westerns that were shown in Thai cinemas and on TV after the GIs arrived.

Whatever heroic tendencies my trusty sidekick—now known as Jason 'Shooter' Lang—and I possessed were blown on the first night. Stumbling down the street of High Hill to our rooms, three sheets to the wind, we spotted an enormous insect smashing its carapace into a fluorescent light above the blacksmith shop that was the façade of our room.

"Dude, that is the biggest bug I've ever seen, Tex."

"Yeah, I know. It's like the vampire bat of the insect world. Shooter! Duck! It's coming for our necks."

As the insect dive-bombed us, Jason ducked and shrieked while I threw up my arms to ward off an imminent attack: a slapstick scene of Keystone cowboys, causing our girlfriends to have a fit of the giggles. Fearlessly, Anchana walked over to the light, reached up and caught the monster in her hands. "Come on, you guys. They don't bite. We used to play with them on the sugarcane farm." Grinning, she threw the insect into the air, where it disappeared into a black velvet night encrusted with stars.

In this spleen of the tropical woods, the womenfolk were making Shooter and Tex look like a couple of greenhorns and yellow-bellied cowards.

DARK HORSES

The last time I went trail riding was up in the mountains of Jasper, Alberta. While cutting through the forest, a branch whipped me across the face. I lost my balance and fell off the horse, but my foot was caught in the stirrup. The horse dragged me along for about 50 metres before it stopped. It was a miracle I didn't break any bones.

Trail riding is dangerous, warned Yuttana.

"If the horse knows you don't have any experience and cannot control him, then he will try to buck you off," the owner said. "Another thing to be wary of is that horses spook easily."

The owner related a cautionary tale of a Thai member of parliament, who was an expert rider, but up in the nearby mountains, he was galloping down a trail when a wild pig appeared in front of them. The horse stopped dead in its tracks, catapulting him into a tree and fatally fracturing his skull.

For the nervous novice, Pensuk Great Western offers riding lessons. All the basics are covered, from saddling up and reining the beast in, to trotting, cantering and how to fall. "When you're falling, you have to pull the horse in that direction to break your fall," said Yuttana.

But you can't really experience the cowboy life until you're galloping down a trail to the percussion of hooves and the tune of the wind sawing through the trees like a fiddle, the forests and streams and sugarcane plantations all dappled with sunlight, cows grazing in pastures and water buffaloes pulling plows in rice paddies—a country mile from the desk-jockey lives most of us live in the city.

Much of the Western's appeal is the scenery: mountains, forests, rivers, deserts and wide-open plains. The grounds of the resort, complete with a small stream and an orgy of tropical botany, rope in city slickers, even though most of the Thais prefer riding around on mountain bikes rather than horses. "They call me and ask if I have horses, but they don't want to ride, only look and take photos," Yuttana laughed.

We were supposed to go trail riding the next morning with Yuttana, but Shooter and I were hungover to the point where we already had horses galloping through our heads. Considering what Ping Pong had told us about how she'd stopped riding horses after getting bucked off four or five times, the three of us settled for the easier and more popular option of having a ranch hand walk us around on horseback while Jason took photos.

At Pensuk Great Western, most visitors prefer shooting photos to blowing off guns; the main afternoon action in High Hill consists of photo sessions among families and friends. The buildings are used as backdrops. One Asian visitor I overheard compared it to Universal

Studios in Hollywood. Nobody at the resort seemed to mind if we borrowed some cowboy hats and toy guns from the souvenir shop to stage our own photo shoot. Going down in a blaze of glory after a showdown at high noon was the usual finale to our childhood games, but as with everything at the resort, there was a weird twist—now it wasn't some lawman or desperado pretending to plug me full of hot lead, it was my girlfriend, foreshadowing darker chapters yet to be written.

Jim and Anchana at Pensuk Great Western, the cowboys and Indians resort in northeastern Thailand.

COWBOYS VERSUS INDIANS

It didn't dawn on me until around dusk, as Shooter and I were moseying along the main drag of the resort's Dodge City section, toy Winchester rifles in one hand and beers in the other, that the anniversary of 9/11 was looming. On a restaurant TV, a news programme showed a retrospective collage of clips from ground zero, as well as sound-bytes from George W. Bush. In reference to Osama Bin Laden and the other members of Al-Qaeda holed up in Afghanistan, he drawled, "We're gonna smoke 'em outta their holes." Talking about John Howard, the then-prime minister of Australia, Bush added, "He's my deputy sheriff in Asia."

Thankfully, nobody at Pensuk Great Western takes the old cowboy rhetoric that seriously. In fact, the big theme show held every Saturday night is full of the ludicrous slapstick seen on Thai TV programmes, so it's easily understood by non-Thai speakers.

The show takes place outside the restaurant. Tables are set up in front of the stage, where a live band in cowboy costumes plays everything from the Beatles and Elvis to Hank Williams and Creedence Clearwater Revival during the dinner buffet. Off to the left is a row of miniature chuck-wagons used for their original purpose: serving up grub. Mostly it's Thai food, although they also roast a pig on a spit every Saturday night.

As you'd expect, the show boasts some gunplay (with blanks, of course), some fisticuffs and horsing around. But as you may not expect, the Indians are central characters with actual speaking parts. The show begins with some drunken Thai cowboys staggering around with beer bottles. They kidnap a lovely Indian princess and threaten to sell her into slavery. It's a far battle cry from the old Westerns, where the natives were usually portrayed as whooping savages, forever scalping decent Christian folks with tomahawks, and setting their wagons on fire with flaming arrows. (Many of the derogatory names for Native Canadians and Americans like 'wagon burners' that we heard as kids came from those movies.)

But the resort does a much more adroit balancing act in its portrayal of frontier America's two great enemies. Inside the old wooden building near the paddock, for instance, are photos of celebrated Indian warriors like Kicking Bird and Two Hatchet from the Kiowa tribe, along with brief descriptions of the famous battles they fought against the US cavalry. Yet another sign in the big barn of a restaurant lists a few Native American beliefs such as 'Remain close to the great spirit', and 'Show great respect for your fellow beings'.

In truth, the Indian iconography at the resort are as plentiful as all the cowboy motifs. And the most colourful and popular accommodations are the elaborately decorated teepees, with TVs and en-suite bathrooms, which sit in a concrete circle surrounded by gaudy totem poles.

During the show's centrepiece, an Indian chief rides in on the front of a train engine to save one of his warriors from being hanged by the cowboys. Accompanied by the owner's young daughter, Shania (who is named after the Canadian country starlet, Shania Twain), the chief walks through the crowd so people can take his photo, jumps on-stage, grabs the microphone and berates the trench coat-wearing cowboys, as if he were a professional wrestler. This was then followed by some corny jokes in English about the 'three hows', like "How are you?"

Then it hit me: the show is a cleverly constructed satire about how the Wild West was tamed, how the cowboys in trench coats are stand-ins for criminal elements, and how the Indians lost their traditions. When you can come up with egghead interpretations like this, you ain't never gonna be no real cowpoke.

The Asians in the audience all warm to the communal rituals, like at the end of the show when everybody gets to carry a lit torch around in a circle, while the band plays the Hank Williams tune about a wooden, cigar-store Indian named 'Kawliga'. Later on, there's line dancing. And you thought square-dancing was goofy? For such tough guys and gals, country 'n' western fans sure listen to some sappy songs and do some flatfooted dances.

The rowdiest folks at the resort this weekend turned out to be our Thai neighbours across the street in the 'bank'. Employees of an insurance firm in Bangkok on a team-building trip, they were only too willing to share their big bottle of whiskey with a couple of pseudo cowboys from the West. At this point in the evening's guzzling, no one was too coherent except their boss, who kept insisting in between guffaws, that "Johnnie Walker is our most important world leader. He makes everybody friendly. Stop war and drink whiskey!" Because he was the boss, nobody dared to interrupt him.

One of the other men in their group said it wasn't a real cowboy town because there was no brothel or all-night saloon. Which is true: the bar closes by midnight and a lot of the guests are families who stay in log cabins named after Jesse James and Billy the Kid.

The weekend hadn't quite worked out the way we'd fantasised—the trail riding had turned into cantering; Shooter and I had been spooked by an insect; we'd both been shot down by our girlfriends (in more ways than one); and neither of us could have hit a barn with a blunderbuss on the shooting range. But in spite of the drawbacks and misfires, we'd still gotten to relive our childhoods by playing costume-party cowboys, staying in a real live ghost town and tying on the feedbag from some chuck-wagons while watching a surreal cowboys and Indians show.

By 1am, I was the last man staggering around High Hill and Dodge City. Even my sidekick and our partners were getting some shuteye. But that's the way it was in the darker Westerns and the rustlers and ranchers novels of Cormac McCarthy like *All the Pretty Horses* and *The Crossing*. The anti-heroes never got the girl, never got rich, never even found a place to call home. Nope. They kept drifting like tumbleweeds, always ending up very much alone. And that's what keeps the old cowboy tales from being put out to pasture for good, because sometimes every wanderer on every continent can relate to that.

THE SEX
FILES

The Black Sex Magician of the Body Politic

Back in September 1995, headlines on the front page of *The Nation* in Bangkok cast a spell over readers: '*Novice Faces Action After Bizarre Baby-Burning Rite*'; '*Defrocked Novice Vows To Carry On With Black Magic*'.

The man in question was a Buddhist monk known as Nen (a novice monk) Aer, and this black-magic ritual made him Thailand's most notorious practitioner of the occult. For the right price, he dispensed curses, sex charms and blessings for the hoi polloi and the elite.

An orphan who grew up in a temple in Saraburi province, Nen Aer first became a household curse after an article appeared shortly before that—complete with gruesome photos—in the Thai weekly magazine *Cheewit Tong Su* ('Life's A Fight'), which showed him performing a series of rituals to grill and preserve a stillborn baby in order to transform it into a magical charm. He admitted to purchasing the baby from a mother for 100,000 baht, not long after the infant had passed away.

According to the magazine, Nen Aer (whose real name is Harn Raksajit) had preserved the corpse in a special potion of chemicals and 'holy water'. Afterwards, he and several other monks recited incantations over the dead baby for nine days at Wat Nong Rakam, a temple in Saraburi province. Then they collected the 'drippings' from the corpse to concoct love potions and produce a powerful 'baby ghost'.

None of these rituals had anything to do with Buddhism, which is why he was defrocked even though he denied that it was the clergy who made him give up his robes. Thirty-five years old at the time of his first arrest, the self-proclaimed sorcerer, whose body and face are covered with magical tattoos, told *The Nation*, "It was my own decision to be defrocked for the sake of Buddhism. Nobody forced me. My practice has tarnished Buddhism and I would like other monks and novices who follow such practises to be defrocked, too." But at the same time, he vowed to continue "performing occult rituals to the best of my ability".

Later in 1995, when I was still working at *The Nation*, a Thai colleague informed me that Nen Aer was in the building for a press conference. We walked over to take a look. He was dressed up like an American gangster (or a jazz musician) from the 1940s, in a black suit, fedora and shades. During the press conference, he compared himself to Khun Paen, one of the two friends and main characters in the fabled Siamese folktale *Khun Chang, Khun Paen*, of which there are many different versions. Like the defrocked Nen Aer, Khun Paen also studied the black arts at a temple when he was a child—a common practice in ancient Siam during the wars with the Khmer and the Burmese when the occult was used as a weapon in the military's arsenal. One of Khun Paen's wives dies in the story while pregnant, so he removes the foetus and 'grills' it to make a powerful baby ghost called a *khuman tong* which can supposedly control people's minds. An effigy of this ghost, in the form of a young boy, is still worshipped on some Thai altars.

To the shock of many journalists at the press conference, Nen Aer announced that he'd been offered two million baht to play the lead role in a film based on his life. Shooting for the film had already begun—deliberately scheduled for the day of a total solar eclipse. Such eclipses are marked by the more superstitious Thais with firecrackers, the banging of drums and pots and pans, and even gunshots as they try to frighten Rahu, the Hindu God of Darkness (often portrayed in India riding a chariot pulled by eight black horses), into regurgitating the sun he is swallowing.

The movie, Nen Aer said, would portray him in a positive light as a practitioner of white or 'sympathetic' magic, which can supposedly ease suffering and cure illnesses. The film would also trace his early studies of mysticism at a temple in Cambodia from the age of nine. The Khmer can be counted amongst sorcery's true believers. Their occultists are among the most respected and feared in Southeast Asia. Many Thai men sport magical, protective tattoos with Khmer script. 'Smoke children' are the Cambodian equivalent of the *khuman thong* and are created in much the same way. Such ritualistic practises have been attributed to the ancient Angkoreans and the more recent Khmer Rouge; documented cases still occur today among the country's backwoods folk.

Fielding a question about what the selling points of the film were, Nen Aer gave a cold-blooded laugh. "The tattoos all over my body, the grilling of children and my background." With the sunglasses on, it was hard to tell if he was practicing his acting by trying on the villain's part, or if he was genuinely villainous. An outcry from the general public and the Federation of the National Film Association of Thailand ensured that the film was later canned. Eventually, Nen Aer was sentenced to six months in jail for damaging a corpse and failing to report a death. He was also prohibited from practicing any form of black magic for five years.

During the press conference, however, the witch doctor boasted that three political parties had already asked him to run as a candidate— not far-fetched in a country where politicians are known to dare their rivals, during parliamentary debates, to swear an oath on the revered Emerald Buddha at the Grand Palace. If either of them is lying, the spirits are supposed to put a curse on them. This is also a fairly common way for Thais to settle disputes of honour or insinuations of thievery. Politicians, too, curry favour, seek blessings and try to appease deities and spirits. Even the more progressive Democrat Party has a logo depicting the earth goddess, Mae Toranee, wringing out her hair in order to drown the minions of the Buddhist devil. Amulets bearing images of Khun Paen on one side and the 'golden child' on the other are easy enough to find, particularly around more superstitious areas like the Khmer-style temple of Wat Khao Phnom Ruang in Buri Ram province, where souvenir stands sell them for as little as 60 baht.

In 2002, Thailand's then-Prime Minister Thaksin Shinawatra and his sister lit the main candles to commence a ceremony in homage to the God of Darkness at the Srisathong Temple in Nakhon Nayok province. The famous fortune-teller Attaviroj Sritula said the pair became believers after Thaksin barely escaped death on a Bangkok runway the previous year. "The plane exploded [on the runway] before he got on board because Rahu protected him." At the time, the prime minister was supposed to fly to Chiang Mai to cut the ribbon for a relaunch of a shopping mall managed by his sister Yaowaret, who had asked Rahu to watch over the place. Unlike in India, Rahu is an auspicious deity in Thailand.

An astrology buff, Thaksin refused to speak with the press for weeks towards the end of 2005 because Mars was not in a favourable position for him, he said. Only a few months later, after a series of financial scandals and a laughable reality TV show about poverty eradication, the premier found himself bogged down in a political quagmire. Battling against the People's Alliance for Democracy, and an ever-growing number of protestors clamouring for his resignation, he once again resorted to the occult. In the northeastern province of Surin (famous for its tuskers and Khmer influence), Thaksin rode an elephant to strengthen his tenuous grip on power, and performed the same ancient rite as Siamese soldiers once did before a big battle: walking under an elephant's belly to absorb some of its might. When he was given a magical elephant prod with which to scare away his enemies, he told the press, "I will use this prod, along with spells and talismans, to control the fierce opponents who are trying to oust me."

At the same time, his political foes tried to use black magic against him. A senator from Buri Ram province named Karun Saingam advised the hordes of female protestors in Bangkok to hold photos of the premier, or pieces of paper inscribed with his name, against their crotches while cursing him three times. Whether such rituals have any power or are mere mumbo-jumbo, the prime minister stepped down in April 2006 after winning an election that all the major opposition parties boycotted. An election that cost taxpayers two billion baht, with no opposition, in which the winning party still ended up losing? Since logic only makes a rare cameo in the tragic farce that is Thai politics, why couldn't a black magician become a premier politico?

Although he boasted about having many big-name politicians as clients, Nen Aer's threat to run for political office back in 1995 never left the starting blocks. For the next few years, I only heard a few anecdotes about him. A female colleague at *The Nation* told me that she'd seen him on a chat show, along with his new bride, and that he appeared to be trying to whitewash his tarnished image. Where else in the world would a practitioner of the black arts and 'serial baby-griller' become a chat-show celebrity? Even sensationalistic American programmes that air shows such as *Single Moms on Crack* would have found that objectionable.

Not long after the five-year ban on him practicing the black arts expired, Canadian photographer Steve Sandford caught up with the sorcerer at his home in Saraburi province.

Did Steve find him particularly evil?

"Criminally evil, cagey... he had a bodyguard in the next room and a kick-boxing ring outside the house. He showed us some of his human skulls—not a real nice guy—and he was braggin' about the photo on his wall of him and the politician Snoh Tienthong."

The black magician showed him some vials of what he claimed were a love potion made from melting the chin fat of corpses. ("It's not like basting a turkey for Thanksgiving," said Steve, laughing.) These vials, known as *nam man phrai*, sell for up to 10,000 baht, because one drop of the potion on someone's skin is said to have enough power to make that person fall in love with whoever put it there.

Nen Aer told Steve that he had 'grilled' a thousand babies, having stolen some of them from cemeteries. The shrunken and mummified corpses could then fit into a trouser pocket or purse. Unless the owner appeased them with soft drinks and sweets, the spirit of the *khuman thong* ('golden child') could wreak havoc on them, bouncing up and down on their beds at night until they went mad.

To show off his purported power, the former novice dripped wax from several candles on his tongue (a classic trick amongst Thai spirit mediums and sex-show performers) and jabbed himself with a long sword to show that it didn't draw blood. The sorcerer warned Steve not to write anything bad about him as he poked coffin nails into the eyes of a tiny voodoo doll. One of the skulls in his home, he claimed, was that of a foreign journalist who had dared to betray Nen Aer's Khmer mentor in the black arts.

Some four years later in July 2005, Nen Aer darkened the pages of the local press once again, after 100 cops encircled his huge compound in Saraburi province to snare him in a dragnet. The police had received a multitude of complaints from women that the magician had violated them sexually while performing esoteric rituals designed to increase their powers of attraction and seduction. According to his conquests, Nen Aer had thousands of female customers. The police also uncovered a stash of videotapes showing him engaged in carnal relations with some of his female clients.

Kamronwit Thoopkrajang, the commander of the Crime Against Children, Juveniles and Women Division (who led the raid along with Paveena Hongsakula, a long-time crusader for the rights of women and children), said these video recordings were used to blackmail the women, and that when the police burst into his house, they found the sorcerer in bed with a 19-year-old bargirl from Bangkok. In the room where he conducted his sex magic rituals, the cops confiscated boxes of condoms, Viagra, firearms, 'love potions' and lingerie. Among other items seized at the large compound—which, in addition to the boxing ring, also included a cock-fighting pit—were a new Mercedes-Benz and passbooks for different banks containing almost ten million baht. Police said that Aer scared up business by promoting his supernatural services in many popular Thai publications. For anywhere from 1,000 to 10,000 baht, he could allegedly mend severed relationships with his brand of hocus-pocus. Some of his female customers claimed they had been raped, but most said they were shafted by a charlatan whose only 'magic wand' in working order was possessed by Viagra, not spirits.

Facing up to five years behind bars and the confiscation of his assets on charges of public deceit—an offense under the Money Laundering Act—the trickster pulled his greatest sleight-of-hand yet, disappearing into the twilight zone after losing some of his assets and serving a brief jail term, from which he recently reappeared.

During the political tumult of 2010 that left at least 90 people dead on the streets of Bangkok, the red-shirted protestors resorted to an ancient, supposedly Brahmin ritual, painting the gates of the parliament buildings and the premier's house with buckets of their blood to put a curse on the government that would force them to resign. But the head of Thailand's royal Brahmin priests complained that these rituals were a blasphemous travesty. "We don't use blood in real Brahmin rites and our rites are designed to promote happiness at different stages of life, like at weddings, blessing a newborn, or going to live in a new house," said Phra Ratchakru Wamadhepmuni. "If they want to donate blood, they should give it to those who really need it." Deputy Prime Minister, and the head of national security, Suthep Thangsuban, also condemned the bloodletting. "The world sees some people in Thailand as believers in black magic and as uncivilised." To counter the witchcraft, the government invited religious leaders from the Buddhist, Muslim, Christian and Sikh communities to perform blessing ceremonies in front of the government building.

In several of the photos published in the local press during the protests, a shadowy figure with tattoos on his face appears off to one side. Was the black magician serving as an occult advisor to the red shirts, or making good on his promise to enter the political fray?

As in the days of ancient Siam warring with the Khmer and the Burmese, and during the time of former PM Thaksin Shinawatra praying to Rahu and practicing occult rituals to strengthen his tenuous grip on power, the country's body politic remains paralysed by a centuries-old nerve centre of patronage, nepotism and superstition. As Nen Aer once said when he first threatened to run for political office, "All politicians are like magicians. They cast a spell on you, promise all sorts of miracles, and then people will believe anything they say. There's no more blood on my hands than there is on any politician's."

For the black magician and all the heavyweight politicos he has advised, power, money and sex continue putting curses on policy-making and democratic reforms.

Empowering Sex Workers

No issue has ever politicised sex the way HIV and AIDS have. In its first stages in the mid-1980s, when most people believed that only gay men and intravenous drug users got it, the disease was used by Christian fundamentalists as an example of an Old Testament-style plague brought down by God to punish the wicked.

The disease sanctioned every strain of racism, as many claimed it came from Africa, supposedly because a black man had copulated with a monkey. Conspiracy theorists claimed that it was bio-engineered by rich Western governments hell-bent on destroying and taking over the Third World, or that it didn't exist, or that it was a group of previously known viruses that had mutated into a new and far deadlier malady. In the pharmaceutical community, the disease spawned a multi-billion dollar industry after Robert Gallo, an American biomedical researcher, and several of his colleagues, first identified and isolated the retrovirus in 1984.

Two years later, the first official case in Thailand hit the front page of the country's most popular tabloid, *Thai Rath*, with a headline that read 'Gay Man Contracts AIDS from Gay Foreigner'.

Chantawipa 'Noi' Apisuk recalled the fear and hysteria sweeping through the bars of Patpong, where she first organised informal English classes for sex workers in the Electric Blue go-go bar, which is still there. "The women working in Patpong were terrified of catching the disease from foreign men and there was a lot of hatred directed towards sex workers for spreading the disease." The NGO she had just started, Empower (Education Means Protection of Women Engaged in Recreation) became the first such organisation to distribute a pamphlet about HIV and AIDS in the kingdom, as well as giving out free condoms to sex workers and the male patrons of these bars. "The profession of sex work is not the cause of the transmission. Unprotected sex is the cause of the transmission. This is education we are doing, not blaming people," she said.

Solely funded by a small grant from a Christian organisation in Tokyo, the NGO faced vehement and vocal opposition. Chumporn Apisuk, a Thai artist who has worked with them since the beginning, recalled, "A lot of people wanted to sweep the issue under the carpet. They didn't like seeing us out there distributing leaflets and condoms. I guess they thought it was bad for business. So Noi and I had to equip ourselves with whiskey, beer and gin before going out to visit the bars of Patpong," he said with a laugh.

As the fatal affliction turned into a full-blown pandemic scything through every sector of society across the world, it became the catalyst for the NGO's multi-pronged agenda. "HIV taught us to look at the conflicts of gender, human rights, sex work and many other issues," said Noi.

At the time, there was only one other NGO in all of Thailand even examining questions of human rights, and no support or recognition from the government. But the pandemic brought

Empower's controversial work to a global audience, winning them as many converts as detractors.

One of the organisation's earliest supporters was the late and legendary tycoon, Udom Patpongpanich, who lent half his family name to the roads of Patpong 1 and 2, the capital's biggest tenderloin and nocturnal bazaar for tourists. Noi may be a radical in some ways, but she remains respectfully Thai in many other respects, adding the honorific *khun* ('Mister') every time she speaks of their benefactor. "Khun Udom came down to greet us and meet the women. He thought that English studies were very useful for the women and he rented us a shop-house for a very cheap price of 16,000 baht a month. Having Khun Udom for a benefactor made us look very good." The shophouse that they first rented back in 1989, hemmed in by go-go bars like Super Pussy on both sides, is still a nexus for sex workers in Bangkok.

Empowerment through education has always been at the forefront of the NGO's approach. "Some people have accused us of promoting prostitution by teaching English to the women. We are giving education to the women. What's wrong with that? If other Thai people can go to English and Japanese classes at many other language schools, then why shouldn't sex workers have the same opportunity? The women in Patpong want to speak up for themselves, they want to express their ideas, they want an education and they want to work, but they don't have time to go to normal schools," added Noi.

To this end, the NGO started its own newsletter in 1986. After several name changes, they settled on 'Bad Girls' with the cheeky sub-head, "Good girls go to heaven but bad girls go everywhere", which is both a line from an old Mae West film and a song by Meatloaf. Leaf through some back issues and the contributions from sex workers simmer with rage and buzz with pride. "I don't care what people say. We give them pleasure and we get money. That's enough!" Another wrote, "Don't call us 'social garbage', because we make this world a paradise on earth."

The newsletter underlines Empower's stance that sex work is just another job that women and men can do. This pragmatic philosophy separates them from many other organisations that issue blanket condemnations of the business of pleasure. Francesca Russo, a volunteer English teacher who spent several years giving classes at the Patpong centre while writing a master's thesis about the organisation, said, "It's very, very alternative in terms of its philosophy amongst NGOs in Thailand, which tend to think of sex work as a problem rather than a career. But Empower supports women who wish to continue working in the industry. The other organisations are trying to get women out of the industry, or even trying to prevent them from entering in the first place." What Francesca said is true of many governmental and NGOs around the world that do not see sex work as a viable profession.

But Empower's endorsement of this career choice comes with many caveats. The NGO believes that *pooying borigan* ('service girls') should be considered part of the wider service industry. For many years, Empower has been lobbying the Ministry of Labour to bring the bar staff in commercial sex establishments—waitresses, doormen, go-go dancers and cashiers—under the protection of existing labour laws, which would grant them health benefits, severance pay and sick leave. All their efforts have resulted in little more than lip service from the Thai authorities and a lot of unfulfilled promises.

Surang Janyam, the former manager of the Patpong office who moved upstairs to found SWING, an NGO for male and transgendered sex workers, said, "We believe that sex work is one kind of valid work people can do, but how can we make them safe? How can we ensure they have the same rights as other workers do? And how can they protect themselves?"

The only laws in existence in Thailand that really protect them are for those under 18 years of age. If underage girls or guys get caught working in the sex trade, she said, they might get put in a state-sponsored shelter, but they're soon back in another bar with a different fake ID, and she understands why. "Yes, we have free school in Thailand for twelve years, but if the young girls and boys don't have the money to pay for food, uniforms, transport, how can they study?" Their newsletters are rife with tales of desperation, poverty and dead-end jobs in factories and on farms that led the women to seek more lucrative alternatives.

For some of these social pariahs, the lack of basic rights has a much more violent impact. Surang has had many run-ins with the Thai police. On one occasion, she took a female sex worker, who'd been beaten bloody by one of her customers, to a police box for help. But when she told the cop that the woman worked in a bar on Patpong, he said they couldn't do anything to protect her. That issue is not the sole province of sex workers. As Chumporn said, "Any time a Thai woman gets beaten up, the police will usually side with the man."

Dee, a male sex worker who drops by Empower and SWING to take different classes, recalled how he and two of his male friends from the bar where they worked were taken to Pattaya by a trio of foreign customers. Once inside a resort bungalow, the men set up a video camera and told them to perform a threesome. They refused and were severely beaten. Fearing persecution and public humiliation, the three Thais did not report the incident to the police.

Under the Prostitution Prohibition Law of 1960, sex work is still technically illegal in Thailand. "The women are not sure whether or not they are workers or criminals," said Chumporn, who hosts workshops on theatre and performance art that mix social and political themes in the Patpong centre. "It's in the interest of the entertainment places to keep this law in effect, because they don't have to pay any benefits to the workers." In fact, it took the NGO three years of lobbying the government to have the application forms at these entertainment venues changed. Until then, Chumporn said, the women did not realise that they were actually filling out the same forms police use after making arrests. So the cops had records of every single woman working in these bars. "The police were not using those records for anything, but they didn't understand that there was anything wrong with this practise or that it was infringing on basic rights."

Frustrated by their lack of progress with the Ministry of

Labour and club owners, Empower opened the Can Do Bar in Chiang Mai in 2006. Nicely lit and tastefully decorated, the bar defies any seedy stereotypes. In the back is a pool table. Out front is a terrace. The atmosphere is laidback; it's not one of those 'hard sell' bars where patrons are constantly pestered by bargirls spewing the same mercenary inanities ("You buy me cola?") over and over again. Billed as the only 'Experitainment Bar' in Thailand, it may well be one of the few establishments in the world run by sex workers for sex workers.

More importantly, the Can Do Bar is a kind of laboratory where Empower has put many of its hypotheses into practise. True to their word, they adhere to the labour laws governing the hospitality sector. All the female staff members, who also moonlight as sex workers, receive social security, sick leave and proper days off.

Because the bar is located on a Thai entertainment strip, far away from the Night Bazaar and other tourist enclaves, they don't receive a lot of walk-in customers. Mostly it's word-of-mouth that brings in patrons from all over the world. Liz Cameron, an Australian national who has worked with the Chiang Mai centre for many years, said they have entertained everyone from European diplomats and UN officials to a contingent of sex workers from a Canadian NGO. These visitors have made their mark in the bathrooms, leaving an array of gushing graffiti and sympathetic comments. One of their Canadian 'sisters' wrote, "The women of Empower are Goddesses!"

Touring the bar's upper floor, it's easy to spot the twin embryos of knowledge and language that have fertilised the NGO from the beginning. Much like the classroom in the Patpong office, the walls of the study centre in Chiang Mai are lined with similar slogans and letters that spell out the language of self-reliance for working girls—'bread winner', 'medicine', 'condom', 'happy'—next to polite expressions the women want to learn, such as "Can you buy me a drink, please?" "Do you want company?"

Empower's founder, Chantawipa (or Noi), was awakened to the power of the written and spoken word when her family relocated to Boston in 1975, around the same time as end of the Vietnam War. Her early days in the United States were fraught with tension. "They called all of us Asians 'yellow'." While studying at Boston College, in between working shifts as a waitress at Pizza Hut, she befriended a number of different Asian minorities and noticed that many women had been leading the protests against the Vietnam War. "It looked to me like women the world over face the same problems of discrimination. We're all second-class citizens." Working with different human rights organisations in New York and Boston, covering everything from the forced sterilisation of women in Third World countries to children slaving away in Thai sweatshops, Noi also schooled herself in the protest songs of Bob Dylan and Joan Baez, making many useful contacts that she put to good use upon returning to Thailand in 1985. She quickly realised that many of her aspirations were well ahead of her time (the Human Rights Commission of Thailand was only founded in the late 1990s). While drinking beer with her American colleagues in bars around Patpong, she became a default English teacher and translator for many working girls who wanted to communicate with foreign men they had become involved with. Noi broke into a rendition of 'Dear John', a popular song of the Vietnam War era that encapsulated the language barrier that the Western man and Asian woman could not surmount.

Teaching the women English and the ideas that inform the *lingua franca* was the starting line for Empower. "When they learn English and get educated on other subjects like human rights, it minimises exploitation at work, and they can make better decisions and regain their pride and self-confidence," said Noi.

The language of dehumanisation that keeps the downtrodden in their place is evident in the way the streetwalkers lurking in the shadows of Sanam Luang in Bangkok are referred to as 'tamarind tree ghosts', while the hookers working the streets around the capital's Lumpini Park are referred to as 'Lumpini ghosts'. Such derogatory terms are hardly unique to Thailand. They are endemic everywhere. In Los Angeles, for example, when a pimp or customer murders a prostitute, the police assign the case a low-priority tag known as 'AVA, NHI', which stands for 'Asshole Versus Asshole, No Human Involved'.

In attempting to rewrite the language of victimisation, Empower, with support from the Rockefeller Foundation, published the Bad Girl's Dictionary in 2007. On sale at the Can Do Bar in Chiang Mai, the dictionary was authored by Pornpit

Puckmai and Liz Cameron, with contributions from all the Empower members across the country. Noi and Liz split the editing credits. It's a fascinating compendium of facts about the sex industry for foreigners in Thailand (although it rarely touches on the much bigger domestic trade), with references to the golden days of Ayuthaya some 400 years ago; the 700,000 GIs from the Vietnam War who came to Thailand for 'rest and recreation'; the first chrome poles in the go-go bars that came from a strip club in Montreal in the early 1980s; and the fact that the business is second only to rice in generating more foreign exchange. They also quote a report from the International Labour Organisation stating that each year, 'sex workers send US$300 million dollars home. This is more than any government rural development budget'.

But the book's core is language, and it's manifesto to challenge stereotypes and clichés. 'Bad girls' they define in both Thai and English as, "Any woman who behaves or thinks outside the space society maps out for them; name of Empower's newsletter". As synonyms they list 'revolutionary or rebel'.

In the introduction of the book, Pornpit, the coordinator of the Chiang Mai office, wrote about how thrilled she was to attend the AWID 10th International Forum (Association for Women's Rights in Development) held in Bangkok in 2005. At the same time, she said, "It was also hard to be labelled a 'victim' and a 'prostituted woman' rather than be respected as the hard working sex worker, family provider, community leader and human rights defender that I am. It was hard to be the only sex worker in a room when the

USAID representative declared that the mighty US government and herself believe that my work degrades all women."

Only a few months before that conference, Pornpit had won the inaugural prize as a 'Women's Rights Defender' from the Thai National Human Rights Commission. That left her wondering, "How could I be both... a recognised women's rights defender and a disgrace to women at the same time?"

The dictionary addresses these contradictions and academic constructs. "The right to define, to create, to adapt words and language is often seen as the right of academics alone. They alone claim the right to invent terms like 'indirect prostitute' and have them accepted even though the very people it refers to do not use, acknowledge or identify with the terms in any way As sex workers, we must be one of the most talked and written about groups in the world, but most of the words used about us have not come from us. We have our own vibrant living language and understanding of the terms used about us."

Incorporating their signature style of cheekiness and outrage, Empower shuns the expression 'flesh trade': "Not our business... we don't cut off our flesh and trade it! We entertain our customers. We sell services not meat. That would be a butcher or abattoir. Preferred: Entertainment Industry." They are quite right in noting that terms like 'prostitute' and 'whore' have become meaningless. Everyone has misappropriated variations on them, from Nirvana satirising themselves on the band's T-shirts that sported the slogan 'Corporate Rock Whores' to Thai politicians flinging the insult at their rivals to label them as 'corrupt' or for buying votes.

Noi believes that their work over the last 27 years has opened up wider channels of communication on the debate about the ins and outs of sex work. Having delivered lectures at universities in New York and Seattle, as well as at many international conferences, and becoming a Harvard Law School fellow in the International Human Rights programme, Noi said the dialogue is not as shrill or scholarly as it used to be. "We can talk about sex work now in universities. Before we could only talk about sexual abuse. Everyone took it that women selling their bodies equalled sexual abuse."

Does she feel much freer now to discuss her pet peeves and passions at conferences?

"Everywhere I speak, I don't care, I don't mind, I will say what I want. People can listen or not," she said with a grin. "But I only accept invitations to speak on the subjects that Empower specialises in: HIV and AIDS, tourism and sex work, and the cross-border migration of sex workers in Southeast Asia, from countries like Cambodia, Laos, Burma, Vietnam and China. It's a growing problem. If tourists can travel freely through these countries, then why can't women in search of work?" (A 2003 report published by the NGO spelled out the differences between 'migrant sex workers' and women forced into prostitution.)

Thanks to their worldwide reputation as iconoclasts, the Empower centres have become hotbeds of intellectual tumult, with scholars, lawmakers, policemen and representatives from both governmental and non-governmental organisations descending upon them. Many visitors have their preconceptions challenged.

Tanyaporn Wansom, a Thai who grew up in America and returned to her homeland on a prestigious Fulbright Scholarship to do work on HIV/AIDS, had some of her feminist theories called into question through teaching English at the centre. "I'd just graduated from a kind of liberal school in the United States which was big on women's rights and women's studies, and I think I had more of a black and white view [of commercial sex], like it's all disgusting and it's all bad. But after working here and meeting some of the people, I can see both sides more and I'm less judgmental."

Having young scholars like Tanyaporn as volunteer teachers has also boosted the learning levels of the students and their self-esteem. Chumporn noted a dramatic improvement in the English and educational levels of the women who come to the Patpong office. "Five or ten years ago some of the women could barely read and write. Today they're much better. I don't think the education system has improved, but women are going to school for longer now." As an art instructor at other schools for the young, who puts on 'imagination workshops' in performance art and socio-political theatre for the women of Empower, he said their creativity is no greater than many of his other students, but "their life experiences are totally different. They're better able to deal with society and take care of themselves. They're also much less shy, and when you're less shy you can produce a lot more."

To keep up with the students' learning prowess and shifting interests, the classes at Empower have changed over the years. "We don't need to teach them so much about IT and computers now," said Chumporn. "They know more about these subjects than we do." He smiled. "But we'd like to do more with 'tourist guide English' as many of the women are escorting their customers on trips throughout the country."

For Empower, and many other such NGOs, decriminalising prostitution is the biggest concern. Doing so, they say, would usher in more protection in the form of laws and rights for male and female sex workers, while ridding the profession of criminal elements and police corruption. In this regard, they have allies in high places. Liz Cameron of their Chiang Mai office pointed out that decriminalising prostitution was endorsed by Ban Ki-moon, the secretary-general of the United Nations, during the UN High Level Meeting on HIV/AIDS in 2008. The secretary-general claimed that this would also help to stem the flow of HIV/AIDS, which has been making a comeback in recent years.

During the 15th International Conference on HIV/AIDS held in Bangkok in 2004, Empower stole the show with one of their performances. They set up a small bar where women danced in bikinis. As Noi recalled, "You should have seen all the different people lining up to watch the women pole dancing. There were religious leaders, NGO people, cops and even the security guards. It was fun and people should have something different at these conferences. But it wasn't like a porn movie and the dancers didn't take off their clothes. It was part of a demonstration about different lubricants, such as water or oil based, and how these can affect or even break various kinds of condoms. Many people still don't know about this."

Among the 20,000 delegates at that conference were more than 100 sex workers from 21 countries, as well as a large contingent from Empower who, in the middle of the 'Global Village', created the 'Bangkok A-Go-Go Bar' with a mamasan, bartenders, MCs and dancers. The multi-nationality contingent of sex workers put on plays and puppet shows, ran workshops, did poetry readings and even presented research papers. Many of them also took part in different demonstrations against pharmaceutical companies, as well as in the official parade.

Quintessentially Thai in many respects (as is Noi with her laugh-a-minute personae), Empower has always coupled entertainment with edification. Besides the dictionary, they have put out T-shirts, a 'Bad Girls' calendar featuring sex workers in provocative poses but sporting serious slogans such as 'Free Trade Agony' stenciled across a mini-skirted bottom. Up north they run radio shows. In Bangkok they sponsored a pole-dancing competition where Thai health officials watched from the sidelines. No matter how earnest their messages are, Noi said, "We still have to make it fun."

In recent years, the NGO has spun 360 degrees. With support from the Global Fund to Fight AIDS, tuberculosis and malaria, Empower has embarked on a new HIV/AIDS awareness programme that includes 50 volunteers handing out condoms and leaflets at hotspots for sex workers and their customers in Bangkok.

But they have also remained true to their grassroots in that their 11 offices across the country still serve as community centres. One of the most demoralising aspects of the job is bearing the social stigma attached to it and the estrangement from families and friends. Dee, the male go-go dancer, said, "I don't trust people outside the 'business' and all my old friends deserted me when they found out I work in a bar." With downcast eyes, he added, "I really wanted to be a good example for my brother and sister, but it was impossible to do so and still make enough money to help them."

Dee and many of the women who come to their offices are drawn by a similar spirit of solidarity. On this afternoon in July 2010, a male and female duo of music teachers was giving singing lessons to about 20 women and several ladyboys in the karaoke room of the Patpong centre, which also serves as the Sex Worker's Museum. Do not expect to be titillated by the sight of a few photos of go-go dancers, a story taped to the wall about the smash hit 'One Night in Bangkok', a few sex toys in a glass case and an enlarged map made in Berlin back in the 1980s that exposed different enclaves of male, female and transgendered sex workers in the capital.

Dressed in casual clothes and chit-chatting about the same subjects that obsess young women all over the planet—clothes, makeup, family problems and gossip—no one would have pictured these women as 'ladies of the night'.

The students had decided that they wanted to learn an R&B hit by one of their heroines, Tata Young, a half-Thai/half-American singer who has amassed a considerable following all across Asia for tunes such as 'Naughty, Sexy, Bitchy'. Lined with lyrics that mock the good-girl fairytales of Snow White and Cinderella, the song the students wanted to learn had struck a few power chords with them through its message of self-determination. As the chorus of 'Cinderella' kicked in, 20 voices rose in an outcry of disquieting harmonies:

I don't wanna be like Cinderella

Sitting in a dark old dusty cellar

Waiting for somebody to come and set me free

I don't wanna be like Snow White

Waiting for a handsome prince to come and save me

On a horse of white unless we're riding side by side

Don't want to depend on no one else

I'd rather rescue myself...

For the 'bad girls' of Empower, it sounded like their theme song.

A Cross-Section of the Third Gender

I'd only been in Bangkok for about a week and was waiting for a bus on a street swarming with passersby and cars. Along the sidewalk sashayed a statuesque ladyboy, balancing a rattan tray on her head piled high with jasmine garlands. Not only was she more attractive than any transvestite I'd ever seen in the West, she also walked in a much more feminine way, without the exaggerated wiggle. But the most surprising thing was that none of the Thais at the bus stop even gave her a second glance. Nobody yelled anything rude at her. Nobody gossiped behind her back. Nobody (and I could easily imagine this happening in the West) pushed her so that the tray of garlands spilled all over the ground.

As I spotted more ladyboys around town, eliciting the same non-reaction from Thais and the same snorts of derision, along with the occasional cock-eyed leer from the foreigners, I had to conclude that Thailand was one tolerant country. But many travellers come to these facile conclusions after only a short time in a new place. It took a few years to realise that Thailand is superficially tolerant of the third sex. Behind the face values of Buddhist compassion, bigotry runs much deeper than bad blood.

Seemingly every soap opera or comedy cabaret has some hideous caricature of a shrieking drag queen (*kathoey*) who is the butt of the jokes and plays a servile role. Strutting around and preening in any of Bangkok's sex-for-sale zones are a few ladyboys and a gaggle of older grotesques who have not aged well and seem bound for the gutter or a fatal addiction.

Few living *kathoey* have experienced more of this persecution than 'Aunty Nong'. Now in her early 70s, still unable to read or write and disowned by her family at a young age, she is not even sure when she was born. Nevertheless, on the first Monday of July, she celebrates her birthday by making merit at a temple. "I pray to the gods to forgive me and to watch over me, because it's a miracle I'm still alive," she said.

Aunty Nong (real name: Suwing Nisgonsen) lives in a decrepit one-room tenement off Surawongse Road. The room, stacked high with her belongings, reeked of stale cigarettes and cat urine. She grew up during the Japanese occupation of Bangkok during World War II. As with architect Sumet Jumsai and many others interviewed for this book, the Allied bombing of Bangkok left deep craters in Nong's reminiscences of adolescence. When recounting the time she carried her young nephew under her arm during one such bombardment, past pulverised bodies, and taking refuge in the Royal Temple of Wat Bowoniwet, her wizened eyes filled with tears. Overcome by a surge of emotions, she brushed the tears away, saying, "I don't want to talk about it anymore."

Bantering with Nong, and the writing duo of Susan Aldous and Pornchai Sereemongkonpol, who were researching a book called *Ladyboys: The Secret World of Thailand's Third Gender*, the conversation wound down a series of ever-darker passageways. Like many older people, Nong's mind has become warped with time, flitting from era to era and episode to episode, in a few short sentences. For the elderly, events of 50 or 60 years ago are often perceived with greater clarity than something that happened last week.

Nong's father was a combat veteran of the Indochina wars. By the time she was born, the youngest of six siblings (all deceased except for one sister), her Chinese dad was a comatose opium addict. Her mother hawked Thai desserts from a pair of baskets she lugged around on shoulder poles. To make matters worse, her older brother beat her up on a regular basis, because of the feminine mannerisms she displayed even as a youngster. There was barely any money for food. There was none for school.

Her only respite from the drudgery of reality was watching the traditional Thai dances and dramas at Wat Saket and the Golden Mount. "I wanted so badly to be beautiful like the dancers," she said, kneeling on the floor of her hovel—which had no chairs—clad in a blouse and a flowery sarong. "I wanted to be appreciated." Besides the temple, her other refuge was the Penang Cinema (which has long since closed) near Khaosan Road, where she liked to watch the handsome matinee idols of the time like Gregory Peck and Tyrone Powers, whenever she could sneak in without buying a ticket.

At the age of 15, Nong's mother told her that their family was imploding and she could no longer afford to take care of her. So the teenager ended up sleeping on streets and in public bathrooms, doing odd jobs like pulling rickshaws and, finally, with the help of a group of transvestites, she began dressing more effeminately. At first the results were hilarious, she said, laughing. After putting on lipstick for the first time, Nong remembered eating a bowl of noodles only to notice afterwards that her entire mouth and chin had turned scarlet.

But the abuse she suffered was not nearly so amusing. Many people called her and the other *kathoey 'seea chat gert'*, or a 'waste of a reincarnation'. "I couldn't help it. I was born this way. I can't change," she said. At least there was more solidarity amongst the transvestites in those days, she said, and the other 'girls' would give her odd jobs like cleaning their apartments in return for free room and board.

She met her first male lover when she was still a teenager. They met by the bridge of Saphan Put, which was a pick-up spot then, and a hyperactive night bazaar now. Although he knew that she was a female imposter, they lived together for a while. But her lover was pathologically jealous—to the point where he used to beat her thighs and legs so she couldn't leave the house, or barely even walk.

In time, Nong's looks, flair for fashion and dancing skills allowed her to remake herself as a professional dancer, performing at funerals, ordination ceremonies for novice monks, private parties and temple fairs. Sometimes they would even put on shows in rural areas, riding buffalo-pulled carts through the moonlit rice paddies. She also worked at the old dance halls in Bangkok. Men would buy tickets and then approach a woman they wanted to dance with. Many of them had no idea that their dance partners were not biological women. "All the men were drunk. Sometimes they'd even fight over the girls and shoot their guns in the air," said Nong, in the craggy voice of a serial smoker. "It was so much fun."

But as a professional dancer, she was always teetering on the edge of destitution. To supplement her income, she used to work as a street-walker along Silom Road. The hookers feared sadistic clients much less than they did the police corps. Many of her sisters of the night ended up doing long jail terms for soliciting or not giving enough bribes to the bullies in brown. One night Nong was chased down a street by two cops. She ran into a construction site, jumped into a pit and covered herself with mud and dirt so the police could not spot her with their flashlights.

Over the course of her 70-odd years, Nong has seen many positive changes for the third sex, such as the installation of special bathrooms in schools and the formation of various self-help groups and NGOs, but her own progress has been scant. The streets of Silom where she once trawled for customers and the tenement where she now lives with a cat as her sole companion are separated by a few blocks and 40 years. To make ends meet, she walks around the red-light zone of Patpong hawking lighters by night. As befitting her status as the grand dame of Bangkok's transgendered underworld, some of the sex workers buy her wares and give her handouts.

When we got up to leave, Aunty Nong gave each of us a personal blessing for happiness, good health and prosperity. "Don't forget about me," she said. "Please come back and visit whenever you want. Sometimes I'm afraid that if I die here alone nobody would even find my body for days."

Looking at the roll call of interviewees in Susan and Pornchai's book—a bank teller, a fashion designer, a PR manager, an economist and even an entire pop group—shows that the Thai transsexuals of today have broader horizons and higher career trajectories than their dead-end 'sisters' of Nong's day.

The first transsexual to break through on a global level was the *muay thai* star, Parinya Charoenphol, better known by her nickname of Nong ('Little Sister') Toom. In 1998, during her first bout at Lumphini Stadium in Bangkok, the 16-year-old—wearing full make up—knocked out a much bigger male fighter. After the fight, she kissed him on the cheek. Soon, the beautiful boxer, whose goal was to make enough money for a sex change and to support her impoverished parents, was notching up knockout after knockout and making money hand over fist. From all over the globe, members of the mass media descended in droves to file features about her. Ever the show-woman, Nong Toom was fond of quips such as, "He was so cute I just hated to knock him out!"

But in 1999 she hung up her gloves and underwent a full sex change. Her singing and acting career rarely got off the ropes. In 2003, the Thai director and Singaporean expat Ekachai Uekrongtham made her story into a powerful film called *Beautiful Boxer* that picked up a few awards at foreign film festivals.

Susan and Pornchai interviewed her for their book.

"I was thinking here was going to be very a muscular jock and aggressive woman, but she was quite the opposite," said Susan. "She was very friendly and sweet and beautiful... sexy but in a tasteful way… a very trusting person too. She drove us back into Bangkok in her car and then took us to meet her parents. She even took us out to eat with her at a local street stall. Everyone recognised her, but she was so down to earth. I came away feeling like I'd made a friend."

The writers found out she's had a few boyfriends but always practises monogamy. Nong Toom told them she was happy with the biopic and thought it was a fairly accurate depiction of her life. The plot, however, is almost like *Rocky*: through great determination, a poor kid rises above adversity to beat the odds. Not surprisingly, the film was more popular in the West, where stories of individualism and self-determination appeal much more to the Western mindset.

In early 2006, she returned to the ring for an exhibition match at the training centre, the Nong Toom Fairfax Gym in Pattaya, where many foreigners come to study the martial art of *muay thai*. She bested the Japanese fighter in that match. In the same year, she starred in the Thai action movie *Mercury Man* (a critical calamity— with a villain named 'Osama bin Ali'—that took a serious beating at the box office). Nong Toom's role in this loony cartoon proved that her fighting prowess was still much stronger than her acting.

The beautiful boxer's international prominence has broken down the door for other performers, who were usually relegated to lip-synching and vamping it up in cabaret shows for tourists in Bangkok, Phuket and Koh Samui, or competing in the annual Miss Tiffany beauty pageant for transsexuals held in Pattaya every February. Following in the slinky footsteps of the first all-transgendered group, South Korea's Lady, came Bangkok's Venus Flytrap, a group of high-society women who wrested the gig from hundreds of wannabes. As you can tell from their stage names like Nok (Posh Venus) and Bobo (Naughty Venus), originality is not their forte. *Visa for Love* (Sony BMG Thailand, 2006), the group's debut album of artificially sweetened R&B was not everyone's cup of treacle. Most of the tunes, videos and dances traversed the same catwalk trodden by the Spice Girls. Declared *personae non grata* on the pop charts, *Visa for Love* was a commercial fiasco. The group eventually disbanded.

But that curtain call may be premature. In late 2009, 'Cool Venus' (Tay Peeraya), who earned a degree in Textile Design from an Australian university, joined a new ladyboy troupe of singers,

actresses and models called Shade of Divas. The leader and founder of the troupe is Teerawat 'Tina' Thongmitr. She told the *Bangkok Post*, "We hope to create a group or an agency for transvestites and transgendered women. For those film or television producers out there, if you are looking for a unique *kathoey* character, you know where to go."

One of the contestants for the annual Miss Tiffany Universe Contest held in Pattaya bares her 'claws' at the press conference. The four-day event features a number of different awards for the Media Favourite, the Friendship Beauty Queen and Miss Silky Sexy Skin.

Tina, who said she has lost jobs as a graphic

designer when clients found out about her 'sexuality', said her best offer so far came in early 2010 when a German theatrical director came to Thailand to stage a play called *Ministry of Truth* at the Patravadi Theatre in Bangkok. The play was based on the reality show *Big Brother*. "The show centred around a mixed group of Thais and foreigners who shared days and nights together in a house, with one to emerge as the winner. My role was to express my thoughts on being a transgender woman. I found it fascinating for a show to dig deeper into the issues of gender, going far beyond the usual portrayal of ladyboys. As my first professional acting role, it was a great challenge but I was so glad to be part of it," she said

After a successful run in Bangkok, Tina and the rest of the cast traveled to Berlin where it was restaged under the name *On Air*. Through her experiences working with the director and foreign cast members, she is hopeful that the third gender will find more mainstream acceptance abroad. "While working on the show, I learnt to appreciate foreigners in the way they respect you for who you are, regardless of your gender. If you have good ideas to share, they will listen to you."

The high-society domain that the members of Venus Flytrap and Shade of Divas inhabit is a penthouse above the seedy streets where many gender-blenders work. Around areas like Patpong, Nana Plaza, Soi Cowboy and Lumphini Park, they cater to the world's oldest obsession. Their reputation, however, has been blackened by tales of thievery and violence. Some practice unsavoury tricks such as coating their breasts with sedatives or spiking the drinks of their customers.

After the client passes out he is stripped of all his valuables. Even Aunty Nong complained to us that some younger ladyboys who use drugs and steal have given the third gender a bad name.

On the so-called 'Boys Soi' off Surawongse Road, rammed with go-go boy bars and fronted by shirtless men pumping iron outside clubs to the tune of cavity-loosening house music, we sat with Bee, a young streetwalker, at the subtly named Dick's Bangkok Café. Bee often stops by a couple of beauty salons at the end of street where sex workers congregate before their shifts.

Strikingly beautiful with long glossy black hair and skin the colour of bone china, she was dressed for work in tight jeans and a cleavage-revealing top. Like many Thai youth, she wore fashionable braces with traces of pink. When she was growing up in northeast Thailand, Bee said she was a normal boy with no feminine or gay urges whatsoever. The turning point in her life came when she met a gang of cross-dressers who introduced her to Patpong and the gay scene. For her, becoming a ladyboy of the evening was a career move, a step up in the service industry where she had been employed as a waitress. Peer pressure exerted an influence, she admitted, as did what Aunty Nong said about how *kathoey* have become trendy.

At first, Bee began dressing up at home. Later, she went to work at the King's Castle 3 go-go bar on Patpong 1, where most of the dancers are transvestites and transsexuals. She began taking hormones to enlarge her breasts, but taped down her penis. It was incredibly painful, she said in a hushed voice that bespoke her fear of sounding too masculine. Many customers still want a sex worker with breasts and a penis, Bee said. At the same time, she figured she could make more money by having gender reassignment surgery. Because she was only 18 then, and Thai law stipulates that someone must be 20, her mother came down to sign the form for her.

The sex change cost 120,000 baht and it was excruciating. Usually, the scars take about two months to heal, but the side effects can be chronic. Commons ailments are difficulty urinating and not being unable to achieve an orgasm. Bee said that she still experiences pleasurable sensations 'down there'—sometimes she will have a sexy dream and wake up moist—but she cannot fully climax.

Almost every night, the 21-year-old scours the streets around Patpong for customers. At 1,000 baht a shot, she usually makes around 10,000 baht per month. "I don't have any other opportunities and no education," she said, reiterating a familiar lament among sex workers, while sweeping her long hair back. "And I don't think much about the future."

What are the differences between real women and ladyboys?

"Real women have uteruses," she said, flashing a metallic grin.

That's it?

Another grin. "That's it."

It was a snappy comment intended to shock and amuse—hardly atypical among the young trying to look cool—but it was revealing on a deeper level: Bee and her friends do not think of themselves as being any emotionally or psychologically different than natural-born women. Sadly, this is generally not the way they are seen by the majority of the straitlaced world.

With a little coaxing, Bee doled out a few blow-by-blow descriptions of her job with all the passion of a secretary talking about spread sheets. Business as usual, nothing to get excited about. More important, she said, after thanking us for speaking with her, was the chance to talk openly about her life for the first time with no judgments levied. For Bee, that opportunity was cathartic.

As politely as Aunty Nong, Bee put her palms together and raised them to the level of her nose to bid us good night and wished us good luck in Thai. She disappeared into a crowd of body-builders, touts and hungry-eyed tourists massing and frothing around the mouth of Boys Soi.

By then it was almost midnight. In an upstairs show bar on Patpong—where the women put on displays of 'vaginal Olympics' using props like darts, candles, cigarettes, razor blades and honking horns—we met Joy, a 30-year-old ladyboy. She was the most vivacious dancer in the bar, gyrating to house music with a 40-karat smile and a zest that went far beyond the zombie shuffle that is *de rigeur mortis* in Bangkok's go-go bars.

As a young buffalo-herder from rural Thailand, Joy was already trying on dresses and smearing ashes on her face to make mascara at a young age. She knew then she was not really a boy. Yet another exile from a state of poverty and provincial attitudes, she came to Bangkok to earn enough money to study dressmaking and subjects such as accounting so she could start her own fashion business and find a husband to settle down with. But lately, Joy said, she'd been doing some soul-searching by studying Buddhism. She wanted to know why she'd been born this way. Karma was the answer. Joy believed she'd raped or abused some women in her past life, and thus had been reincarnated as a ladyboy to know how women feel, and repent for the errors of her ways.

Over the top of the throbbing dance beats (which is music that never rises above the groin), Joy said she didn't want to have her sexual organ amputated because she worries about having her sex drive curbed, but in her work she has found a spiritual calling: giving pleasure to others is a good deed not so different from other acts of Buddhist compassion.

Over the course of that hard day's night, we had encountered a grandmotherly type in her 70s—scarred by memories of World War II and terrified of dying alone, and a striking young streetwalker who claimed 'ladyboys' is an oxymoron because, uteruses aside, they are much more feminine than masculine. We'd swapped anecdotes about a gracious celebrity kickboxer and a pop troupe of high-society singers with less 'balls' (but more testosterone) than the Spice Girls, and we'd discussed Buddhism and reincarnation with a seamstress-cum-business student-cum-bargirl, whose first experiments in cross-dressing were witnessed only by water buffalo on a rice farm.

All of them were kind and decent folks. Any of the usual labels like 'tranny', 'drag queen' or 'ladyboy' had been stripped of their negative connotations and sleazy merchandising, because it's always much easier to judge than it is to empathise. That's what all the people we chatted with were looking for—empathy.

Just like everyone else.

Erecting a Tribute to
A Fertility Goddess

Thai vendors put them at the bottom of their plastic money baskets to reap a greater cash harvest. Some men wear belts strung with them under their trousers as a kind of supernatural Viagra. Magazines devoted to amulets advertise miniature ones carved from ivory and inscribed with Khmer incantations, and Buddhist monks will bless them for you. Tucked away behind the Swissotel Nai Lert Park Hotel on Wireless Road in Bangkok is a shrine that's almost literally overflowing with them.

Yes, the phallic symbol stands tall and proud in Thailand.

Behind the Swissotel is an 'alfresco hothouse' of tropical flowers and shrubs, with a shrine devoted to the fertility goddess Tubtim. The walkway leading to it is studded with wooden phalluses in all sorts of shapes, sizes and shades. Some of them stand two-metres tall and one even has the hindquarters of a pig, which is a Chinese symbol of fertility. Many of these offerings have been placed there by both men and women whose wishes have been fulfilled by the goddess. Married couples come to ask the spirit-in-residence for a child. Single women pray for a husband who is prosperous and faithful. Men entreat her to help them rise above impotence.

Behind the sanctuary, shaded by a natural umbrella of foliage, is Khlong Saen Saeb. Until the mid-1970s, this canal was one of the area's commercial bloodlines where floating brothels once trawled for customers, to and fro from different piers. When the hotel was constructed in the late 1980s, they renovated the decades-old spirit house, right beside the canal, under a sacred ficus tree garlanded with sashes. One woman who prayed for a child there became pregnant, which—for fertile imaginations—gave birth to the shrine's legacy.

The Fertility Shrine in Bangkok gives rise to the spectre of phallic power.

The ficus or bodhi tree (held sacred by many Thais because it's the tree that Buddha sat under to attain enlightenment) is still there. As with many Thai ghosts—especially the female ones—Tubtim's spirit is said to reside in the tree. That's why there are offerings such as women's clothes hanging from the branches. Around the trunk of the tree are other gifts such as make-up and dolls of classical dancers.

Smaller versions of these phallic totem poles are known as *palad khik*. One of my regular motorcycle taxi drivers keeps one attached to his keychain for good luck. The *palad khik* are the ones advertised in Thai magazines devoted to amulets; the more elaborate talismans sell for thousands of baht. But the market beside the Tha Tien Pier in Bangkok, close to the Temple of the Emerald Buddha, has a whopping selection of them, most costing only a handful of spare change.

Fertility goddesses, however, demand bigger tributes, like the ones at the Swissotel shrine, or the poles wrapped with colourful sashes in the Princess Cave on Krabi's tourist hotspot Railay Beach, where there's a spirit house dedicated to the ghost of a drowned Indian princess whose ship sank off the coast. She later became something of an oceanic fertility goddess—local fishermen began to leave offerings so she would help them reel in a big catch. The phallic symbols left for female apparitions are also meant to provide them with sexual gratification.

But if these shrines are supposed to be presided over by female deities, then why are their only feminine aspects these offerings of clothes, dolls and make-up? That's because, in phallocentric Thailand, where men won't walk under a laundry line strung with female undergarments for fear of losing their virility, the dick has been deified and the vagina turned into a hot commodity.

The Swissotel's sanctuary in Bangkok for the limp, lovelorn and luckless is mostly visited by Thais, primarily on weekends, but it also attracts a few travellers. "For some reason," said one of the security guards, "a few of the foreigners think the shrine was built by desperate, horny women. So they come here and wait for them."

The renovated spirit house is buttressed by an ancient Khmer design which reveals how the shrine is rooted in the Hindu faith, as does the formal name used in Thai for these talismans: *shiwa leung* (literally, 'Shiva's penis'). Which means they're offshoots of Shiva's *lingam*. Centrepieces and objects of reverence at many Indian and Khmer temples, the *lingam* (Sanskrit for 'symbol', 'the image of a god', 'phallus' or 'the mark of a disease') represents the invisible omnipotence of God as well as the thrust of primal energy which started the world, and the human race, with a big almighty bang.

One of the most prominent Hindu scholars of the late 20th century, the American-born Satguru Sivaya Subramuniyaswami defined the *lingam* in his book, *Dancing with Shiva*, as 'the most prevalent icon of Shiva, found in virtually all Shiva temples. It is a rounded, elliptical, aniconic image, usually set on a circular base, or *peetham*. The *lingam* is the simplest and most ancient symbol of Shiva, especially of Parasiva, God beyond all forms and qualities'.

The late sage notes that these symbols are often carved from stone, but can be made from wood, precious gems and metal, or more temporary structures can be formed from a variety of substances, from rice and cow dung to butter and flowers.

On a quest for the roots of these phallic fetishes, I launched a few research trips to Cambodia. Anchana refused to accompany me. She was vehemently anti-Cambodian as many Thais are. The two countries and peoples have a long-running blood feud that goes back centuries. As many know, the name of the town Siem Reap, near the temples of Angkor, means 'Siam Conquered'. And the temples were finally abandoned to the jungle because the Siamese kept razing and sacking them so often. The Khmers were no angels either. One of their favourite ways of dealing with enemy troops was to carve out their eyes while they were still alive, and then pack the empty sockets full of spices, before burying them alive. Most of the temples of Angkor, like the pyramids of Egypt, were built on the backs of slave labourers.

Upon returning to Bangkok, I took malicious pleasure in taunting her about all the similarities between the two countries in terms of phallic symbols, temples and traditional dance. She retorted, "That's because they stole everything from Thailand."

"Actually, no. They say that a Siamese king loved Khmer dance so much that he kidnapped a bunch of the *apsara* dancers and brought them back to his royal court so they could teach his teachers how to perform. The royal barges came from the Khmer too, and I read that even a lot of Thai dishes like sweet green curry were invented by the Khmer, but the Thais added a lot of chilli and other spices to them."

Like most Thais, she did not believe any of those claims.

When we finally made our first pilgrimage to Angkor in early

2004, we couldn't have picked a worse time. It was almost a year after a group of Khmer men had torched the Thai embassy in Phnom Penh, destroying and looting many other Thai businesses, after a Cambodian daily made false allegations claiming a Thai actress said that Angkor Wat belongs to Thailand.

On the first anniversary of the carnage, high-ranking politicians and both prime ministers convened for photos taken in front of Angkor Wat, to prove that all the simmering grievances and recriminations had once again been put on the backburner. But the photo-op propaganda did not dispel any of the angst in the atmosphere. Like the prelude to an electrical storm, the air was charged with tension. In the booth where we had to buy our three-day passes, the swarthy Khmer guy behind the desk saw Anchana's passport and looked up at her. "So, you are from Thailand." It was not a statement. It was an accusation.

"Yes, I know Cambodians hate Thais."

"No, Thais hate Cambodians." With that, he dropped her passport on the table and shooed us out the door like a couple of human flies.

That was not the only problem to contend with. In the temples of Angkor the *lingams* had been castrated and pillaged long ago, although some of their bases—resembling the female genitalia and representing *shakti*, or the life-bearing power of the womb and the divine feminine—were still visible. After two days of trudging through tons of temples in brain-sizzling heat, following months of reading and researching, we had seen only one intact *lingam* at the cliff-top temple of 11th-century Khmer vintage, Wat Khao Phnom Ruang, in northeastern Thailand. I was sick of the whole subject and equally sick of the age-old 'dick contest' between the warring men of Thailand and Cambodia that was causing us friction wherever we went, forcing Anchana, in a fit of karmic retribution, to pretend she was Khmer.

No one I had spoken to, in either country, could confirm or deny that phallic charms possessed any fiscal or physical potency. My growing doubts about their efficacy was comically summarised by Eric Weiner in his brilliant travel book *The Geography of Bliss: One Grump's Search for the Happiest Places in the World*, when he wrote about the prevalence of such fetishes in Bhutan. "As the owner of a penis myself, I can tell you that no body part is less qualified to ward off evil than the penis. Most of the time it seems to welcome every form of evil, vice and temptation."

The testicular temples of Angkor encompass some of the most macho and muscular architecture on earth. So it was strange to see that two of the most prevalent motifs there are female: the heavenly *apsara* dancers and the guardian angels known as *devatas*. Until then, I had never seen anyone grope a statue before, but this Khmer guy was rubbing the breasts of an *apsara* dancer on a bas-relief. So many times had her breasts been rubbed—in what was another ancient fertility rite—that the stone was worn smooth and shiny.

Our attempt to balance out the yin and the yang, Shiva and Shakti, sent us off on another tangent—examining Angkor's feminine mystique and fertility rites. The Temple of Women, however, was not actually built by women. As immaculately preserved as it is, the name is derived from the use of pink sandstone in its finely hewn details and lintels. After a dinner show starring a dozen *apsara* dancers, we tried interviewing them. Onstage, these 'celestial nymphs and muses', garbed in golden finery and wearing pagoda-like crowns on their heads, were visions of languorous grace and sensual beauty. Backstage, they were a group of giggling teenage girls wearing jeans and T-shirts. All the questions I asked them through the interpreter were immediately answered by their middle-aged male teacher, who forbade them to say anything.

On the last afternoon, we went to the Apsara Massage Parlour in Siem Reap, staffed by tough-looking Khmer women from the countryside. Beside the mattress a traveller had written on the wall with a marker pen, "Don't mess with these women. They will rip you from limb to limb." Not a bad disclaimer for the heavy kneading and contortionist-like postures of traditional Khmer massage, similar to the invigorating yet agonising bodywork of the Thai school. Only a few minutes into the massage, Anchana said something in Thai to the masseuse who was working on her. The woman repeated it to my masseuse. Then she yelled something in Khmer to the women working in the next room. Within a minute five or six of the masseuses had surrounded us. My first thought was, "Oh no, the Cambodians have formed a lynch mob to kill the lone Thai!" But that wasn't the case. As she repeated this expression in Thai, the Khmer ladies began smiling and talking excitedly.

Outside the massage salon, they all wanted their photos taken with her. The masseuses were pictured sitting on her lap, hugging her, kissing her on the cheek, all of them smiling and laughing.

I finally had to ask what she'd said to them.

"I quoted this old expression about how Thais and Cambodians are like big brothers and little sisters. We're all from the same family."

On her part, this was a remarkable turnaround. I suppose it was an act of repentance for nursing a grudge, nourished by schoolbooks and teachers, against Cambodians. But with the exception of the man at the ticket booth, and a couple of other minor incidents, she had been impressed by how nice the people were and alarmed by all the poverty and limbless beggars. As an antidote to xenophobia, there's no cure like travel.

This joyful reconciliation outside the massage parlour left me thinking that if the women of Thailand and Cambodia got together to work through these bilateral dilemmas (like the ongoing dispute over the Preah Vihear Temple on the border), they would come to an amicable conclusion in no time. But in two countries where the few female politicians are shunted off to posts deemed 'insignificant'—typically the Health Ministry—and where the phallic symbol still looms large, any such reconciliations will have to remain reveries for the time being.

The spectre of phallic power raised its ugly dickhead once again on our first trip to the Fertility Shrine behind the Swissotel. En route, the taxi driver moaned about all the Thai women dating foreign men. This was not common but it wasn't out of the ordinary either: plenty of Thai women catch flack for hooking up with foreign guys. In yet another 'dick contest', there has been a recent trend for Thai men to undergo all sorts of penile enhancement treatments, so that they can join the so-called 'Top Guns Club'. None too pleased with her terse answers, the driver snapped, "Why are you with him? Is it because he has a bigger dick or a bigger wallet?"

So we got out of the taxi and walked the rest of the way. Since there was nobody around on the weekday afternoon that we visited, I asked her if she'd kneel in front of the spirit house for a couple of photos. I promised not to shoot any close-ups, or mention her real name in the story that I was writing at the time. Anchana frowned. "But I don't want a baby."

"You don't have to ask for anything. Just pretend like you're praying, I'll shoot a few photos and it will be cool."

Eventually, she relented. After taking a few shots of her kneeling before the shrine, I asked her if she had put in a request to Tubtim for anything—maybe a new designer handbag?

"No, Mr. Sarcastic Man. I told her, 'I don't want to offend you, but I don't need a baby now. My boyfriend must do this story and take photos. So please make *him* unlucky... not me.'" Then she laughed.

The weirdest thing about our visit to the shrine is that it did serve as an aphrodisiac and Anchana also forgot to take her pill that night. That had never happened before. A week passed and her period still had not come. That also hadn't happened before.

Like Shiva's *lingam*, which represents the unseen forces at work in the universe, there was something going on here that eluded the eye. Or perhaps the shrine exerts more of a psychosexual, rather than occult, influence on its visitors.

Whatever it was, we spent the next few days in a state of agitation. In the end, she didn't get pregnant, even though her period was ten days late, and that had never happened before either. So we both suspected that 'something' had occurred at the shrine that day. Anchana was convinced our actions had angered the goddess.

I've never been sure of that. Maybe it was only the power of suggestion. Maybe it was a series of coincidences. Maybe it was a surge of erotic electricity that briefly short-circuited the neurons and synapses of our brains.

Maybe it was none of the above.

But since when have love and lust ever inspired anything akin to common sense and rationality?

STRANGE
CELEBRITIES

The Artist Of Bizarre Architecture

Anyone who has ever peaked on hallucinogens (or air pollution) in Bangkok has probably thought, when staring at the skyline from on high, "Wow, that robot must be about 20 stories tall! And is that a ship or a hotel? Man, this is some good shit…"

But these are not hallucinations—they are the surreal byproducts of Sumet Jumsai's imagination. For this National Artist, the cornerstone of his bizarre architecture is his long-abiding interest in painting, cubism and surrealistic art. Looking at photos of his artworks and buildings, it's easy to draw parallels between them: the pigments of imagination, the serpentine lines and the techno-geometric forms of The Nation buildings in Bangkok also form the blueprints for his artworks.

It's not surprising then, that his first ambition was to be a painter, not an architect.

"I started drawing and painting from an early age, but my father didn't want me to be an artist, which meant being a pauper," said Sumet, sitting on his terrace with a glass of 16-year-old malt whiskey in one hand and a pipe stuffed with cherry tobacco in the other. "There was no market for modern art in those days. So I decided to compromise and study architecture because it was the nearest thing to art. But as I discovered, architecture—real architecture, is art. It's a very important form of art, and it's also a form of poetry in concrete and steel, wood and glass."

Although he's been painting for most of his life, he didn't begin exhibiting his works until his first solo show at the Galerie Atelier Visconti in Paris towards the end of 1999. Judging by the reviews and the lengthy guest list of European aristocrats invited to the *vernissage* (which also included his old friend, the renegade filmmaker Roman Polanski), Sumet's debut exhibition *Guernica, Typewriter, Racing Cars, and Einstein* was a major artistic event.

So why did he wait this long to have his first solo show?

"I don't like the idea of selling my paintings, because they're part of my flesh and blood, so I don't want to part with them. But there's no room to keep them in my house now, and my children think they're hopelessly conventional and outdated," he said with a cultured British accent echoing his Cambridge education. Even with a guest list like that, Sumet denied getting a case of the pre-exhibition jitters. "Oh no, I'm too old for that," he laughed.

From a young age, Sumet's view of architecture and the world was shaped and coloured by painters and sculptors.

"Picasso was my great hero when I was a student, and Le Corbusier [a sculptor, painter and architect]. The two of them went hand in hand for me. They were part of my generation in the early '60s, with Vivaldi and modern jazz. And I'm still at it because I come from that generation," he said.

On display at his exhibition in Paris (and many exhibitions since) was a series of paintings based on Picasso's massive *magnum opus* about the Spanish Civil War: '*Guernica*', the name of a town in the Basque country that was all but annihilated by the fascist forces of General Franco. Likewise, Picasso's Cubist period exerted a tremendous influence on Sumet's design for the two Nation buildings, situated in the southeasterly extremities of Bangkok, alongside the highway to Pattaya.

"On the west side, quite recognisable, is the anthropomorphic: the chief editor sitting at his computer. But as you come around to the east side, the cut out, the shape of the editor becomes more and more abstract, until you come right round the building and he becomes a completely abstract shape permeated by electronic circuitry, which is an image of communications. So that's Cubism. When you look at a Cubist painting or sculpture you see other sides at the same time. Like when Picasso painted his girlfriend and she's divided into different sides," he said with a laugh.

A model of these two buildings was exhibited at one of the world's biggest exhibitions of contemporary art, the *Venice Biennale*, in 1996. Ten years earlier, his designs were featured in *The 50 Leading Architects in the World* exhibition in Vienna.

It was 9pm and we were sitting in the garden of the home he designed on Sukhumvit Road, listening to Ornette Coleman's be-bop jazz, smoking Cuban cigars and drinking malt whiskey. When he's sober, Sumet is more of an upper-class Englishman—subdued and composed. When he's drinking, the Thai side of his character comes out to play and he starts telling a lot more jokes and spinning tales about a spectre he encountered in a Victorian mansion in England.

Whether sober or tipsy, he is a namedropper, forever talking about encounters he's had with everyone from Prince Charles to Nelson Mandela and Roman Polanski—the Polish filmmaker whose pregnant wife was knifed to death by Charles Manson's 'Family' and who could not pick up his Oscar for directing *The Pianist* in 2003, because he was still wanted on statutory rape charges in the US. Sumet loves to be seen with other celebrities. So there he was, resplendent in a pale yellow suit with no tie, right beside Polanski as he emerged to meet the press and the fans after the Asian premiere of his version of *Oliver Twist* at the Bangkok World Film Festival in 2005. That night Polanski also received a lifetime achievement award, trading quips with the award presenter Meechai 'Mr. Condom' Virajit, who owns the Cabbages and Condoms restaurant on Sukhumvit Soi 11. Alluding to the director's libidinous reputation, Meechai said, "Roman was handing out condoms in Bangkok's Chinatown back in the '70s," to which Polanski quipped, after being handed the award, "I thought Meechai would've sealed it in a condom."

But the architect actually met the filmmaker many years before that when they "were trekking in the Himalayas and I came down with a really bad case of altitude sickness, so Roman had his porters jettison the cases of wine they were carrying for him and helped them to carry me back down to the base camp. He really helped to save my life and we've remained friends since then. He used to come to Bangkok quite often for reasons you can probably imagine, but he's happily married and a family man now."

The architect also described an odd yet very friendly encounter he had with Nelson Mandela at the World Economic Forum in Davos, Switzerland back in 1999, when Sumet won a Crystal Award for his colossal contributions to the art of architecture over the last four decades. During a banquet, Mandela was seated at the next table. "He kept smiling and waving at me, and I thought he must've mistaken me for somebody else. But then he came over, put his arm around me, and said, 'You're from Thailand. I was so well received there. Please give my thanks again to the king.' I thought, 'Who am I to deliver such a message?' He's such a warm and charming man, Nelson Mandela, such a humanist. I later found out he's charming to absolutely everyone: the doorman, taxi drivers, the chambermaid. He charms them all."

It was an encounter tinged with a measure of irony. For back in his Beatnik days at Cambridge University in the early 1960s, the aspiring architect took part in an anti-apartheid march, striding behind the philosopher Bertrand Russell. A photo from this period shows Sumet dressed up like an archetypal Beatnik in jeans, a black turtleneck and black wraparound sunglasses.

After interviewing him on several occasions, I came to the conclusion that Sumet is less of a namedropper than a born raconteur. Two of his biggest charms are that he simply hates to bore his company and that he'd rather talk about his friends than himself. The artist who lurks behind his aristocratic façade is not an egomaniac, though. When I mentioned how I used to live in Barcelona and that the surreal buildings, the park and the church they're still building—La Sagrada Familia—designed by Antoni

Gaudi loom the largest in my memories of living in the city, and that similarly, Sumet's architecture has come to define the skyline of Bangkok for me, he waved off the compliment. "I really don't consider myself to be a genius like Gaudi."

Out of the hundreds of actors, musicians, supermodels and titans of industry I've profiled over the last two decades, Sumet is the only one who has ever called me up to personally thank me for writing a story about him. Not only that, he had his secretary send a thank-you present. The perfect gift for any wordsmith, it was a poster for his Paris exhibition featuring one of his paintings: a Burroughsesque image of a typewriter with a human face.

But Dr. Sumet Jumsai na Ayudhya is much more than an architect, painter and a gentleman. He has also produced a scholarly book about the archetypal serpent king of Buddhism, titled *Naga: Cultural Origins in Siam and the West Pacific* (Oxford University Press, Singapore, 1988). In the introduction he writes, "Possibly no other region in the world possesses as many water symbols as East and Southeast Asia culture. Particularly in Siam, whether it is in ritual, literature, dancing, folk art, painting, sculpture, architecture or city planning, a host of aquatic attributes underlies them all. The scope of this work is to attempt to explain them."

Working with the Thai government's Fine Arts Department since the 1960s, Sumet has saved many historic buildings, houses and temples from demolition. Without his conservation efforts, it's debatable whether or not the ancient city of Ayuthaya would ever have been preserved enough to attain World Heritage Site status.

Somehow he has still managed to find the time to be a family man, an avid skier and to pursue humanistic work—he despises the word 'charity'—such as being the chairman of the Duang Pradeep Foundation. Named after the Thai woman widely known as 'The Slum Angel', this grassroots organisation runs a wealth of programmes for the slum-dwellers in Bangkok's shantytown of Khlong Toei—not the kind of place you would expect to find a direct descendant of King Rama III (1788–1851).

Sumet was born in Bangkok around the outset of World War II when Thailand was under Japanese occupation. He still has vivid memories of the Americans dropping bombs around the district of Dusit, where the family house was located, near the Japanese military's headquarters. As a young boy he cheered when the Japanese shot an American bomber out of the sky. But one day he came out of the family's bomb shelter to find that all the houses around theirs had been flattened by an Allied *blitzkrieg*—there were many casualties. His first flights of artistic fancy—and his life-long obsession with painting tanks and airplanes—took off around then.

After living and studying in France and England, returning to his abandoned homeland in 1967 was extremely difficult for him. "I couldn't speak Thai very well and my written Thai is still quite bad. There were American military bases in Thailand for bombing Vietnam, so I was very angry when I first came back. But I could only write articles in English so I suppose our generals—dictators —must've thought, 'Oh, he's quite harmless', because nobody read English here. That was the first big boom period in Thailand and the red-light districts in Patpong and Pattaya got started because of all the American GIs. It was much more negative than positive, but we've only adopted the negative side of America here. I know the good side of America more than most Thai people because I've been there." Then Sumet smiled wryly and remarked in that dry, British way of his, "America is a wonderful concept."

But he is not a myopic patriot. Ask him about the penchant in art and architecture for 'Thainess' and watch his eyes narrow, his lips pucker and his voice drip with vinegar.

"That form of national identity is archaic. I don't subscribe to that at all. If you try to force it you get pastiche like the buildings along Ratchadamnoen Avenue with their Thai roofs. They're really atrocious. You can't set down a formula for contemporary Thai architecture or art. It's a process, a progression, you can't stop it. But what is important is that the younger generation ought to know their own history. History is not learning by heart what happened. Those are chronicles. History is an accumulation of experiences from our forefathers, and you have to build on that, and I think that's very important in art, architecture, and of course literature."

At this point in his career he feels he's done enough architecture. Most of his waking hours are devoted to painting.

"I've been in semi-retirement from architecture for many years now, because I wanted to get away from the business side of architecture and running the office, which is a hassle. Some new partners are running the show so I could be free of it. But the more I try to retire the more work I seem to be doing. The supreme aim in my life is to do nothing, which is the most difficult thing. When I say nothing, I mean going back to art... pure art."

Has working in Paris, where he rents a painting studio, been a big influence on his new artworks? "Paris is free. There are no constraints. It also means going back to my childhood because I went to school in Paris before I went to England. The older I get the more infantile I become and I like to go back to the old places, the school where I used to study, and there's the desk with my initials carved into it." These are sentimental journeys for him, not attempts to touch up old memories for the sake of future paintings. But certainly you can see more than a few dabs of child-like whimsy in a lot of Sumet's semi-abstract, semi-figurative, and very expressionistic, canvases —a whimsy reminiscent of Joan Miro at times in the use of primary colours and the sense of playfulness that is also distinctly Thai.

These touchstones of his work were made concrete in the architect's design for the so-called 'Robot Building' on Sathorn Road in Bangkok. The original inspiration for the edifice, replete with eyes, antennae and the biggest nuts in the world, came from his son's toy robot; but the philosophical cornerstone of this twenty-floor android—a desire to humanise instead of demonise technology—is hardly child's play.

Would it be fair to say that there's an element of satire in this building and his paintings of tanks, typewriters and racing cars? The sense that technology can be extremely infantile?

"Most definitely."

After a few more glasses of malt, Sumet (a wee bit tipsily) wove his way into the house he designed to get a photo of a robotic hand picking up an egg. Ever the entertainer, whose boyish enthusiasm forbids him from boring his company, the architect was eager to get my opinion on this technological breakthrough.

"Wow! This is great, Sumet. Modern technology has now accomplished what cavemen could do 50,000 years ago." He chuckled and poured us another round.

His detractors, who have set out to demolish his achievements, claim that his work is a triumph of 'form over function', that his buildings are proof 'there should be mandatory drug testing for architects', and in a fraudulent feature from the satirical online newspaper *Not The Nation* in 2010, that he had designed a new structure based on his own penis. That story came after a controversial event at the Foreign Correspondent's Club of Thailand. Sumet sat on a panel discussing whether the Western media coverage of the 2010 protests on the streets of Bangkok had been biased or not. Noticeably drunk, the architect lambasted foreign correspondents for not being 'intellectual enough' to understand the complexities of Thai politics, claiming they got too much of their information from go-go bars and sleazy strips like Soi Cowboy. It was odd to hear him repeating accusations he had once flung at the American GIs through newspaper columns he wrote back in the 1960s. One foreign journalist at the event said, "Maybe Sumet's acerbic wit masks his deep-rooted snobbery and nationalism."

But that's not really true either. Sumet has often spoken out against the local trends in art and architecture for 'Thainess'. On the other hand, Sumet took a former Miss Thailand, Areeya 'Pop' Jumsai, to court to prevent her from using his family's surname, which is exclusively reserved for descendants of King Rama III like him. She caved in and dropped the surname. Yet, his radical stance against apartheid in the 1960s and days as a Beatnik are not consistent with the views of the old guard.

In interviews, Sumet sometimes refers to himself as 'schizophrenic', meaning he's divided between his Western education and artistic influences and his allegiances to his homeland. This happens to many Asians who study and work abroad for years, only to return home and find they're not purely Asian anymore, nor are they really Western. It's a widening rift and a growing identity crisis. In his case, that schism has produced some remarkable artworks and buildings. For all his triumphs, though, Sumet's dalliances with dipsomania and occasional outbursts suggest that this is a deeply divided Renaissance man.

To some he may come off as arrogant, but I've found him only too willing to satirise his own work. In a career teeming with awards and accolades, his proudest accomplishment is "my proposed design for the Museum of Contemporary Art in Bangkok, which was rejected. I'm very proud of that," he said with a smile. "I wanted to make a colourful public sculpture because the area around the Mah Boonkrong mall is full of all this concrete spaghetti."

As he gets older and still keeps creating—Sumet designed the set for the horror-opera *Mae Nak*, as well as the marvelously surreal 'Bird Building' off Sukhumvit Road in 2009, and keeps doing solo shows of his paintings like *Weapons of Mass Destruction*—does he worry about posterity and what future generations will think of his work?

A scowl flitted across his face. With a drop of tartness in his voice, he said, "I really don't think that's important. At this stage in life it's important to go on creating, and enjoy the process of creation, and family, and good friends. If you don't enjoy what you do then you're not contributing anything to the world. But I still take pleasure in creating and that's my contribution."

The Angel And She-Devil Of Bang Kwang Central Prison

An 82-year-old Australian woman was visiting a prisoner at Bang Kwang Central Prison on the outskirts of Bangkok, when he introduced her to Susan Aldous. She told Susan that she'd been writing to different convicts for many years, but had never thought of visiting one until she saw a show on TV about an Australian lady. "She'd been a horrible person... a drug addict and a Playboy bunny, and there she was hugging all these prisoners and AIDS patients. And I thought that if she could do it, so could I."

Dubbed the 'Angel of Bang Kwang', Susan Aldous is best known for her altruistic endeavours in the country's biggest maximum-security jail.

"I told her that was me," said Susan, her voice chiming with laughter. "And she said, 'That programme changed my life. You have no idea how much of an inspiration you've been to me.'"

For the last few decades, the nomadic philanthropist has been an inspiration to many: Cambodian refugees and terminally ill prostitutes; Thai cops, drug addicts and mental patients; disabled children in Laos; foreign prisoners in Bangkok; and senior citizens moldering in old folks' homes in Malaysia. A mighty impressive CV of achievements for a high-school dropout and teenaged troublemaker who rebelled against her suburban upbringing in Melbourne because, "I wanted my life to have meaning. I didn't want it be just three meals a day, getting married, having kids and dying," she said at her apartment in Bangkok.

Driven to the brink of suicide and drug addiction when only 16, Susan found a spiritual calling in social work. "Some people challenged me and that's what I needed. They said if you're going to throw your life away you might as well give it away."

She conceded that her grandmother, who received a medal from Queen Victoria for charity work, was an early influence. "She told me about Joan of Arc and angels, and she was a very down-to-earth Christian who loved to have a drink and watch the horse races." In turn, Susan told her classmates at school about Joan of Arc, who teased and bullied her. "That's when I realised you either believe or you don't. And if you do you're going to get burned at the stake. I always thought that was going to be my destiny." She laughed. "A martyrdom complex." Susan, however, dropped out of Sunday School when she was only seven because they couldn't give her any answers. "So if we came from monkeys then Adam and Eve couldn't be real."

Because of her blond hair, blue eyes, svelte physique and extroverted nature, Susan was recruited to work at a high-class Playboy bunny club in Melbourne after the manager saw her handing out religious pamphlets on a street corner. "I just thought, 'Where do people go when they're lonely and have problems?' They don't go to church. They go to a bar. So I thought this was the perfect place to reach people." Working the quiet nights, Susan proved herself to be honest and reliable enough for the club to offer her a position as the manageress. "But Asia was already calling me, and when they said they didn't want me to talk about God with the customers anymore, I thought, you've just given me my answer—I'm off to Asia."

This was not atypical of an Australian generation who came 'of rage' in the 1970s—tripping on rebellion, drugs, booze, anti-conservative politics and music, before fleeing to Asia to escape the life sentence of what the Aussie journalist Jim Pollard called 'death by suburbia'. Like Susan, Jim and many others travelled through, or relocated to, different parts of Asia. For them, the grit and openness of Thailand is infinitely preferable to the hermetically sealed sterility of the Sydney and Melbourne suburbs. Many of these Aussie expats have become activists in altruism. "It gives their lives meaning and they get a buzz out of it," said Jim, a former crime reporter and 'Consumer Watchdog' columnist in Australia, who has been bastioned in Bangkok for the past decade.

In a book he is hoping to complete in 2010, Jim is chronicling the lives of a multi-nationality contingent of humanitarians working with refugees along the Thai-Burmese frontier. He wants to turn the project into a three-book series, profiling the expats doing social work in Bangkok, Laos and Cambodia. Susan will be mentioned in one of the books but Jim also wants to underwrite the efforts of more publicity-shy stalwarts like Denise Coghlan, whom he said is "possibly the only female head of a Jesuit relief centre anywhere in the world." Asked if she was Australian, Jim wisecracked, "Whack a jar of Vegemite in front of her and if she picks it up, she's Australian." He laughed. "Yeah, she's Aussie. She started working at the refugee camp called Site #2 back in the mid-1980s and returned to Cambodia with many of the refugees."

Susan also worked at Site #2. With a population of 150,000, the camp was a virtual no man's land for Khmers who could not return home for fear of political persecution and could not be sent to a third country. Stripped of their political might but not their firepower, the Khmer Rouge launched mortar shells and sneak attacks on a regular basis. "You'd be standing there talking to a family one week, and come back the next week to see that their hut had been shelled and the whole family had been killed," said Susan.

Another time, the NGO she worked for had 2,000 pairs of shoes to give out. Once they announced the news on the loudspeaker, refugees gathered for kilometres around while guards with M-16s stood by to keep the peace.

"It was the most horrendous thing I've ever been through... it was bedlam, it was madness. How do you say no to someone? How do you choose? So we had to throw them into the crowd. Finally, after I don't know how many hours, I stood there with one shoe in my hand, and I was an emotional wreck." Then she looked down to see a woman who'd lost her leg to a landmine and didn't have a shoe on her other foot. As it turned out, the shoe in Susan's hand was a perfect fit. "I just burst out crying. It was too much."

By the early 1990s, Susan had founded her own one-woman NGO, One Life at a Time (entirely funded by private donations), and moved to Bangkok. Her work in Thai jails and police stations aroused the suspicions of the authorities, so the secret police kept her under surveillance 24/7 for three months. When an undercover agent finally showed up at her front door, he admitted that, not only had they been unable to dig up any dirt on her, she moved around the capital at such a frenetic pace that they couldn't even keep up with her. Succumbing to her bubbly charm, the secret police hired the chatterbox to teach them English.

Some 'spooks' from another cloak-and-dagger organisation followed Susan and her daughter into an ice-skating rink in a Bangkok shopping mall. They had walkie-talkies hidden in their shirts. "When cops go undercover they either look like drug addicts or journalists…" Susan laughed. "Oh, I'm sorry."

"Don't worry. We writers are used to the abuse."

Susan smiled at me and continued. "But when I have a fear I have to confront it. So they were all sitting there with no skates on in a skating rink, and I went over and said in Thai, 'Where are you from?' And then I listed all these different branches of the Thai police and the army. 'Oh, and they make you work on Sundays, you poor things.' They couldn't speak. They were just flabbergasted. I wasn't sure what I'd done, or if they'd kill me. But one of them spoke into his walkie-talkie and they all just dispersed."

True to the spirit of her late grandmother, Susan's unorthodox views on Christianity have fuelled the ire of fundamentalists who work for other NGOs. "God had a penis because he made us in his exact image and told us to be fruitful and multiply. One theologian told me that there are no sexual desires in heaven. Excuse me, but I don't want to go to heaven if there's no sexual desires. If Jesus came back today he'd wear Levi 501s, have long hair and be very sexy. Jesus never went to church. He was a radical, he was a revolutionary, and they killed him for it."

A Christian who does not believe in organised religions, her work is inspired as much by righteous indignation as what she calls 'touching lives', "You just have to go by faith all the time because feelings are faith, your moods go up and down, especially if you're a woman and you're pre-menstrual. Then you can't do anything except maybe kill someone. I know I could chew someone's head off. But sometimes you need to be angry. Anger is not a bad thing."

The supernatural 'visions' she experienced as a child have continued to provide her with secular wisdom. When a young woman was brutally slain in Bangkok, Susan remembered feeling upset and sitting down on her bed, when the woman's face appeared before her. "The dead girl told me, 'Dying is not difficult. Once you cross the threshold, there's no more pain or fear'. She told me lots of things about herself that only came out in the press later, so I knew they were real. Then she asked me to go and forgive the man who had killed her."

"When I went to see him in prison after he'd received a life sentence, I could feel the compassion and forgiveness she had. So I told him she'd sent me and he was blown away. We ended up praying together and he asked her and God to forgive him. The inmate really did well in prison after that, so they used this as an example in the Corrections Department and asked me to talk to the guards about compassion and how to look beyond the crime and examine the motives of the criminals. Like this murderer, who came from a family of ten children; his parents never had time for him, he was uneducated, etc. These things don't justify the killing, but they do help you to understand it better."

Susan is renowned for her work in Bang Kwang Central Prison: a squalid, maximum-security jail on the outskirts of Bangkok, which, when she first started going there, only had a medical budget of around 80,000 baht per year for some 7,000 inmates. Because of all the AIDS and tuberculosis cases, the budget was completely spent only a few months into the year. So if you were admitted into the rundown prison hospital, full of vermin and bloodstains, you'd have to bring your own pillow (assuming you had one) and be lucky to get an IV drip and a single aspirin. Working with a group of Singaporean dentists, Susan saw that the prison's rundown hospital was outfitted with proper mattresses. And in conjunction with the Causarina Prison in Perth, Australia, where inmates fix around 20,000 pairs of broken glasses each year and distribute them to Third World countries, Susan helped dozens of elderly convicts—the majority of whom had never been to an optometrist before—to sharpen their vision.

On one occasion, Jim Pollard was an eyewitness. "For these old men who couldn't see and got their first pair of glasses late in life, seeing the expression on their faces was incredible. It really improved the quality of their lives."

Watching Susan in action at the prison while he was out there doing different stories, Jim was struck by the fact that "she speaks the language fluently and understands Thai culture and that they like fun. A lot of her work concentrates on the prisoners who are neglected there, but she does a great job of lifting their spirits. I'm sure she has her mood swings, but she's just a very positive person. Susan has done some terrific stuff. I take my hat off to her. But we need a lot more crossover from the well-to-do world to the less fortunate countries."

In Bang Kwang, Susan struck up an acquaintanceship with an American inmate named Garth Hattan, who was serving a lengthy sentence for drug trafficking. "It took a long time to convince him that I wasn't out to do a good deed at his expense and then, he opened up and said, 'I'm very vulnerable now, don't hurt me.' It just came out of my mouth—'I'm gonna love you in ways that you've never been loved before.' I blew myself away with the depth of conviction, because I wasn't really in love with him, but I made a commitment to myself and to his mother to see him home."

Impressed by the eloquence of his letters, Susan told him that he was going to become a writer and that his experiences behind bars would touch the lives of countless others. Garth laughed at her. "But I told him, I'm starting to have feelings for you that I've never had for anybody, and he went ballistic. 'How can you say that? You don't even know me.' And I'd never sworn around him before, so I said, 'Go and fuck up and have fun then.' So I went away thinking that he didn't feel the same about me, but when I came back a week later he confessed that the feelings were mutual."

Once again, Susan's intuition was bang on, because he eventually began contributing a monthly column to *Farang Untamed Travel* magazine called 'Letter from the Inside'. In his first column, Garth wrote about what it's like being locked up in a cell intended for four people that actually held twenty. "Aside from the sweltering heat, you'd be deploring the lack of sufficient ventilation and be desperate to just get out for a breath of fresh air, and you'd discover that your physical proximity to the guy you're meant to be sleeping next to defies every law of your heterosexual ethos." Even though he had to write out the columns in long hand, his sweaty hand smudging the ink, Garth was our most punctual and reliable contributor. Susan smuggled the columns out. The prison officials didn't care, because they realised that his writings were cautionary tales for travellers about mixing high times with lowlifes. "There's no glamour here, just a sweaty inanimate existence riddled with the futile dreams of what could've been, mingled with the aching regret of having let so many good people down—especially yourself," he wrote in another column. "Enjoy your travels, and never put yourself in a position that would jeopardise your freedom to do so."

For the first three years of their relationship, Garth and Susan didn't have a 'contact visit' because Garth thought he wouldn't be able to control his longings, or act like himself in what amounts to a 'monkey cage', with some 60 prisoners and their kin sitting around at tables. Most of the Asian inmates, overwhelmed by the emotional reunions, do not hug or kiss or do much more than stare at their food. Eventually Garth agreed to a 'contact visit' and they'd sit in the corner, hugging, kissing and making love, using her long skirt as a veil. During one hands-on visit—the prison guards would tease her mercilessly on those days—Garth asked her to marry him. She said yes and he gave her a ring that once belonged to his grandfather. The stone was missing, so he asked her to replace it. She refused. The missing stone was symbolic of their relationship. Not until after he was out of jail would she find a replacement.

Because of a prisoner-exchange agreement with the United States, Garth was sent back to Los Angeles in late 2002, where he served only a few months before being let out on parole. (Every year served in a Thai jail counts for three in America.)

Late in 2003, the couple was married on a deserted beach in California as a flock of pelicans flew past. The wedding photo shows the two of them in front of a gold and crimson sunset, which 'turned' the seawater into volcanic lava. Garth is holding her up in his arms. Both of them are clad in denim pants and jackets, and their smiles are on high beam.

In an email she wrote, "We will eventually be having a larger ceremony with family and friends in 2004, when we can wear something a bit more spectacular than thermal underwear."

That ceremony never took place. In the middle of 2004, she sent a newsletter from her own NGO to all the people on her mailing list. "I did not wish to break up with Garth. He left me, he had numerous affairs and to this day, participates in recreational activities that are not in accordance with my lifestyle or convictions. I did state, however, that I would go on with or without him and have done so. He had fallen in love with another woman and decided to leave me very soon after I returned to the States.

"It was an extremely trying time for me, I held on, did not move away from him or stop loving him, forgave him and eventually let him go free with my blessings and hopes that he will find true happiness and real love—perhaps one of the most difficult things of my life to do and some of the hardest choices to ever make.

"Then in turn I was left as a foreigner in a strange land with no rights and for the most part, alone without sufficient money to survive. On top of it, my health failed to where I nearly died, due to uterine polyps and the life-threatening anaemia that followed. At one point I was without food or water in the apartment where I lived, and had it not been for the intervention of a friend in Norway, I may have not made it out alive. Ironic to have to face possible death, feeling so alone in a first world country after caring for those in dangerous situations in the third world, ha! Eventually I wound up for a time with nowhere suitable to live, Talya [her daughter] was admitted to a mental ward and diagnosed as bipolar and it was a real slice of personal hell for her as well for a good many months."

Susan felt devastated and rejected. She also felt blamed by Garth for this break up. "It's enough to feel bitter about, and many would, but it's not worth feeling such soul-destroying thoughts and I believe that these forces would do me more harm than the supposed injustices that I have suffered would."

In a few terse emails I exchanged with Garth, he complained that Susan's intensity and religious zeal were too much for him. After years in jail, the only work he could find was as a caddy. Garth soon started dealing drugs again. Caught violating the rules of his probation, the former rock drummer was sent back to prison. As of 2010, he is out of jail and on a 12-step programme. In a spirit of reconciliation, he and Susan are now friends on Facebook, but she ignores his more sentimental overtures, saying, "I don't trust him anymore."

One has to wonder why so many intelligent women are attracted to such incorrigible criminals and why someone like Charles Manson gets dozens of love letters, and even marriage proposals, every month. Is it because the women like playing to a captive audience? Or that old rock 'n' roll cliché about good girls loving bad boys?

Even though she hadn't reaped what she had sown, Susan returned to live in Thailand, completing and publishing her autobiography, *The Angel of Bang Kwang* (an honorific bestowed by the press) in 2007. My suggestion to the petite dynamo that her angel wings have been clipped, her halo tarnished, and that she should have called her book *The Angel and She-Devil of Bang Kwang* made her laugh.

The book opened a new chapter in her life as Susan began a sideline career as a writer. In 2008 she co-authored two books: *Ladyboys: the Secret World of Thailand's Third Gender* and *Bad Boy*. Splitting the writing credits and royalties was Pornchai Sereemongkonpol. What surprised him about working on the book was that "because I'm Thai they wouldn't open up to me like they did to Susan. She isn't judgmental and she shared with them a lot of unhappy moments from her own life and that encouraged them to open up. Her charm is disarming, so the interviews were more of a sharing process than a typical Q&A. And she's a lot of fun to work with."

The biography of a tout, male prostitute, alcoholic, dope fiend and actor in scat-porn videos, *Bad Boy* is one of the grimmest and most sordid reads to come out of Bangkok's red-light strips of Patpong and Boys' Town. Towards the end of the book, the titular character was pummelled to a pulp and left for dead on Patpong 1. Even his own wife did not recognise him in the hospital. When Susan and Pornchai went to visit him, "She got down to pray with him. Because we were around the nurses and doctors thought that he wasn't just another bum, so they waived the medical bill of a 100,000 baht and put it on his 30-baht health care card. He had a lot of time to think in the hospital, and now he's quit drinking, gotten back together with his wife and wants to become a forest ranger."

From scat-porn actor to forest ranger—not the kind of career moves Susan's neighbours in the shrink-wrapped suburbs of Melbourne would have ever considered—but once again her benevolent influence, and that of her co-author, has brought a measure of redemption to the life of another lost soul.

Asked how he would describe Susan in a few sentences to someone who had never met her, Pornchai paused. "That's a difficult question because she's complicated. If you only knew her from the things she's done you would think she's lofty, but she's not, she's real." He paused again. "I respect the fact she believes in Jesus but she's never brought up the subject of religion unless I mentioned it first. She's not preachy and has never tried to impose her views on me."

For the past few years, the Aussie expat has curtailed many of her prison visits, citing the failed marriage and emotional burnout as reasons, in favour of working at a shelter for battered women and giving classes in 'laughing yoga' at the Chest Disease Institute in Bangkok. The postures and eruptions of mirth stimulate the respiratory systems of more than a hundred patients per class. To amuse them, she dresses up as a clown and cracks quips in Thai. "I get to dress up as a lunatic for free and help a charitable cause," she said with another laugh.

Susan has also been working with the Don Muang Home and Emergency Shelter for battered women and girls as young as 12, who have been raped, impregnated and cast out of their family homes, under the aegis of the Association for the Status and Promotion of Women. In a country where domestic violence runs rampant, and not a single complaint of sexual harassment has ever been lodged with the authorities since a law ostensibly protecting women from such was first promulgated in the mid-1990s, the shelter is a sanctuary and safe house for a floating population of anywhere from 150 to 200 women and children.

When she first started working there, many of the girls and women were almost mute from battery, estrangement and a serious shortage of self-esteem. Through scripting and staging dramas about the traumas they have suffered, many of the women have found they do have a voice and means to express their woe and call for justice. "I don't work with them in the Thai tradition of a teacher dictating to their students. They have an equal say in everything we do, and they also decide what other skills they want to learn, such as public speaking. I'd also like to start a blog with them so they can voice more of their concerns and connect with other women who have similar problems." Sunday evenings are devoted to the children; some of them are HIV-positive and have opportunistic illnesses such as tuberculosis. "I get covered in snot and vomit and wee. I call it my 'Sunday night perfume'. Don't take me out on a Sunday night!" Her eyes twinkled as she laughed. (Susan must have more laughs per day than any person I've ever met.)

Having interviewed and bantered with her many times over the years, it doesn't seem like her personal philosophy has changed very much since I first spoke with her back in 2002, when she spoke of a Jewish rabbi who worked with the terminally ill in America.

"He said that most people can get used to the idea of dying, but what they can't die with are all the regrets. And I'm one of those people who can't stand living with regrets, so I really want to live my life as if I could die any day. That's not a morbid thing. It just means doing your best, and it doesn't have to be great big things, but just passing those little tests every day—like not losing it with the taxi driver, making the right choices, or giving that extra tip. I think those things prepare you for a good death."

She laughed again, which seems to be her antidote to all the different strains of misfortune and mortality she's been infected with over the decades. "I think you die as you live."

Susan's website is: http://onelifesusan.homestead.com/OneLife.html

The Scorpion Queen and Centipede King

I have often wondered: what compels a person to bathe in maggots for two weeks straight? Is it just to get their name and photo in the press? Will it create a 'viral video' on the internet that becomes the first rung on the ladder of reality TV stardom? Should it be classified as a form of mental illness? Is it an 'accomplishment' anyone would want listed on a CV or tombstone? 'Here lies John Smith, devoted husband, father and world champion maggot bather.'

But for money and notoriety, people will do the strangest things. Before reality TV, homemade videos on YouTube and the asinine antics of MTV's *Jackass* turned the sideshow into a series of digital and primetime showstoppers, the *Guinness Book of World Records* was the Bible of the bizarre and the A to Z of outlandish behaviour, where maggot bathing is still a hotly contested category and highly prized title.

Thailand has notched up quite a few entries in the book: as the birthplace of the person with the longest hair (a hilltribe man with a seven-metre-long mane who died in 2002); the longest name of any city on earth (the Thai moniker for Bangkok is either 164 or 171 letters, if you want to quibble over semantics); Betong, a town-cum-bordello straddling the Malay border, posted the record for the biggest mailbox; and for a brief time in the late 1990s, the city of Nakhon Pathom hosted the world's tallest joss-stick. As another obituary for haphazard Thai workmanship and shoddy safety standards, it soon toppled like a redwood, killing several people.

That's why some doom prophets were predicting catastrophe would do an encore when Kanchana Ketkaew, a sideshow performer already billed as the 'Scorpion Queen', set out to demolish the Guinness record by living with 3,000 of the arachnids in a glass room outside the Ripley's Believe It Or Not Museum in the seaside resort of Pattaya in 2002. Considering that this creepy-crawly is fiercely territorial and the only living creature besides humans which commits suicide (rather than conceding its turf to a rival, the proud scorpion will sting itself to death), it's no wonder that some of us yellow journalists were already dreaming up tabloid-lurid headlines the likes of 'Death of a Hundred Pricks'.

Nocturnal by nature, scorpions usually emerge from their moist habitats when darkness descends. During Kanchana's stint in the glasshouse, the arachnids—due to the noise and light—didn't come out of hiding from under her bed, or in a small garden beside it, until 1 or 2am. Then they went on a mad search for food, even crawling around on her bed, so she got little sleep. Around 500 died and Ripley's replaced them on the fly. But for a while the organisers didn't notice that several hundred more scorpions had been born. The young are white, and use their pincers to latch onto their mother, so the female can carry the young around on her back.

Although she did suffer nine painful stings, Kanchana prevailed, spending 32 days in the twelve-square-metre glasshouse and entering the *Guinness Book of World Records*. Afterwards, in the museum's conference room, her eyes bruised from sleeplessness and her skin faded to a fluorescent shade of pale, the newly crowned and now official 'Scorpion Queen' granted me an exclusive audience.

Surely the creatures' presence, and malodorous waste products, must have darkened her dreams?

"The only nightmare I had was about eating live worms," Kanchana said. "But on the 21st night I dreamt that I saw a beautiful temple surrounded by a rice field. So I knew something good was going to happen. The next day, Her Royal Highness Princess Soamsawali came to visit me. She encouraged me to keep going and to break the record for the sake of our country." As she talked about the princess, her face lit up like an angel crowning a Christmas tree. It must have been the most exciting thing that had ever happened to her.

When asked about the worst part of her ordeal, the petite performer unsheathed her cutting wit. "Having to answer the same questions from journalists over and over again," she said, softening the stab with a smile.

Kanchana was born into a poor fishing family in Chumporn province, where she also fished for a living. In the mid-1990s, she attended a show at the Snake Farm on Koh Samui where she met the centipede-handler, Bunthewee Sengwong. Blushing and looking at the floor, Kanchana said it was love at first sight. In order to be with her new boyfriend (a former pig farmer from Ratchaburi province), Kanchana had to develop her own act for the Snake Farm's still-running, twice-daily shows—so she choreographed a unique routine, dancing around in sexy outfits with scorpions crawling across her breasts, before pulling live ones out of her mouth and dangling them by their stingers.

According to Kanchana, being stung by a scorpion results in about three or four hours of intense agony and a swelling that lasts a couple of days for a normal person. Actual fatalities are rare. Since she began doing the shows on Koh Samui, she has been granted a physical immunity to the scorpions' poison-tipped tails. All the same, she likened their sting to being jabbed with a needle.

Kanchana's act is charged with the same erotic electricity that the old 'snake enchantresses' used to charm their audiences during the American sideshows of the 1920s and '30s. But as three-ring circuses flourished, these sideshows of old—unable to compete otherwise—ramped up the gore-and-cleavage quotient with strippers and so-called 'geeks' who bit the heads off live chickens. Through these spectacles, Westerners who never got to travel—either physically or through fibre-optics—were able to see Siamese twins, Fijian mermaids, African dwarves and voodoo icons.

The Ripley's museums, with their shrunken heads from Ecuador, skull bowls from Tibet, and perfectly preserved three-legged horses, trade on this nostalgia and all the taboos that have since become kitsch. After all, when much of the world has access to a constant stream of smut and violence on the Internet or cable TV, watching a woman in a bathing suit swallow a sword isn't quite going to cut it.

At temple fairs in Thailand, however, the curtain has yet to fall on the traditional freak show. During the country's biggest and longest fair, held annually at Bangkok's Wat Phu Khao Thong—the 'Golden Mount'—during the Loy Krathong festival (usually in November), there's still a tent with a girl in a rubber mermaid's costume, the corpses of doll-like babies pickled in formaldehyde, and a female ghoul with a pretty face and a body made out of rubber entrails.

Once banished to the boondocks of politically-suspect obsolescence and outright hokum, the sideshow has slowly been creeping back onto pop culture's centre stage, thanks to the notorious Jim Rose Circus— which has amassed a global cult following of punk-star proportions, and the late HBO series *Carnivale*—a gritty drama with supernatural set pieces that follows a Depression-era carnival run by a midget and starring jugglers, sword swallowers, strippers and a 'snake enchantress' played by horror-movie vamp Adrienne Barbeau.

When did freaks become so normal and mainstream?

For Valentine's Day in 2006, Ripley's Museum in Pattaya ushered in a new annual event intended to upstage its rivals with a group wedding ceremony and publicity stunt called 'Till Death Do Us Part'. The nuptials commenced with a parade down Beach Road. Leading the pack was a marching band in black outfits playing a brassy, hilariously off-key version of the go-go bar standard, 'Final Countdown'. Behind them were the seven grooms, dressed to chill in black tuxedos and ghoulish make-up, replete with blood and fake scars. Bringing up the rear was a train of typical Thai wedding guests, holding traditional fertility symbols such as sugarcane and bananas.

On a stage between the Ripley's Haunted Adventure House (with the façade of a 19th-century American casket company) and

The Scorpion Queen and the Centipede King got married at the Ripley's Believe It or Not Museum in Pattaya on Valentine's Day in 2006.

a stall selling pairs of handcuffs and lingerie (just what a roaming Romeo needs in Pattaya), the couples sat before a row of chanting monks. The guests of honour were the newly betrothed Scorpion Queen and Centipede King, Bunthewee, who had just broken his own Guinness Record by living in a glasshouse with 1,000 centipedes for 28 days. He sported a tuxedo and a facial tattoo of his totemic arthropod, while the bride wore a bloodstained wedding dress and tarantula legs of rouge around her eyes.

During the wedding they reprised some of their capers with the creepy-crawlies (Bunthewee even had a 20-centimetre-long centipede hanging out of his mouth), and they proved to be the most constantly venerated couple during the blessing ceremony. True to Thai tradition, guests emptied conch shells of holy water over their hands and offered their blessings—or, in my case, condolences. The only foreigner getting married was Darren Hammond from Manchester, England. Darren said that he and his Thai girlfriend were "always doing crazy things together, but it'll be hard to top this".

Right you are, Darren, I thought, as they cued the dancing zombies. All actors at Ripley's Haunted Adventure House, they whirled and shuffled around to a dance number with two uniformed nurses in skimpy outfits holding up stakes with rubber heads on them, as if George Romero had been invited to choreograph a Vegas revue of *Dawn of the Dead*.

The plan for the mass wedding was dreamt up by Ripley's general manager, Somporn Naksuetrong, and his team. He said they want to keep it going as a yearly event.

The climax of the ceremony—when love copulates with death in a display of fidelity to Saint Valentine's lovelorn martyrdom—came when each couple took turns getting into a coffin fit for two. This macabre twist on a Thai rite of matrimony—usually enacted in the bridal suite, with the parents of the recently betrothed first sitting or lying down on the bed—is supposed to ensure a long and blissful union not only in this life, but future reincarnations, too. Such beliefs and practises are difficult for most Westerners to grasp, but essential if you want to court, bed and marry a Thai partner.

Most of the spectators at this reincarnated sideshow—backpackers, ageing package tourists carrying saddlebags of cellulite, local office workers and ladyboys—were more amused than anything, taking shot after shot with their mobile phones and digital cameras. But it's hard to freak out an audience these days—especially with competition like MTV's *Jackass* or the Jim Rose Circus, with its cast of performers such as the 'Human Serpent', who has a real forked tongue and scales tattooed on his face; Mexican transvestite wrestlers like Low Blow Ventura and Trailer Trash Guerro, who wear strap-on dildos in the ring as they grapple for the 'Panty Weight Belt'; and the 'Amazing Mr. Lifto' who hoists car batteries with a chain attached to a piercing in his tongue. And there are probably a huge number of puritans who are grateful for the fact that the concrete blocks he lifts with his pierced penis should ensure he doesn't pass on any trade secrets to his progeny.

By comparison, the performances of Kanchana and Bunthewee seem quaint and subdued. They would never consider doing anything as extreme as Mr. Lifto or Low Blow Ventura. "We have to respect Thai culture and traditions," she said. "So I can't wear any outfits that are too revealing. We're not so different from most people in this country. Thais love putting insects in their mouths." Kanchana smiled. "But we're good Buddhists so we never harm any of the scorpions or centipedes."

I sighed. "Do you think you two could start acting a bit weirder and throw me some sexier anecdotes? I'm trying to write a tabloid exposé here and you guys just aren't playing along." This elicited a laugh from them, but alas, no juicy tidbits.

For the pair, the shows they perform at the Snake Farm on Koh Samui are a well-paid escape from the drudgery and penury of fishing and pig farming. To celebrate her first smashing of the Guinness Record, Kanchana's sole desire was endearingly banal: going out for a bowl of her favourite Thai soup at a small restaurant. After she set a world record for holding an 18-centimetre-long scorpion in her mouth for two minutes and three seconds in 2008, and again after she reclaimed her title from a Malaysian woman by living with 5,000 scorpions for 33 days the following year, Kanchana returned to the very restaurant to order the same soup on both occasions.

Any first impressions of them being salt-of-the-earth folks were seconded by Ripley's manager, Sompong, "They're not Bangkok people, you know. They're much friendlier and more humble than that. Sometimes they call me just to see how I'm doing, not because they want something."

The Centipede King is a polite if sullen young man. Out of shyness or perhaps deference (she's eight years older than him), he let her answer most of the questions. Whenever he was asked a direct question, his body turned rigid, he looked down at his hands and murmured a word every few seconds. It was rare to hear him speak more than five or six words at any given time and even rarer to see him smile. Had the centipede's bite—much more toxic and painful than the scorpion's—wrought havoc with his brain chemistry? Given the high rate of injuries and occasional fatalities suffered by the country's freak-show fraternity, snake-handlers in particular, it would not be surprising if he'd suffered some neurological damage. For the sideshow performers of today or a century ago, not much has changed in this respect. Danger pay does not figure in their salaries and many will bow out to early retirements and premature demises.

But the couple is well aware of these potential perils. In the next few years, both of them are planning on retiring, for fear that all the accumulated poisons in their systems will do irreparable damage to the children they want to have.

Could they really give up their lofty titles as the reigning Scorpion Queen and Centipede King? Kanchana responded to the question with a playful smile that said she doesn't take her career too seriously, and it would take a lot to try her patience. "Sure. We'd love to live normal lives again and open a small Thai restaurant on Samui. That's our big dream."

That's it? Suffice it to say, anyone who has ever interviewed or encountered the country's most infamous 'freaks' since the original Siamese twins Chang and Eng became the 'Eighth Wonder of the World', has probably been touched by their humility, politeness and the modesty of their ambitions. At heart they are not very odd at all: millions of working-class Thais share their humble dream to start a family and run their own small business.

In a final, desperate gambit to provoke an outrageous reaction, I enquired if they had seen any of the stunts in the movie version of *Jackass*, such as shooting fireworks out of one's sphincter. And would they ever consider laying their love life bare on a talk show or reality programme like Westerners do?

The Centipede King blushed and picked at his nails. The Scorpion Queen frowned and paused. Her forehead creased with puzzlement. Realising that the query was serious and not a jest, Kanchana rolled her eyes. "Those people are *weird*."

After setting two world records and performing for some 15 years at the Snake Farm, Kanchana's most cherished memories are meeting her husband and chatting with the princess. Growing up as a fisherwoman mired in dire straits surrounding a speck of a village on a rocky coast, she was always well aware of being looked down on by the middle and upper classes of urbanites (which always makes the unfortunate look down on themselves too). Getting to meet and receive encouragement from a member of the royal family had bolstered her spirits and enthroned her self-respect like never before.

And so it is with all the seekers of publicity and chasers of fame, would-be record-breakers and reality-show hopefuls—vain as they are, and yet driven by a basic and very human need to be loved and admired—to be the best at something, no matter how ludicrous, like bathing in maggots.

Thailand's First Lady Of Forensics

When a nine-year-old boy was caught in the crossfire of the Thai government's 'War Against Drugs' that resulted in more than 2,500 extrajudicial killings over three months in 2003, Dr. Porntip Rojanasunan investigated the shooting. When the tsunami laid waste to the Andaman coast in December 2004, the forensic doctor worked for 40 days straight to identify thousands of corpses. After Hurricane Katrina inundated New Orleans, she and her team flew to Louisiana. During the political tumult of 2010, when a glitzy area of Bangkok was under siege and fire, the doctor's department launched an investigation—mostly stymied by the powers-that-be—into the most contentious killings.

Dr. Porntip's outspoken nature and run-ins with the police have created numerous bones of contention.

High-profile cases like these, constant run-ins with the Thai police and her unique Goth-punk image have made Dr. Porntip a celebrity and cover woman in Thailand. She has also been profiled in numerous women's magazines around the world. But it was the Asian tsunami that first swept the Bangkok-born doctor into the global media's searchlight following her interviews on CNN, the BBC and Fox News.

Not long after the ten metre-high waves slammed into the coastline of Thailand, Dr. Porntip and her team established a makeshift morgue on the grounds of Wat Yan Yao, a Buddhist temple in the most deluged province with the highest body count—Phangnga. Within days, thousands of corpses with salt water and bodily fluids leaking from their mouths were laid on the ground outside the temple. To keep the bodies from decomposing too quickly, the volunteers used blocks of dry ice, so an eerie mist drifted over the dead. The ice also prevented chickens from pecking at the maggots wriggling out of wounds and eye sockets. At times the volunteers would gasp and reel back in terror as the corpses moaned; they thought the dead were coming back to life. But, as Dr. Porntip explained, when gases escape from corpses, they wheeze past the vocal cords.

Kelly May, the original publisher of Thailand's version of the celebrity scandal sheet *OK!*, was one of the volunteers assisting in identifying the deceased and doing translations for people looking for loved ones. She remembers walking into the temple grounds and being horror-struck. "There were limbs poking up everywhere, and these hideously deformed bodies so swollen and black that they didn't even resemble humans but something out of a bad horror movie.

"Dr. Porntip stayed on the temple grounds, and although she was working from 7am until midnight for 40 days to help identify thousands of bodies, I never saw her lose her temper once. I just have so much respect for her. She came in, got down and dirty, and she always looked great. It was funny, but some of the volunteers even got their hair cut like hers."

On an emotional level, how did the forensic specialist cope with such an unprecedented catastrophe? This was a question put to her by freelance photographer Steve Sandford as they stood in the middle of the temple, overwhelmed by the eye-watering stench of bodies putrefying in 35-degree heat—which soon made it difficult to tell whether they were male or female, Asian or Caucasian. "She told me, 'We just have to do the best we can', and it's typical of her cool and professional manner," said Steve. "I've photographed her doing an autopsy in her lab; she's very quick and methodical. She sliced up the body of this guy who'd died in a motorcycle accident in about 30 minutes and removed the top of his head to show me some of the injuries that had caused his death. She also pulled out his liver and put that on the table to show me that he'd been an alcoholic. I think I skipped breakfast that day and stopped drinking for a while."

***

At the Central Institute of Forensic Science (CIFS), Dr. Porntip sat on a black leather couch, the only concession to trendiness in her clutter-free, grey-carpeted office. She summed up her career with a grin, "I'm a lady of disaster." That's a typical example of her morbid sense of humour, colour-coordinated with a stylish black outfit, matching boots and a porcupine hairdo with quills of tinted red hair sticking out.

Speaking about the post-mortem identification of more than 5,000 bodies after the tsunami, the doctor gave more credit to her ad hoc team than herself. "It was the hardest work of my life, but we were happy to help them [the victim's families]. Ninety per cent of my team were volunteers and they did a great job. From the tsunami, I think our government has learned a lot about Critical Incidents Management, before which we had no idea about."

Still, she admitted that the situation was completely shambolic—trying to co-ordinate volunteers and experts from many different countries; dealing with frantic and grieving relatives; cutting away pieces of flesh to bag for DNA samples; examining mouths for dental work and bodies for scars and tattoos. She had to sleep in a van at night and lost three kilos during the first couple of weeks.

To make matters worse, Dr. Porntip was caught in the backwash of allegations from the forensic unit of the Thai police that she had wrongly identified some of the bodies. In retaliation, she accused them of trying to steal the credit from her team. But the general public remained firmly on her side. In surveys taken at the time, Dr. Porntip was second only to then-Prime Minister Thaksin Shinawatra as the country's most popular non-royal. Having already received the regal title of *khunying* (the equivalent of dame), from His Majesty the King for her contributions to the country, she was promoted to the position of acting director of the CIFS in late 2005. Once again, rumours made the rounds that she would forsake forensics for a prominent position in the body politic.

"Many political parties have invited me to be a member, but I will not be a politician. No, never. I just want to be an ordinary person and establish the institute for the people, but I don't want to be the director. But at this time, we don't have anyone else to do the job." Later she relented to public pressure, becoming the director in 2008.

Decades of dissecting cadavers and poring over the minutia of crime scenes have imbued the doctor with intense concentration. Whether speaking or listening, she made constant eye contact. Her stare was unnerving, partly because it's so uncommon coming from a Thai woman. But in a justice system almost completely dominated by men, she has also seemed wary of acting too feminine or showing any signs of vulnerability. Any questions that missed the mark were immediately shot down with an impatient "No, no, no", before she clarified the matter.

The forensics specialist was chatty and affable, but kept her professional distance. Personal questions received terse answers: her Thai husband is a bank manager; her teenage daughter spends five days a week at a boarding school; the doctor still listens to a lot of Western music "but only female singers". Elaborations were not forthcoming.

What she relished talking about most was the science of death and the cases she has worked on. Khunying Porntip first became a household name in Thailand in 1998 when she was working at Bangkok's Ramathibodi Hospital and Faculty of Medicine as a pathologist investigating unnatural deaths and as a consultant for medical students. When a female student disappeared for a week, the doctor theorised that her boyfriend, Serm, another medical student with very high grades, had killed her.

"The chief of the police forensic department knew that I had knowledge of DNA; it was the first time in Thailand that we used DNA testing on a case. There was blood in Serm's car, so I asked the police to give the bloodstain to me to do the DNA test, but they told me they believed Serm's statement that this was the blood of a fish because his mother worked in the market."

The bloodstain matched the DNA of the missing woman, Janjira. So did another droplet of dried blood found in the bathroom of Serm's apartment. These clues led to a ghastly discovery: the medical student had indeed killed his girlfriend and, with a surgeon's skill, dissected her and flushed her remains down the toilet. Photos in local papers, and video footage on TV, showing Dr. Porntip trawling through the drains in search of the young woman's remains became indelible images in the public eye, and soon led to a series of true-crime books about her cases, such as *Sop Phut Dai* ('Corpses Can Speak'). All of them have been bestsellers in Thailand.

Ever since she showed up the notoriously corrupt police by providing the body of evidence for Serm's conviction, Dr. Porntip has had numerous roadblocks put in front of her crime-scene investigations. "I don't have a problem with the police, but they have a problem with me," she said, smiling in a manner that seemed both mischievous and a little arrogant. "When they claim a man has committed suicide and then we find two bullets in his skull, what should we believe? That he was a bad shot?"

This was why, as the director of the CIFS, she wanted to set up mobile labs for crime-scene analyses so her department can conduct investigations that are independent from those of the police. Her motives for doing so were selfless; it's not like she needs to win any more popularity contests in Thailand, where she was named the country's 'Most Trusted Person' in a survey by the Asian edition of *Reader's Digest* in 2010. "I'm already popular enough with the Thai public," she said.

So it seems unlikely we'll get to see her hosting any pop concerts or being captured by TV cameras dancing enthusiastically with her husband to the tunes of Thailand's most enduring pop star, Thongchai 'Bird' McIntyre.

* * *

The doctor's growing fame in the rest of Asia and the West, where she has been dubbed 'Dr. Death', is an outgrowth of forensic medicine's rise from basement morgues to the mainstream media. Bestselling novels by Patricia Cornwall and Kathy Reichs, along with mega-popular TV shows like *CSI*, have proven that the first commandment of TV news producers, 'If it bleeds, it leads', has been a 'blood bank' for the makers and merchants of pop culture.

In late 2002, while she was doing a promotional tour for her gruesome thriller *Grave Secrets*, I interviewed Kathy Reichs in the plush Author's Lounge of the Oriental Hotel in Bangkok. As one of only 50 forensic anthropologists certified by the American Board of Forensic Anthropology at the time, Kathy Reichs toiled at 'Ground Zero' in the aftermath of the World Trade Center conflagration;

testified at the United Nations Tribunal on Genocide in Rwanda, and sifted through the remains of Guatemalans butchered by government soldiers and buried in makeshift bone-yards. The latter experience inspired the first chapter in *Grave Secrets*.

Like Porntip, and like the heroine of Kathy's novels (forensics expert Temperance Brennan), discussing the emotional hangover of the job is too close to the bone. "It's hard... especially when what you're digging up are women and children who were shot and macheted [in Guatemala]. Another colleague who was interviewed for a documentary down there had a very good answer when he was asked about this: 'If you have to cry, you cry at night when you're home alone. During the day, you have a job to do.'"

Kathy noted that people now have a better understanding of the world of forensic pathology than they did in the early 1980s, when she started out in the profession. But while the science of *CSI* is realistic, "one of the downsides of those shows is that there's always an answer and an explanation, so unsophisticated viewers think that's reality. *CSI* is also not realistic in the way that it shows crime-scene technicians doing all the work—at least not in the jurisdictions where I work."

Dr. Porntip, on the other hand, is a fan of *CSI*, partly because she said it's inspired many young Thais to consider taking up the career. At present, Thailand only has five forensic pathologists and 50 lab technicians. Most of them are women. Many Thais are afraid of working with the dead, she said, because they fear ghosts. Yet another disincentive is lousy pay.

But is *CSI* realistic?

"Thailand is so far behind the West in forensics that the question isn't really important," she said, a smile flickering across her face.

As a teenager, it was a different TV show that triggered her interest in crime-fighting: the 1970s detective series *Colombo*, starring Peter Falk as the cigar-smoking private investigator whose rumpled trench coat and rutted features made him look like a drunk coming off a three-day bender. At the time, her two favourite publications were *National Geographic* and the fashion magazine *Glamour*. So she was torn between becoming a doctor or an interior designer. Her father cajoled her into pursuing medicine.

"When I finished medical school, I was an intern in the northern part of Thailand, and I wanted to dress in this style and listen to the music I like. Thailand only had a few pathologists back then. I worked up north for ten years so I could stay away from my father and he couldn't control me. I wanted to work independently from other people, because to work for the government in Thai society means you have no power. I can dress in this style because my office is in the autopsy room and no one will complain," said the doctor, whose stylish appearance and high profile have made her a natural model for fashion shoots, such as when she dressed up as Cleopatra for the Thai-language magazine *Image*. The red-haired heroine in popular Thai thriller *Body of Evidence* also looks like a carbon copy of the doctor.

The country's first lady of forensics has the slump-backed posture of a life-long academic. When seated, she slouched forward with her elbows on her knees, as if the deadweight of all those unsolved cases weighed constantly upon her shoulders. Or it may just be the constant weariness that comes with her workload, and her plans to establish a Missing Persons Bureau and another agency to investigate the thousands of unexplained deaths in Thailand each year.

During this interview, I mentioned an anecdote Kathy Reichs had told me. At one of her book signings in America, a fan showed up with a big plastic tub containing the bones of a deceased relative. She wanted the author and forensic anthropologist to pinpoint the exact cause of death.

Dr. Porntip smiled and nodded—she's had many similar experiences. Every week, her office is called upon to perform autopsies for murder victims. Some have died under very suspicious circumstances—like the Buddhist monk-cum-environmental activist found dead during a land-development dispute, or the three young hilltribe men who allegedly hung themselves from the bars of a police cell with their own shoelaces. Often, she only has time to examine the bigger bones of contention. In 2004, for instance, she performed autopsies on 78 Muslim men in southern Thailand who died after being stacked on top of each other like cordwood—six deep for five hours in the back of army trucks, during the so-called 'Tak Bai Massacre'. The soldiers had tied the victims' hands behind their backs. Dr. Porntip's autopsies revealed that the men died of suffocation so severe that they bled from their eyes.

Every weekend, Dr. Porntip still heads down to the three southernmost provinces of Yala, Pattani and Narathiwat, where several thousand civilians and soldiers have died since the beginning of 2004 in a spate of shootings, bombings, and arson attacks that the Thai government has blamed on everyone—from Muslim separatists to al-Queda terrorists to drug traffickers diverting attention away from their illicit dealings. As one of the few public figures trusted by the Southerners, the doctor tried to contact the former premier, Thaksin Shinawatra, a one-time policeman who earned a PhD in Criminal Justice from a Texas university, to tell him that the country must use forensic science to carry out proper investigations. "But the staff around him never allowed me to speak to him," she said.

In the entire south of Thailand, she added, there are only two forensics specialists, both based in Hat Yai, who refuse to do field work because it's too dangerous. The fractures between the Southerners and the government have only been compounded by the fact that Muslims bury their dead quickly and don't like autopsies to be performed on them.

On her desk sat a copy of the book, *Mass Fatality and Casualty Incidents: A Field Study*. It's a checklist for calamities, covering areas such as 'Sustained Morgue Operations', 'Release of Deceased' and 'Coping with Response to Mass Death'. She picked it up on a trip to New Orleans, where she studied the Federal Emergency Management Agency's rescue efforts in the aftermath of 2005's Hurricane Katrina. She tries to read for at least an hour each day to keep up with the latest developments in her field, and publishes a few medical papers each month, as well as newspaper columns on subjects such as Buddhism and even astrology (the doctor is a Sagittarius).

Although she claims to have never had any nightmares and never been spooked by any ghosts, Dr. Porntip still believes in life after death in a Buddhist way and karma. "I believe that the spirits of the dead want me to help them, so we have to fight for justice. And when I'm faced with a problem, I will try to pray to the spirits of the dead to help me, or lead me in a good way. And every time they will help."

Catching up with the doctor in mid-2010, after the political tumult on the streets of Bangkok left more than 80 people dead and at least 2,000 injured, was a chance to launch an investigation into her findings. On 19 May, soldiers overran the barricades of tires fortified with bamboo stakes and brambles of barbed wire erected by red-shirt protestors around the intersection of Rajprasong. Six bodies were found on the grounds of the Wat Pathum Wanaram Buddhist temple. The morning after, Dr. Porntip and her team from the CIFS were on the case. "We were doing an 'external examination' of the crime scene. Since the bodies were moved by the police, we had to examine and match the DNA from blood stains to get a clearer picture of what happened. It's standard practise to check for gunpowder residue on hands to see if the victims had been armed. In this case, some people had claimed the victims were shot because they were armed, but we didn't find any traces of gunpowder on their hands. Some of the victims were hit many times so it was difficult to tell the trajectory of those bullets, or find out the truth about stories of snipers from different sides."

Yet, her team had no authority to pursue any further inquests or do the autopsies. Two weeks after the shootings, the forensics unit of the Royal Thai Police released the results of their post-mortem examinations. Among the six Thai victims at the temple, most in their 20s and 30s, there was only one female. Kamonkate Athart, a 25-year-old helping out as a volunteer nurse, and the sole rice-winner in a large, impoverished family, had been shot ten times. The autopsy report listed the cause of death as 'damage to her brain stem. A trajectory study cannot be performed, because of excessive damage to muscles and bones'. Dr. Porntip was disappointed with these inconclusive results, referring to the police as 'tomatoes' (Thai slang for red-shirt sympathisers). "The police have much better equipment now [for autopsies and crime-scene investigations], but their guidelines and practices have not improved." At the same time, she was just as disappointed with the government's equally inconclusive probe into the shootings on once-hallowed ground. In doing a form of post-mortem on the major, multiple murders she has investigated, the doctor zeroed in on an unchanging miscarriage of justice. "It doesn't matter whether it was the 'war against drugs' or the Tak Bai Massacre, or the killings during the political protests. Evidence disappears or is tampered with, so afterwards anybody can claim whatever they want. I hate to see politicians take advantage of this."

Many of her brainchildren—such as the Missing Persons Bureau and establishing an independent body to serve as watchdogs and coroners—are stillborn, but she is still trying to reanimate them. "I've been fighting for these developments for ten years, but with no progress," she said, smiling with a weary resignation tempered by steely resolve. As always, the doctor and author refused to play partisan politics or subscribe to any party lines. "In my work I still follow a Buddhist middle way. I might work for the government, but it doesn't mean I have to believe everything they say." In her case, facing death threats and constant obstructions from the powers-that-be (even having to defend herself against charges—later dropped—of 'misappropriating state funds' to bring her team to New Orleans after Hurricane Katrina), it is remarkable that her idealism and defiant streak remain intact after a decades-long career. And still, she perseveres. "I want to change the justice system in this country permanently."

In one corner of Dr. Porntip's office is a shrine where she prays to a Buddha image depicting him 'in the position of subduing evil', imploring the spirits of the deceased to help her. Behind the doctor's desk are statues of her other idol, King Naresuan the Great (1555–1605 AD), one of Siam's most fabled monarchs and a phenomenal *muay thai* boxer who, legend has it, was captured by the Burmese but regained his freedom after beating their best fighter in a bout.

Perhaps these conflicting images sum up the extremities of her personality and career—a kindly sister of mercy who claims that her work, no matter how grisly, 'is all about love'; and the hard-as-bullets crusader for justice who continues to combat the most powerful politicians, policemen, businesspeople, military officers and criminals.

It's never easy to tell who's who in the country.

CREATURE
FEATURES

Going Ape in Simian City

The macaque scampered down a power pole and scurried past a convenience store, a gold shop and a tailor, before stealing into a Chinese pharmacy. Behind the counter, the monkey snatched several bottles of medicine off the shelf and ran back outside, where it drank a bottle of codeine-laced cough syrup. Several minutes later, the monkey fell asleep on the street. A car swerved around it, narrowly avoiding a head-on collision with a motorcycle, but severing the thief's tail.

In Lopburi, 160 kilometres north of Bangkok, the city's 1,000-plus population of monkeys are both miscreants and mascots. Some locals believe the animals are godsends from Kala, a Hindu divinity who holds sway over time and death, because many of them live around the 10th-century Khmer-style shrine devoted to him. But for most of the city's residents, the monkeys are nothing more than pests and petty thieves.

The old section of Lopburi, studded with ruins from the Khmer Empire, as well as a 17th-century Siamese palace, is a breeding ground for three different species of macaques—the pigtail, the rhesus and the crab-eating variety. They have lived in the city since the late 17th century, when Lopburi was Siam's second capital. Some people believe that the monkeys are soldiers of Hanuman, the monkey god and warrior who led simian armies to great victories in the epic Indian tale, the *Ramayana*.

The monkeys are divided into three different factions: those who live at the Phra Prang Samyod Temple and sleep on its roof; those who roam free around the nearby Phra Karn shrine; and their arch enemies, who loiter on the streets nearby and sleep on the tops of apartments and Chinese-style shop-houses.

The two groups that live around the places of worship largely subsist on handouts from visitors and have it easy. As with other primates like humans, comfort does not necessarily breed content. On the contrary, it often inspires discord and in-fighting. The macaques living on the streets and buildings have to forage for themselves, so they tend to be the worst troublemakers. Living in unhygienic conditions, they are also prone to a great many skin diseases and even leprosy.

All three factions are as territorial as LA gangs. For instance, if a member of the street gang tries to gatecrash the shrine, it is immediately chased away or attacked, and vice-versa.

In attracting foreign tourists and day-tripping Thais, the animals have been a boon for Lopburi's economy. On any given day, you can watch visitors gawping at the macaque's high-wire antics or having their photos taken with them at the shrine. The youngest macaques are the naughtiest. Outside the Angkor-era shrine, on a morning gilded with sunlight, Anchana had four or five of them leap on her back. She grabbed a bamboo stick, coaxed them to jump on it and then started swinging them around in circles while pulling monkey faces and cackling. Born in the Year of the Monkey, she has a similarly hyperactive, chatterbox nature. Sensing they had met their mischievous match, the juvenile macaques leapt from the stick and scampered back into the shrine. The monkeys don't usually bite, but they are notorious for picking pockets and stealing sunglasses and cameras.

As a tribute to the town's mascots, and a way of fattening local coffers, the authorities prepare a huge buffet of fruit and vegetables for them in late November every year. This wacky tribute often turns into a few-hour food fight between the macaques, who sometimes pelt tourists with their foodstuffs. To prevent this from happening, local authorities have started putting the fruit and veggies in blocks of ice, so that the monkeys have to lick and scrabble their way to the goodies and visitors have some great photo ops with the shrine in the background.

The world's first Monkey Hospital, located in the city's zoo, provides first aid and re-training for rogue primates—like the thieving junkie whose tail had to be amputated. The hospital also helps to spin some positive public relations for these victims of bad press, by proving they can be put to more positive uses like helping the blind.

The latter programme, the first of its kind in the world, came about by accident. A local soldier who volunteered at the hospital noticed that when he put a rope around the waist of a three-year-old female macaque named Cindy, she liked to stand upright and lead him around. Manad Vimuktipune, the president of the local branch of the Wild Animal Rescue Foundation of Thailand

(WAR), saw this and thought they might be able to use monkeys as a substitute for seeing-eye dogs.

Cindy, the hospital's mascot for the programme to help the blind, had been attacked by other members of her pack at the Phra Pang Samyod Temple. "She was almost completely immobilised by bites," Manad said, shaking his head in dismay. "She didn't have any energy left to fight them off. So the security guards there brought her to our hospital."

At first, Cindy was terrified by the walking sticks the blind use, so the trainers had to leave a bamboo stick in her cage. During the training, it was necessary to tap the stick on the ground constantly to reassure her. For test runs, they used the yard at a local school for the blind, so she would not be distracted by the city's racket.

Sitting behind the hospital's front desk, in front of a black-and-gold painting showing one monkey pushing another in a wheelchair, Manad conceded that the programme was still in its infancy, but he was encouraged by an organisation in Boston called Helping Hands. Since 1979, the group had trained more than 100 capuchins (a tiny, agile monkey found in South America) and placed them in homes with quadriplegics. The monkeys, after two years of training, could fetch food from the refrigerator, change CDs, and even comb their owner's hair. Helping Hands now has a waiting list of 500 quadriplegics who want their own capuchins.

One of the main difficulties in training the Lopburi macaques is that "they have short-term memories, so the trainers have to use short verbal commands and repeat them constantly". As the middle-aged Manad spoke, a young nurse scooped up a two-week-old monkey running around at his feet and fed it milk from a baby bottle. Meanwhile, an older macaque whose back legs were paralysed in a fall from a building propelled itself around on the tiled floor with its arms.

After they trained her for several months at the school for the blind, Cindy passed her first big test by guiding a blind teenager through the city. Since then, she has appeared on national TV in Thailand and put on a command performance for Her Royal Highness Princess Chakri Sirindhorn.

She also became the role model for a small group of orphaned macaques who live at the Lopburi Zoo, where Cindy performs tricks on a daily basis in order to draw visitors and raise desperately needed funds for the programme. The cost of training a monkey for the necessary two years is a minimum of several thousand dollars.

"The monkeys have constant contact with people coming to the zoo, and that's crucial for them being able to work with the handicapped," said the beaming Manad, who has been at the helm of the US$45,000-dollar hospital since it opened in December 2003. "It's also important that they're orphans and don't have other family members around to distract them."

The Monkey Hospital also functions as a kind of rehabilitation centre for wayward macaques. It receives numerous phone calls from irate citizens about monkeys breaking into their homes, stealing their food and even biting them, said the head veterinarian, Juthumas Supanam. When this happens, the hospital uses some of their volunteers—paratroopers from the nearby Royal Thai Airborne base, armed with tranquilliser darts—to track them down. "It's an exasperating task," Juthamas said. "They are so agile and clever that they often make monkeys out of their pursuers by pulling the darts out of their flesh and scampering away." As pack animals with a ferocious loyalty to their kin, the other monkeys, seeing one of their own in trouble, will race in and try to bite the paratroopers with teeth as sharp as broken-glass shards. It often takes ten soldiers to round up just one of them.

To retrain the rogues, Juthamas said, "We talk to them, use a lot of eye contact, and you have to be very patient. We can only keep them here for about a week—any longer and they wouldn't be able to return to their pack."

Despite the monkeys' hyperactivity and penchant for hi-jinks, what bodes wells for the future of the primates-leading-the-blind programme, the veterinarian continued, is that they "are far easier to train than other animals. They display so many human characteristics that they pick up on your emotions very quickly."

Repeat offenders—namely, the more temperamental and aggressive macaques—who do not respond to training, are castrated. About 50 per cent of the time, this calms them down. Together with the male orangutans at the nearby zoo, they are taught how to use pieces of watermelon, punctured with holes, as sex objects.

Behind the hospital's front desk are three rooms full of different primates in cages; out in the back are several bigger cages. For the full-time staff of three, much of their workday is spent caring for the maimed and the wounded. A three-year-old macaque had gone blind in one eye because of a rock from a child's slingshot. "It hates children and women," Manad said. Another monkey was electrocuted on a power-line and they had to amputate its right arm. As if still in shock, it sat there on a tree stump, looking forlorn and almost motionless. Yet another monkey, along with four of its friends, tried to hitch a ride on a train bound for Chiang Mai, some 500 kilometres north. The others returned home but this one got lost in a neighbouring province and was brought back to the hospital. Most of the other 'patients' had been involved in car accidents or taken tumbles off buildings.

Sitting in the biggest cage was a baby orangutan named Joi. Like a child craving affection and attention, he kept reaching through the bars in the cage, trying to touch and shake hands with every visitor who entered the room. His palms were black, but they felt like leather and looked human. The staff was teaching him tricks for the special show at the zoo, such as riding a tricycle, throwing his arms into the air and how to balance a grape on his nose before letting it roll down into his mouth. Demeaning, yes, but certainly preferable to being hunted down in his native Sumatra, where orangutans (the only great apes indigenous to Asia) are a nearly extinct species.

Before we left the room, Manad squatted down beside the cage. A big grin illuminated his face as Joi gave him a kiss on the cheek. Anchana laughed and knelt down beside the cage. Joi gave her a kiss, too.

On Manad's desk in his office were wallet-size calendars showing the Chinese 'Buddha of Wealth' with a monkey sitting on his shoulder. For Thais and Chinese, the monkey is an auspicious sign auguring a year of great, predominantly positive changes. That was certainly true at the Monkey Hospital, where they initiated a fund-raising drive aimed at people born in the Year of the Monkey. The donations went towards a facility to care for elderly and injured primates. The plan was a prelude, Manad said, to building a massive dome enclosing a jungle-like environment, where they can move all of the city's macaques to in the future.

Thumbing through a photo album, Manad explained how Cindy had now been trained to clean up garbage and fetch food for her blind master. One photo showed the macaque walking a blind teenager across a street in front of the Phra Prang Samyod temple.

Buddhist compassion is the soul of the hospital's philosophy and plans of action. Also depicted in the album and promotional pamphlets is one of the main benefactors for the self-funded hospital. Phra Khru Udom Prachthorn, the elderly abbot of the province's famous Wat Phra Baht Num Phru, is well-known across Asia for his work with the temple's hospice for AIDS patients. Back in the early 1990s, when other monks and even family members were ostracising those infected with HIV or full-blown AIDS, the abbot set up a special area in his temple and arranged for medical personnel and volunteers to care for the dying.

The hospice is still running, but now the abbot also donates medical supplies to the Monkey Hospital every month. When one of the macaques at the hospital dies, or a local brings in one that has passed away, the abbot presides over a special cremation ceremony at the hospital. Like at a person's funeral, he chants Buddhist and Pali mantras to wish the creature a safe and speedy trip into its next life. After it has been cremated, the ashes are put in an urn and buried in the hospital's special graveyard for simians.

"Some Thais believe that monkeys will become humans in their next reincarnation," Manad explained. "But the abbot also says that in Buddhism you must make merit and do good deeds for everyone—the rich, the poor and animals, too."

In the Glass Ring with Siamese Fighting Fish

It was 10am on a Wednesday morning in the 21st century, but it may as well have been a thousand years ago. In the hinterland, under the shade cast by a jackfruit tree beside a grove of bamboo, a millenium-old contest and gambling game was about to begin. From their bags, men pulled out small whiskey bottles half-filled with water. Inside the bottles were male Siamese fighting fish, creatures so viciously territorial they will even attack their own reflections in a glass surface.

One of the 'referees' held up two bottles to properly match the opponents by size. When the owners agreed it was a fair fight and made a wager, the fish were put into a square glass tank that stood a half-metre high.

Immediately, the gill covers on each fish shot out like protective armour and they charged at each other. Their iridescent scales shimmered as the blue-and-green fish nipped at the fins of its red-and-purple rival. Like boxers, they circled each other, making quick strikes and then retreating. But unlike human combatants, these fish can fight like this for three hours or more.

They can fight like this to the death.

This morning's session out in Nakhon Pathom province, an hour northwest of Bangkok, had pulled in a crowd of about 30 men, watching a like number of matches going on at once. Some of the men bred fighting fish (better known as *betta splendens* or *bettas*). Some were wholesalers. And a few were professional gamblers. One of them said that the matches also attract gangsters, drug dealers and other criminal elements who gamble on fighting cocks during the dry season and *pla gat* ('biting fish') during the months of the monsoon. Sensing our nervousness, he reassured us that these rough-and-tumble characters holster their firepower and rein in their homicidal tendencies when gambling. "Well, most of the time anyway," he said, laughing in that gleeful Thai way that strikes a discordant note with the seriousness of what they've just said.

In the middle and upper echelons of Thai society, the 'sport' is looked down upon as a no-class pastime for 'pricks from the sticks'. Most of the spectators and fish owners, even in Bangkok, which has around 20 fighting rings, are migrants from rural areas, and have never attended high school. At Bangkok's weekend Chatuchak market, where they sell Siamese fighting fish, visitors can sometimes also see gambling matches.

But one man in attendance shattered all these stereotypes: Precha Jintasaerwong holds master's degrees in both philosophy and computer science. Through his website (www.plakatthai.com), he exports the fish around the world. Precha said that gambling on fighting fish is also popular in Vietnam, Cambodia and Malaysia, with smaller followings in Singapore and Hong Kong.

Like many Thai boys, Precha remembers playing with the creatures when he was a kid. In those days, the freshwater fish could still be found in the canals of Bangkok. Nowadays, they thrive in ponds, rice paddies and irrigation ditches in the pastoral parts of the country. Because the fish has both gills and a 'labyrinth organ' in its head, it comes to the surface now and again to breathe oxygen, and can live in small jars with no filtration system or even mud puddles. (One of my bettas jumped out of his tabletop jar while I was away for the weekend and I found his withered corpse lying on the floor about five metres away from the table—an astounding feat of strength and endurance.)

The short-finned species has been bred to fight for centuries now, said Precha, who served as the scientific advisor for a Discovery Channel programme on them in 2002. However, the fancier kind, such as *pla kat jeen* ('Chinese fighting fish', because their long fins resemble the ancient robes of China's nobility), while still aggressive, are strictly bred for aquariums. And they're a large part of the reason why Thailand has become the world's second largest exporter of tropical fish.

What attracts fish fanatics to the betta, however, is the incredible variety of hues, patterns and at least 12 different kinds of tail. The International Betta Congress estimates that there are more than 26,000 different varieties of the fish. Breeders are coming up with new hybrids all the time and new colour combinations like gold and copper. Some species sell for up to US$150 each.

At today's matches in Nakhon Pathom, many breeders came to show off their fighters and trawl for new customers. Also in attendance was the province's biggest breeder. Sandit Tanyaporn has 230 big clay tanks at his nearby farm. Each tank can hold around 200 fish; and each month he sells around 500 of them for 50 baht each. When he's breeding the fish, Sandit leaves the male and female in opposing tanks. The female can begin producing eggs just from looking at the male, and her ease of fertility has given rise to a slang term that rural Thai women use: *Mai chai pla gat* ("I'm not a biting fish")—meaning they are not easily seduced. On the eve of spawning, the males are particularly territorial, so the breeders get them to relieve their sexual tension by taking some nips out of an opponent in the glass ring.

Once the male and female fish are finally put together, the male builds a bubble nest to store the eggs. The mating dance of the two fish can last for three hours, as they swim slowly to and fro with their fins wrapped around each other, which allows the male to fertilise the eggs. Then the two fish take turns pulling out her eggs. Occasionally, the female tries to eat her own offspring, so she is usually taken out of the jar while the male guards the bubble nest until the fry are born. Even afterwards, the male plays a matronly role (rare in the realm of the wild), helping the sliver-sized newborns stick to the bubble nest as he protects them against predators.

At the age of six months, the short-finned breed is trained to fight. The owners use ancient techniques such as putting them in a big tub and splashing the water around to increase its strength and stamina. Another technique is putting a male with a female to let him 'exercise' by chasing her around. Different herbs, such as Indian almond leaves, are added to the water to toughen the betta's scales. Some owners also have their own trade secrets for breeding winners. Sandit, for instance, feeds his fighters shellfish—as supplements to their staple diet of mosquito larvae and live bloodworms—in order to make their tiny teeth stronger.

Although it's a 'sport' for men, Thai women don't mind it, Precha claims. "The women aren't interested in playing, but they think it's okay because they know that when a breeder is training his fish, he's not fooling around with a second wife." The businessman laughed. "He must stay home and train them—every day for two or three hours, same time morning and night."

This is not entirely true; some Thai women hate it. At one point during the fights, Anchana, who was the only woman present besides an older lady selling food and drinks, picked up my dictaphone and pressed the record button, saying, "This is Thai men... sitting around, gambling, drinking, smoking, talking shit. They don't do too much. Now you know why I have a *farang* boyfriend." We shared a smile. She looked around at the 30 glass rings under the jackfruit tree beside the stand of bamboo, wrinkled her nose and swore in Thai. She went back to reading her celebrity gossip magazine, stopping occasionally to read me headlines she liked, "'Robbie Williams Romp'... what does romp mean?"

Training only accounts for about 20 per cent of any fight, Precha estimated. The most important thing is the bloodline. Even that does not guarantee any blood money, though.

For professional gambler Gai, the X factor is the most exciting thing about the fish fights. "One day, a fish from a particular family wins a match," he said, "but the next day he'll lose."

Gai (or 'Chicken'), who preferred to go by his nickname, estimated that he is one of around 1,000 full-time gamblers on fighting fish, laying down bets six days a week in and around Bangkok. The 40-year-old explained that he makes a living off his obsession, but he won't be buying a BMW any time soon.

Before the match begins, said Gai, the gamblers put down a stake of around 300–500 baht—though he's heard of tycoons placing as much as 500,000 baht on a single match. After 30 minutes, once they've had a chance to assess the strengths and weaknesses of the two aquatic adversaries and look over their wounds and mobility, they might choose to raise the stakes, or other gamblers can get in on the action.

Gai reckoned the floating number of gamblers and fighting dens is actually increasing, even though the pastime is technically illegal and the police sporadically bust them. For gamblers like him, the attraction lies in the fact that it is "not like playing cards, because it's very difficult to cheat when you gamble on the fish. And you actually have a chance to win sometimes, not like when you're in a casino, where the odds are stacked against you."

According to the rules, if a fish swims away and refuses to fight, then the match is over. This is what usually happens in the wild, but rarely in captivity. Also rare is a quick kill. They only occur when one of the contestants tears the gills of his rival so the fish can no longer breathe and slowly sinks to the bottom—dead in the water. More likely is that one of the gamblers will concede a match, because if he refuses to give up and his betta dies, then he'll be fined 100 to 200 baht. Losing fish—if they survive (and most do)—are released into local rice fields, where they disseminate their combative genes.

Some of the matches we saw went on for three hours until the fighters' fins and tails were in tatters. Even so, the two combatants could still lock jaws for minutes at a time, barely moving, while trying to tear the lips off the other fish. Transfixed by this 'death kiss', the gamblers stared at the glass jars. Minutes passed. Lit cigarettes smoldered. Energy drinks went untouched. And still we stared.

There was something very primeval going on here that reminded me of Chuck Palahniuk's novel *Fight Club*, which provided the framework for the film starring Brad Pitt and Edward Norton. The satirical depiction of a man so bored of being an office lackey—and stressing out over the purchase of a new living room set—that his only safety valve and sense of satisfaction comes through physical violence, may put a more human face on the perennial appeal of blood sports and martial arts.

But is it cruel?

Precha, the businessman with degrees in philosophy and computer science, paused for a long time and looked down at the dirt. Many of the people posting messages on his website have levelled this accusation at him. "I don't consider it cruel, but I consider using cheap labour, breeding pigs and selling drugs very cruel... that's the way of this fish. People breed pigs to eat. So you have to kill them. We breed fish to fight, so they have to fight. And why do you Western people not think boxing or wrestling is very cruel?"

Asked the same question, Sandit, the province's biggest breeder, shrugged it off.

"Some people are cruel and some aren't."

And other people just like reading and writing stories about cruelty, so we can close the book and leave it between the lines and the covers.

The Water Buffalo's Tombstone

In Thailand, buffalo may bear the brunt of jokes and insults about their stupidity, but some people are convinced that they're far more useful than some human beings. One such person is the abbot of Bangkok's 'Buffalo Head Temple' (Wat Hua Krabeu), located on the outskirts of Bangkok near Samut Sakhon province, the only district of the city with an ocean-view and a beard of mangrove forest.

"Buffaloes help us in the rice fields and their manure is good for the soil. Even when they die, their skins and horns are still useful.

But bad people contribute nothing to society," said the elderly Phra Khru Wiboon Pattanakit at his temple on Bangkhuntien-Chai Taley Road. "Why do people call buffaloes stupid? Bad people are much worse."

As a tribute to these once ubiquitous beasts of burden, who served as steeds for Siamese soldiers to ride into battle, the abbot is building an

The temple's abbot is planning on building a pagoda out of buffalo skulls as an epitaph for this dying breed.

eight-metre-high pagoda of buffalo skulls with a tunnel at its base so that cars can drive through it. So far, the 260-year-old temple has collected about 8,000 skulls, but they need 10,000 to construct the pagoda and tunnel. Many of the skulls were donated by villagers in the surrounding district of Buffalo Head. They are scattered around and piled up in front of one of the main halls of worship.

The memorial could very well serve as an epitaph for what is already a dying breed in Thailand. According to the government's Livestock Department, the buffalo population has plummeted from around 6.7 million heads in 1990 to 1.2 million in 2008, as farmers rely increasingly on the gas-powered ploughs introduced to Thailand in the 1960s. Sharpening the horns of this dilemma is the fact that around 300,000 animals are butchered in the name of protein every year, while only 200,000 calves are born. Most of the beasts that end up in the slaughterhouse are females, an unhealthy number of them pregnant. What has further reduced the population is the fact that the males, favoured for their brawn, are castrated to make them even brawnier.

A few projects have bulked up the thinning herds. His Majesty the King established a seminal 'Oxen and Buffalo Bank' which loans draft animals to villagers, who have to give back some of the offspring after the females give birth. In the northeast, several monks have started similar initiatives.

In tourism, the most prominent festival keeping the animal off its last legs is the annual Buffalo Races, held every October in front of City Hall in Chon Buri province. Using a bamboo switch for a riding crop, the jockeys ride their charges bareback down a

100-metre-long course. In every heat, five or six of them compete for a grand prize of around 20,000 baht.

Or at least that's the premise. But some of the beasts are content to mill around the starting line. Most of the races have a minimum of three or four false starts. And a fair number of the bovines buck their riders off only a few metres down the track. Once they get running, however, the buffalo charge down the track with a velocity that could be measured in double-digit horsepower, and watching the riders dismount near the finishing line with breakneck leaps from their backs is an act of dare-devilry. To keep the crowds on their toes, now and then a buffalo runs amok, charging into the crowd so people scatter like pool balls after a break.

The competition is more than 130 years old. When it was first held, Chon Buri was the biggest market place on the eastern seaboard. After 'Buddhist Lent', when the farmers came to town, the races first began as an informal joke, spurred by booze and macho bravado. In the decades to come, more events were added to race day: a beauty contest for the beasts—their fur dyed with different colours and horns bedecked with flowers, and a 'Miss Farmer' beauty pageant for young women. Now, it's a full-fledged spectacle attended by thousands of locals and a few hundred tourists.

Running a distant second in the bovine tourism sweepstakes is the Buffalo Villages near the capital of Suphan Buri province, a few hours north of Bangkok. During the bus trip there, Anchana and I scanned the ride paddies and farmyards but didn't spot a single buffalo.

The village itself is a déjà vu of Siam's bygone days—minus the squalor and the machetes that villagers used to keep beside their sleeping mats—with wooden houses on stilts, carefully coiffed gardens, a fortune teller's abode and a Siamese merchant's place of business. The signs and brochures impart history lessons in animal husbandry; archaeologists have unearthed evidence that farmers used the domesticated breed of water buffalo in the area some 1,300 years ago.

The twice-daily 'Buffalo Shows' take place in a dirt arena with a grandstand overhung by a thatched roof. On a weekday afternoon in the soggy season, I was the only Caucasian in a 'crowd' of seven or eight people, mostly older women. The first buffalos were led into the arena, ambled up a wooden stairway, and then, in a death-defying feat, continued ambling along a wooden beam through a couple of hoops nailed to the platform.

Another man, wearing the blue cotton outfit favoured by rural folks, led a brown beast by a rope through its nostrils. After much coaxing and pushing down on its neck, the animal knelt on its forelegs to the astonishment of absolutely no one.

For what was supposed to be the showstopper, a young boy laid down on the dirt and a bovine performer, lured by a handler with a fistful of bananas, walked up, ate a few of them, nosed around in the dirt, flogged some flies with its tail, ate a few more bananas and then… defecated. But wait, the show wasn't over yet. The buffalo then wiggled its ears, looked around and, following the bananas in the trainer's hand, walked over the boy without actually crushing him to death.

The choreographers of the show have their hearts in the right place, but not their minds, because these animals are never going to replace dancing bears and leaping tigers in circuses. Unlike elephants, they can't be taught to play football and wiggle their rumps and flap their ears to the tune of the 'Hippy Hippy Shake' like they do at other tourist distractions in Thailand. Unless buffalo are pulling a plough, or served on a plate, they are sadly and tragically useless. To think that any tourism spectacles (even the Buffalo Races) are ever going to save herds of them from the abattoir is futile.

My disappointment with the show was diminished somewhat by getting to feed them out of my hand afterwards and laughing when they licked me with their sandpapery tongues. Not even fawns have such large, liquid eyes. When one of the male staff members helped to prop me up on the back of a beautiful albino female for a ride, I was leery of getting bucked off, but buffalo lack the skittish temperament that marks all equines as 'dark horses'.

On occasion, the creatures have unwittingly saved lives. Shortly before the 2004 tsunami struck the coast of Ranong province, the local press reported how a group of buffaloes stampeded for higher ground. The villagers followed them and managed to outrace the water.

At the Buffalo Villages, after feeding time, an old rice farmer with a conical hat and plaid shirt took Anchana and I for a bumpy ride in a buffalo cart. As he urged his two animals onwards with a bamboo switch, we bantered about the 2001 historical drama *Bang Rajan*, starring the most famous Thai buffalo of them all, Boon-lert, who acted as the 'warhorse' for the film's hero. The historical settlement of Bang Rajan is not far from here in Sing Buri province. Outside the town is a monument to the battle and slain heroes.

Set in the 18th century, *Bang Rajan* is based on a real-life story of heroism, in which a rag-tag group of Siamese villagers, fighting with homemade weapons, staved off eight different attacks by a total of 100,000 Burmese soldiers before finally going down in defeat. The film garnered some impressive plaudits when it was released in the United States in 2004 and presented by Oliver Stone. One American critic called it 'the *Saving Private Ryan* of ancient Thailand'. Another compared the climactic battle scene to Colonel Custer's last stand at the Alamo.

At the age of 32, Boon-lert died only a few months after *Bang Rajan* was released. One of the film's leading men, Bin Banluerit, paid credit to his co-star, saying that his incredible three-metre horns and huge presence helped to make the movie a blockbuster in Thailand. The actor arranged a funeral for the buffalo, during which crowds of mourners came to see the corpse held upright with a rope and draped in white cloth. As an elegy, Bin arranged for a troupe of Thai classical musicians and dancers to perform in front of the corpse. After the cremation, rock star and energy-drink pimp Ad Carabao (his surname is the Filipino word for buffalo) offered to buy the beast's horns, but was shooed away.

Bumping along in the cart, the old rice farmer told us that he remembered ceremonies called *phi tee su kwan* that paid tribute to living buffaloes when he was a boy, but that hardly anyone performs them nowadays. After the farmers had reaped another rice harvest, they would wash and comb the fur of their draught animals, attach flowers to the horns of the females, and put out special food for all of them.

In a voice as craggy as his face, the farmer and Anchana did a duet of an old Thai country lament called '*Tui Ja*' about a young girl who loses her buffalo during a flood; and then a verse from another old song that translates as '*The rice liquor and buffalo are my only friends*'. Never content to play 'the hind legs of the elephant' (as the Thai expression about a woman's place in society goes), Anchana sang twice as loud as he did, their voices ringing and clattering together like a beggar sifting through garbage for cans and bottles.

A monk holds up a skull at the Buffalo Head Temple.

The farmer claimed that Boon-lert was actually a wild water buffalo. These animals are much bigger than the domesticated breed and have the largest horns of any bovine. While wild water buffalos were once found all over India, Nepal, Vietnam, Cambodia, Thailand, Burma and Malaysia, conservationists speculate that there may now only be 4,000 of them left in the wild. Around 40 to 50 are believed to remain in the Huay Ka Keng Wildlife Sanctuary in Uthai Thani province near the Burmese border. Mostly placid, they use their horns, which can span up to four metres and are shaped like a sickle, as shields or battering rams when attacked by tigers; their only enemy other than humans.

Within a few years, the wild water buffalo will be extinct. Their domesticated cousins probably have another few decades before they die out too, or so Phra Khru Wiboon Pattanakit, the old abbot, believes. "This area used to be full of them," he said, before pointing towards the jumble of skulls in front of Buffalo Head Temple. "Now these are the only ones left."

The pagoda of horned skulls he is planning to erect in their honour may end up as a kind of tombstone for the dying steed, as well as all the rituals, songs and history yoked to these gentle creatures.

When the US cavalry rode out to exterminate the American bison (a related species) in the 19th century, they knew that not only would this deprive the Native Americans of their most important source of food and shelter, it would also tear out the very marrow of their animistic creed and culture.

In this spirit, the abbot's memorial-in-progress is similar to the altars of buffalo bones built by Native American hunters who bowed before them and intoned this prayer:

"Let us honour those who gave their flesh to keep us alive."

Reptilian Ménage à Trois:

COBRA VILLAGE

Outside of Thailand's national parks, only in the northeastern province of Khon Kaen are you likely to see road signs that read, 'Warning: King Cobra Crossing'. It's a sure sign that you're on the right track to see the 'Cobra Village', where most of the villagers breed and raise snakes for a living. At Ban Kok Sa-nga, they also put on daily shows of derring-do where snake-handlers wrestle with king cobras up to five-metres long.

The majority of the 700 villagers raise snakes, and some even keep them as pets, said Sirisak Noi Lek, the president of the village's Cobra Conservation Club. "The tradition started back in the 1950s when a man named Ken Yongla from this village began travelling around the countryside selling herbal medicines. To attract more people, he started doing regular shows with cobras, but these snakes were too dangerous because they can spit venom for several metres. So he used king cobras instead. They're still dangerous, but the venom is delivered through their fangs. Ken trained many of the locals to do the performances and how to raise snakes."

The chiming of cow bells heralded the arrival of a shepherd directing her charges down the dirt road as Sirisak led us to the back of his house. Curled up in a wooden box was a python as thick as a fire-hose. The locals catch them in their gloved hands when the snakes are sleeping during the day. Every few days, Sirisak feeds the python smaller snakes or a frog. Some of the serpents have their gall bladders removed for Chinese potions—even mixed with whiskey for an aphrodisiac. Others are cast as performers in shows that pit man against serpent.

Far from the sinister figure in the Garden of Eden that encourages Eve to eat the forbidden fruit of knowledge (thereby bringing about the downfall of humankind), the seven-headed 'Lord of the Serpents' (*Phaya Nak*) opened his hoods to protect the Buddha from the elements as he attained enlightenment while meditating under the sacred ficus tree. For many Thais, Phaya Nak, whose long body forms the balustrades of many Buddhist temples, is a figure of reverence.

So it's not a revelation that the monks incubated a special laboratory to breed king cobras in the Buddhist temple near the zoo and the venue for performances. On this afternoon, sitting in the bleachers surrounding the stage, was a group of Buddhist monks draped with orange robes, among a smattering of Thais and tourists. Behind the stage was a gigantic billboard for Pepsi, framed by photos of the King and Queen of Thailand.

To the tape-recorded tune of hand-pummeled drums, the *clink, clink, clink* of finger cymbals, and an Indian oboe playing melodies serpentine enough to charm a cobra—the same traditional tunes played live during *muay thai* boxing matches—three dancers took centre-stage. Dressed in pink sarongs, each of the young ladies wore live garlands of sinuous pythons, jaws wired shut with string. Shooting off flashbulb smiles, and moving as gently as palm fronds in a breeze, the dancers' slow-motion body language spoke volumes about the tranquility of traditional Thai culture, and its nature-borne birthright.

At the back of the stage, a snake-handler used a long metal pole with a hook to pull a writhing king cobra out of a box. Black with silver bands, the three-metre-long serpent slithered towards the front of the stage. In the crowd, spines straightened and a hush descended. The venom of a single king cobra bite is enough to kill a man—or a hundred rodents—unless treated immediately. Many of the snake-wrestlers take herbal concoctions daily to lessen the possibility of fatalities. Just in case, a local medic equipped with anti-venom attends every show.

On his knees, the snake-handler crawled towards the king cobra. The snake reared up into the striking position, its forked tongue flicking the air. (Snakes use their tongues for sniffing out their quarry and their enemies.) Quick as a whip, the king cobra lunged at him. The snake-handler dodged the attack. Distracting the snake with one hand held in the air, he crawled beside it, lowered his head and kissed the cobra on its head.

TORTOISE TOWN

In Asia, few creatures are mythologised like the turtle, partly because of its longevity, and the symbolism of its shell in the Chinese vision of the earth and the cosmos. Turtle soup is enjoyed by many East Asians as an anti-ageing tonic and delicacy, but it's usually the soft-shelled kind, because the hard-shelled variety have too much spiritual significance.

In Vietnam, the mascot for its many wars of independence is a turtle that still lurks in Hanoi's Hoan Kiem Lake. To this day, Vietnamese schoolchildren learn the 15th-century legend of a rebel soldier named Le Loi whose troops repelled Chinese invaders. After he became the emperor of a dynasty named after him, Le Loi was boating on the lake when a turtle snatched his sword and dove beneath the waves to protect the weapon for future battles.

Nowadays, there is only one turtle left in the lake, weighing around 200 kilos. The so-called 'Turtle Professor', Professor Ha Dinh Duck of Hanoi University, is the foremost expert on the reptile. He claimed the turtle has surfaced some 400 times since the early 1990s, often coinciding with state visits by Chinese presidents and even the unveiling of a Le Loi statue. "It's something we can't explain," the academic told AFP, adding that every appearance of the creature has caused an upsurge in crowds.

The government spent US$2.4 million to clean up the polluted, algae-plagued 'Lake of the Returned Sword' for Hanoi's 1,000th anniversary celebrations in 2010.

At Suvarnabhumi International Airport in Bangkok, one of the first sights to greet visitors is a colossal statue of the Hindu creation myth, detailing the seminal 'Churning of the Milky Ocean' from which all life arose. Standing atop a sacred tortoise is the deity Vishnu. At Angkor Wat, bas-reliefs depict similar tableaux.

An hour's drive from the Cobra Village in Khon Kaen province is Mu Bahn Tao, or Turtle Village, a town crawling with tortoises which have also been blessed with a divine lineage. Locals believe these yellow-headed tortoises are protected by the village's guardian spirit, Chao Khun Pa, the late abbot of a local temple who befriended the creatures. (Consider him a Siamese equivalent of Saint Francis of Assisi, the patron saint of animals.) At the entrance to the village are two models of its totemic figure, burnished with gold, draped with garlands and housed in a wooden pavilion. Down the main road is Tortoise Park. Bridges span the park, affording an overview of the creatures trudging around.

The adults of this species (*Indotestuda elongata*) weigh around three kilos. Their shells, a patchwork of black and yellow, span 30 centimetres. The reptiles' staple diet is grass and fruit. Some visitors feed them slices of watermelon by hand.

In this hamlet, the 400 residents living in weatherworn houses propped up on stilts with cows underneath them, and fenced in by pickets of bamboo, are outnumbered approximately three to one by tortoises. The prime times for tortoise-spotting are early in the morning and late in the afternoon. They are everywhere then: chewing up the greenery in the fields, crawling down the dirt roads and trudging into houses where they are treated like pets. In a hamlet almost 250 years old, even the dogs do not pester them.

Picking up a tortoise in his front yard, Prasong Sutwiset, a local who runs a home-stay for overnight visitors, said, "The males have flatter stomachs and rounder shells. The females have concave stomachs and a capsule-shaped shell."

The 48-year-old, who was born in the village, is one of many locals with weird tales to relate about the creatures. "A Taiwanese film crew came here and one of them put his foot on a tortoise. Only a few minutes later all their equipment started malfunctioning. Some Thais and foreigners who stole baby tortoises later brought them back after experiencing ill health. But I guess the strangest case was a Thai tourist who accidentally ran over a tortoise in the village. Later that same day, he got into a serious car accident that almost took his life," said Prasong.

Are these coincidences? This is the question I put to the former editor of *Hyper* magazine, Veeraporn Nitiprapha, who said, "You Westerners destroy so much with that word. Everything that cannot be rationally explained you call a 'coincidence'. Thais don't believe in coincidences."

These cold-blooded reptiles warm up during the mating season from June to December, when they are quite literally doing it in the streets, the backyards and the park. Like stags in rut, the males square off in head-to-head duels, butting shells to subdue their rivals. The battle-hardened winner then mounts the female from behind. When copulating, the males make strange croaking sounds. Stoically bearing the brunt of these intrusions, the females are silent.

Until watching this orgy erupting all over town, I had not realised the true significance of the Motorhead song, 'Love Me Like a Reptile'.

ON THE ROUTE TO EXTINCTION

Bulleting down the highway in a fossil-fueled car, en route to the Phu Wiang Dinosaur Museum and national park, we encountered one of the most deadly reptiles in all of Thailand: a police officer, who ran out into the middle of road to flag us down. If it wasn't for the driver putting a lead foot down on the brake pedal, the cop could've ended up like many snakes—road kill—though not the kind that is reincarnated in a pungent curry.

Still wearing his sunglasses and grinning at the Thai lady in the front seat, the policeman (who reeked of alcohol) said the radar trap had red-flagged our vehicle breaking the speed limit. Discretely, she handed over her driver's license along with 200 baht—the going rate for traffic violations—tucked inside it. He pocketed the money and cheerfully gave us directions to the dinosaur museum. Then he told her, "There aren't any more radar traps on the way, so drive as fast as you like." The policeman laughed and wished us good luck.

Along the way we spotted many life-size models of dinosaurs, in front of hospitals, beside banks, hovering above traffic islands. These statues are primers for the museum and the park, advertisements for the province's main draws.

The centrepiece of the Phu Wiang Dinosaur Museum is the metal skeleton of a *Siamotyrannus isanensis*. Unearthed in 1976, this 15-metre-long monster was the first of its genus and species to be discovered. It's a forebear of the much bigger Tyrannosaurus Rex. Off to one side of the museum is a kind of Jurassic Park, filled with built-to-scale dinosaurs baring sabre-sized teeth, amid jungles of foliage.

As the museum illustrates, this area was Thailand's stomping ground for dinosaurs. Other species, like the *Phuwiangosuarus sirinhornae* (named after Princess Chakri Sirindhorn) and the *Siamosaurus suteehorni*, were also first discovered in the region. Over in the nearby national park, visitors can get down to the bones of these discoveries and see the pits where paleontologists unearthed them, as well as dinosaur footprints, a 9th-century Buddha image carved into the cliff buttressing Phu Wiang Mountain, and caves with Stone Age artworks.

Many children come to the museum on field trips. Their enthusiasm brightens the gloomiest of days. Running around screaming or sitting on the wooden walkways of the jungle to sketch pictures, the kids are loud testaments to the creatures' primeval pull.

While the boys gravitate towards the monsters, the girls orbit around the cuter creatures, like a massive tortoise in a glass case. Many sea turtles and land tortoises—of which some 28 different species are found in Thailand—date from 200 million years before the first season of *Survivor* was shot in southern Thailand. A display in the museum calls this the 'Age of Mammals'. From that epoch also came the distant ancestors of elephants, dolphins, rabbits and snakes.

In the midst of global warming, rising seas, and the second greatest mass extinction of species the world has ever seen, the museum invites comparisons to the natural calamities that killed off the dinosaurs. It would be ironic if, from the fallout of an environmental apocalypse, what crawled out of the wasteland in 2500 AD were not human survivors, but tortoises, serpents and lizards with the DNA of dinosaurs—prehistory coming full circle and the reptilian brain outsmarting Darwin's descendants.

For the museum bears little evidence of humankind except for one drawing on the wall showing a portrait of evolution: from the naked *homo erectus* to the Neanderthal carrying a club and swaddled in animal hides to a pale-skinned woman in a mini-skirt at the end of the line. Compared to the dinosaurs that survived for tens of millions of years and the reptiles which still thrive, the *homo sapien* looks frail by comparison—the human race but a flash in a primeval reptile's eye.

THE
SUPERNATURAL

Modern Primitives
and Ancient Shamans

A young male traveller with a radioactive-looking suntan, colourful tattoos and enough earrings to set off an airport metal detector stepped out from behind a new Toyota, snapping a shot of a Thai man who had a metre-long sword pierced through both of his cheeks. Behind him was a Kodak photo shop, an ATM machine and the off-white façade of one of Phuket's oldest examples of Sino-Portuguese architecture, the On On Hotel.

This bizarre juxtaposition of the modern and the primitive is the most photogenic feature of Phuket's annual Vegetarian Festival. These Taoist Lent celebrations are held in some of the southern provinces of Thailand for nine days during the 9th lunar month of the Chinese calendar. Of all these movable feasts, Phuket's is the grandest.

Throngs of tourists crowd the sun-glazed streets for the processions on the last three days of the festival. In particular, a healthy contingent of rich Chinese fly in for the festival, as this is the only part of the world where Taoist Lent is celebrated with such colourful and grisly abandon. While the snap-happy tourists gawk in disbelief and take photos, the *mah song*—'entranced horses'—willingly stop and pose for them. The faces of these Thai men, women and even a few transvestites, are skewered with everything from swordfish to cymbal stands to tennis rackets and small bicycles. In a trance, they walk in the middle of small entourages, shaking their heads from side to side, while their eyes roll back into their heads.

Both shirtless and shoeless, and wearing bright silk smocks emblazoned with fanciful dragons baring fangs and claws, the devotees claim to be possessed by a pantheon of spiritual entities—from Hindu gods like Shiva and the elephant-headed Ganesha to Chinese and Taoist divinities. It is these deities and a strict vegetarian diet, they say, which gives them the power to undergo the painful rites of penance, passage and purification through self-mutilation.

Many of the local onlookers, dressed in white as a symbol of purity, put their hands together to *wai* the participants—also known as 'spirit warriors'—as they pass by, while other locals cluster behind makeshift shrines on the streets. Draped with red cloth, these wooden tables are set with bowls of burning joss sticks, plates of oranges, pineapples and candies, and nine tiny cups of tea—one for each of the Emperor Gods or Immortals of Taoism, who also represent the seven stars of the Big Dipper constellation and two others (from earth the formation resembles a yin-yang symbol). The deities are believed to attend the festival each year.

An elderly Thai woman standing among these streetside supplicants explained that their offerings and shows of respect for those possessed by the gods would bring them good luck.

But some of the tourists stared at the people in the procession like they were freaks. Raymond Jones, the aforementioned photographer with the tattoos and earrings, noted some similarities between the 'modern primitive' body-piercing trend and these ancient rites.

"They used to pierce their navels in ancient Egypt as a sign of nobility. And Roman centurions used to do it to show how virile they were. Some people may do it strictly for fashion's sake today," noted the young American computer programmer. "But my piercings and tattoos mark important turning points in my life. I got one when I graduated from high school, another when I got my first apartment, and then my tattoo of Isis [the Egyptian Goddess of Love] when I finished university."

The coming-of-age rites that he spoke of also play a part in the Vegetarian Festival. Some of the devotees, both male and female, are still in their teens. Prasong, a 15-year-old fisherman, said, "It's important for a man to show how strong he is, how much pain he can take." By participating in the festivities, Prasong also believed that he could bring good fortune to himself and his community.

Some of the participants, however, are professional spirit mediums, or like Prasong's father Veerawat, a *mor phi* (literally, 'ghost doctor'). The 63-year-old—who had his face pierced by a steel bar draped with a garland of jasmine flowers for one of the processions—pointed to the Khmer script emblazoned on his back, and described in painful detail how a Buddhist monk at a temple in northern Thailand had stenciled it into his flesh while reciting magical incantations. As a latter-day shaman in Phuket, Veerawat consults various spirits for his clients, reads palms and dispenses herbal remedies. According to Veerawat, his magical tattoos have protected him against illnesses and accidents. "Look at me," he said. "I'm still alive and I've never been seriously ill or in a car accident."

In contrast, inked into his son's skin was a tattoo of rock band Guns N' Roses' skull logo. In his left ear was a silver stud. "I am the new generation," Prasong said with a grin.

The term 'modern primitives' was first coined by Roland Loomis in 1978 to define the neo-tribal movement of the tattooed, the pierced and the branded. Better known by his adopted name of Fakir Musafar, Loomis is a former advertising executive with a degree in electrical engineering and an MA in Creative Writing. He also founded the first school for body-piercing in the United States. A lecturer, shaman and legend in the fetish community, Loomis' most famous and well-documented feat was performing the excruciating 'Sun Dance', a Native American spiritual rite that involves being hung from two big hooks piercing the chest and nipples. (The Ripley's Believe It or Not Museum in Pattaya has a life-size tableau of a tribesman undergoing that rite of passage.) Much of the inspiration for his experiments with body modifications came from the indigenous peoples of the United States, and various Southeast Asian tribes and sects. For instance, the Hindu festival of Thaipusam, held outside Kuala Lumpur around February each year, attracts upwards of 100,000 people. The really devout have hooks put in their backs so they can drag chariots bedecked with flowers and Hindu idols up to the caves in a nearby mountain.

Many locals in Phuket are upset that the more extreme elements of the festival—walking on hot coals, scaling razor-runged ladders and spirit mediums licking hacksaw blades until their white smocks turn scarlet—have upstaged all the ascetic aspects, and that many travellers only come for the last three days of bloodletting and pyrotechnics.

When I first attended the festival in 1997, people were already complaining that it had gotten out of control. A woman working at the Tourism Authority of Thailand's office in Phuket said that the antics of the devotees had become imcreasingly outrageous over the years to impress the tourists and the gods. "Many foreigners who come to the festival only want to see the piercings and fireworks. They forget about the purity side of the festival—abstinence from alcohol, sex and eating meat. They don't bother watching all the Chinese operas and dragon dances. I don't like the piercings. They're very, very boring," said the woman, who asked not to be named.

To a certain extent, however, the shamans' showmanship is in keeping with the festival's first act. In 1825, a visiting Chinese opera troupe agreed to eat a strictly vegetarian diet and perform acts of self-mortification in the hope that the gods would stop the malaria epidemic that was decimating the local populace. After they performed these rites of atonement, the number of deaths mysteriously declined.

In Marlane Guelden's informative and lavishly photographed book, *Thailand Into The Spirit World*, she linked the history of the performing arts in Southeast Asia with shamanism—many of the first performers were also traditional healers and practitioners of magic. The same is true in the West, where Greek tragedies evolved from magical ceremonies and the mythology of the country where the first Olympic Games were held to honour the gods.

Some of the expat community on the country's largest island and second richest province find the festival's lunatic fringe revolting. "Watching some of the men whipping themselves, or dancing with

Wrenches, swordfish, cymbal stands and the odd AK-47 are all used during the world's grisliest celebration of Taoist Lent, when 'spirit warriors' go into trances and become possessed by different deities.

rows of safety pins stuck into each arm, that's offputting to me," said Alan Morison, the owner of local news website Phuketwan.com. After relocating to the island in 2002, the Australian has even seen "one or two people wrapped in barbed wire. It's hard to dance when you're wrapped up like that." He laughed. "Authorities try to discourage the excesses but every year you still see a few people who have been pierced with the barrel of an AK-47 or have a BMX bicycle stuck through their cheeks with their friends carrying it as they walk."

Those 'extreme elements' also include more than a few members of the fetish scene, both Western and Asian. Mistress Jade, a Thai-Chinese dominatrix living and working on Phuket, said, "I think it's the sexiest festival on earth. I always get some good ideas from it about what to do with subs in my play space," before she burst out laughing. More seriously, she elaborated on the most piercing part of all the great faiths and status-quo systems of social control—guilt. "The rituals of penance that the warriors are doing are similar to some of my customers who feel guilty about having certain fantasies and fetishes. So they want me to make them suffer to absolve their guilt."

In its penitential aspects—according to the 'ghost doctor', the warriors take on the pain and suffering of all their fellow humans—the Vegetarian Festival draws blood from the same vein as Easter in the Philippines. During Holy Week, surrogate 'Christs' are nailed to crosses on a volcanic Golgotha outside the town of San Fernando de Pampanga, where the streets are filled with hundreds of men, some dragging crosses, some wearing crowns of thorns and many flagellating themselves with cat-o'-nine-tails made from bamboo. In 1997, when I went for Holy Week for the first time, all foreigners were banned from being crucified because during the previous year, a Japanese man had been nailed to a cross. Only later did they find out he was an actor shooting the first scene in an S&M movie.

Taoist Lent in Phuket is nowhere near as gory or sorrowful as Easter in the Philippines. Many of the piercings are mundane. They demarcate certain professions. The man who installs satellite dishes has a TV antennae stuck through both cheeks. The gardener has a tree branch. The factory worker is skewered with a pineapple-laden shish kabob that has an ad for the local cement company where he works.

But some of the shamans are synonymous with shysters, who walk around with bars through their faces draped with Thai baht and pestering people to take photos of them to make a donation. By way of thanks they hand out a few 'blessed candies' (read: Hall's lozenges).

In 2009, the authorities launched their biggest effort yet to crackdown on the frauds and extreme elements. Each of the 350 'spirit warriors' was issued a special ID card with their full name and details, the name of the deity that possesses them, the temple to which they're attached and a list of friends assisting them during the processions. That year also saw two more of the island's Taoist temples join in the free-for-all (one on Rawai Beach, another in the Tungka district of Phuket city), bringing the total to 18 as occupancy rates soared to 70 per cent of the island's 40,000 rooms—incredible for the soggy season. All the hotel rooms in Phuket city, where many of the rites are held at the elaborate Jui Tui Temple, were booked solid for months before the festival commenced with ceremonies on a deserted beach to welcome the gods ashore. For the traders in tourism, the windfall—according to TAT estimates—was 200 million baht.

As a high-voltage fixture on the travel circuit, it is surprising that the festival has not become more shockproof. But Alan noted, "The reason all the tourists keep coming is that it hasn't been compromised. The believers still think that the gods come to visit, so for them it's real. There's no pretense about it. The Taoist communities in Singapore and Malaysia have their own versions, but without any of the incredible feats. So those nationals will come to Phuket. There probably was such a festival in China once, but it has now disappeared. So many of the visitors come from different parts of China." The ladies in the TAT office said that the local version of Taoist Lent has never been celebrated like this in China; the piercing rites are spiked with Hindu influences from the Thaipusam Festival.

As popular as the Vegetarian Festival has become, there are still bastions of Chinese traditionalism and 'demilitarised zones' in the war-zone cacophony of exploding fireworks. Alan recommended the "old parts of Phuket city where there are some delightful parades and many of the older Chinese people come or sit outside their houses to watch". Over the first few days of the festivities, the rituals of raising lanterns and praising the Emperor Gods are considerably more subdued, with not a drop of blood shed.

On a culinary level, Taoist Lent is celebrated all over Thailand. Just look for the restaurants and food carts flying yellow pennants. Many of the usual Thai dishes, liberally spiced with chilli, basil leaves and lemongrass, are on offer, as well as Chinese fare. The only difference is that the meat has been replaced by chunks of tofu that have been marinated so they look and taste like chicken, beef and seafood.

Some of the Taoist temples in the southern provinces of Phang-nga, Krabi and Trang celebrate the return of the Immortals, but only the capital of the latter province features any processions or feats of self-mortification.

On Phuket, the 'spirit warriors' who stick to a meat-free diet, wear white clothes and abstain from alcohol and sex, claim to be possessed on and off throughout the festival by the same entity.

"It's quite surprising," said Alan, "to see someone who works as a bank teller and suddenly they're possessed and become this supernatural being for a short time. You do see people around with scarred cheeks, but it's amazing how quickly they heal. It depends on the individual of course, but some of the warriors are back leading normal lives the next day with only a couple of bandages on their cheeks."

For Western visitors, this is the most baffling part of Thailand's extreme take on Taoist Lent. How can a person have both cheeks pierced with a sword and walk around for hours in the tropical heat and not wind up with hideous permanent scars? True believers claim that the gods who possess them, and the strict regimen of diet and asceticism, protect them. Most Westerners do not believe this.

Peter Davidson, the director of International Services at Phuket International Hospital, is one of the disbelievers. In an article for the *Phuket Post* in 2008, he wrote, "The cheeks predominantly consist of soft tissue; mostly skin, fat and some muscle which are used for facial expressions and eating. There are no large blood vessels in the cheek area, however, like all areas of the face and head, there is a complex blood vessel network with abundant small vessels. Because of this anatomy of the cheek, it is unlikely that significant bleeding is present when the cheek is pierced. With piercing, a puncture wound is made, which typically bleeds less than a laceration or other type of wound. This, coupled with the anatomy of the cheek, could explain why bleeding is minimal. Over recent years it has been a requirement that a doctor be available at the temples where *mah song* are pierced, and it is not unusual for these doctors to have to perform some suturing and wound repair where the puncture or piercing practice elicits too much bleeding."

In his opinion, the fact that most of the participants are young men means that their wounds heal faster. Medical precautions have also diminished the high-risk stakes. All the men and women taking part are now required to have HIV checks before they get pierced, and the paramedics on hand at all the temples where the piercing is done wear gloves and sterilise the objects to be inserted. The main risk is that the wounds will get infected.

Some of the feats the *mah song* perform are not as easy to explain. At night, the 'entertainment' includes demonstrations of walking through beds of glowing red coals—that are a good ten-metres long and 20-metres wide—in front of Chinese temples ablaze with shades of gold and scarlet, while some warriors scale ten-metre-high ladders runged with razorblades sharp enough to shave with. In 2009, one of the fire-walkers at the temple of Tharua fell face first onto the coals. In a flash, flames engulfed his white trousers and the traditional apron. Several spectators ran to his rescue. They dragged him to safety but not nearly quick enough to prevent serious burns that kept him in the hospital for weeks of treatments, followed by months of physiotherapy so he could learn how to walk again.

"That man clearly did not have the spirits inside him," said Alan Morison. "It should satisfy the skeptics that these 'warriors' are doing some incredible things."

Of all the spirit mediums Alan has met or interviewed, one man stands out. "He's a Buddhist but becomes possessed by the spirit of a Muslim religious leader who was highly respected in that area. He has Taoist and Muslim shrines in his house. A Thai woman I know regularly consults him as a kind of oracle, often for big decisions she wants to make, such as the best time to buy a new car. She's not an ignorant or superstitious woman. Nor are the other people who go to see him. They respect his wisdom. It's really quite strange to see this man who only speaks Thai go into trances where he speaks Arabic and recites lines from the Koran."

Allan was right about that. Watching the devotees go into trances before they are pierced is strange. At first, they start twitching and shaking their heads, then they approach the metal altar in the temple, banging on it with their fists and making high-pitched noises. As they begin to shake more violently, one or more of their minders sneaks up from behind to tie on a special smock emblazoned with Chinese dragons and yin-yang symbols. But the devotees' Thai name *mah song* ('entranced horses') is telling—the gods are said to ride them like horses. That is not unique to Thailand. The dancers in the white magic rites of Haitian *vodou*—as opposed to the black magic of Hollywood voodoo—were captured undergoing similar transformations by filmmaker and ethnographer Maya Derin in her riveting book and documentary, *Divine Horsemen: The Living Gods of Haiti*.

Many Thai ceremonies revolve around men and women being possessed, like the underground gatherings of spirit mediums and the now infamous Tattoo Festival at Wat Bang Phra, near the town of Nakhon Chaisri. There, a motley crew of gangsters and blue-collar workers are taken over by the animal deities inked on their skin—roaring like tigers, hopping around like monkeys and snaking across the dirt on their bellies.

In Phuket, some of the wildest spectacles take place on the last night of the festival during the 'Farewell to the Gods' ceremony, when the backstreets of the island's capital are cloaked in darkness and illuminated only by a few streetlamps, the golden glow of candles on makeshift shrines and firecrackers exploding everywhere. (Bring earplugs and flame-retardant headgear is the best travel advice.) Overhead, the sky was an *aurora borealis* of pyrotechnics, the smithereens fading as they fizzle out and fall. At the same time, the warriors—unpierced and carrying black flags emblazoned with sacred incantations that are supposed to protect them, and cracking whips to drive away malevolent spirits—strode through the streets with their entourages. Behind them came men carrying sedan chairs that housed icons of the Taoist divinities so they could be released back into the sea, as standard-bearers hoisted golden dragons on poles.

Watching Veerawat, the middle-aged 'ghost doctor', dancing under a streetlamp while teenagers threw lit firecrackers at his bare feet, was mesmerising. Balancing on one foot like a Thai classical dancer while holding the black flag aloft, he slowly and gracefully arced in a circle. An older Chinese man lowered a string of firecrackers on a pole just above the warrior's head. A single spark set off a chain reaction of big bangs. One after another, the firecrackers exploded in his face. He did not flinch or even blink; and kept spinning around in a circle like a whirling dervish. This was one of the most incredible acts of endurance and grace under pressure that I've ever witnessed. Whether he was actually possessed by a higher power, or whether it was his faith that gave him the power to withstand such a deafening bombardment, it did not really matter. Either way, it was an athletic and artistic feat of Olympian proportions. With that kind of willpower and indifference to pain, what other achievements are possible?

On this night, Veerawat's entourage consisted of Ray the computer programmer and two Chicago punk rock girls who were tattooed and pierced from ankles to eyebrows. Ray, who has tattoos of Isis, Osiris and John Lennon to mark turning points in his life and a Prince Albert piercing in his nether regions, said, "Kelly and I went to this 'Spirit and Flesh' workshop run by Fakir Musafar, where you go through ecstatic states of shamanism through rituals of body modification and piercing. We had all sorts of trippy visions and revelations. But it was more like, rising above the pain and purifying yourself, finding something bigger and better—kind of like this festival."

Fakir Musafar, the man who coined the term 'modern primitives' and who, at the age of 79, still runs his own body-piercing studio, explained during one of his lectures, "Intense physical sensations create focus which gives one the ability to do things in life that you couldn't do with unfocused attention."

Ask any virtuosic musician or martial arts expert and they'll tell you much the same thing.

Unhurt and unfazed by all the pyrotechnics, the modern-day shaman strode down the street like a warrior going into battle. His entourage of three young punks—who were on a spiritual and psychological mission to transcend suffering and rise above middle-class mediocrity through this ancient and arcane wisdom—scurried to catch up with a Thai man old enough to be their grandfather.

In a way, that's exactly who he was.

Oral Hexes and Shock Airwaves

The radio show's first caller began his story:

"The owner of a company that screens movies at temple fairs and outdoor festivals received a phone call from a man named Vinai to show ghost films at a Buddhist temple fair near Korat. When he arrived, the owner met Vinai, who asked him to screen the movies behind the temple. While the films were playing that night for an audience of 50 or 60 people, the projectionist noticed some women in really old-fashioned clothes and wondered why they were dressed that way. That night, the projectionist slept at the temple. The monks woke him up the next morning, asking why he'd shown films behind the temple—no one had asked him to do so. The monks were perturbed because some people had died under mysterious circumstances nearby. So the projectionist told them about Vinai. The old mortician at the temple, who prepared the bodies for cremation, then showed the projectionist a memorial plaque for a dead man named Vinai..."

And so began another eerie evening of ghost stories on one of Thailand's most popular radio shows—'Shock Radio' on 102 FM. Hosted by Kapol 'Pong' Thongplub from the witching hour until 3am every Saturday and Sunday, the programme mostly involves callers sharing tales of the supernatural which they've personally experienced, or heard from friends and family members.

Most of the stories deal with traditional Thai spectres such as *phi pop*—a supernatural parasite that possesses people—and *phi kraseu* ('filth ghost'), the villainess in many Thai horror movies. This ghoul, which flies around rice fields at night, has a hideous female face and a flashing green or red light in its head, while its body consists of dangling intestines. Its staple diet is blood, human excrement and the entrails, placentas and foetuses of pregnant women.

Since its first broadcast in 1992, the programme has built up an audience of more than 100,000 listeners per night. Before allowing callers on the air, Pong and his staff first screen the calls. Although there is a long tradition in Thailand of comedic ghost movies starring such satirical phantoms as 'Miss Sexy Ghost' and 'Miss Universe Ghost', the Shock Radio programmers are only interested in the hell-and-hair-raising tales. Listeners sometimes call in with anecdotes about aliens and paranormal phenomena, but mostly they tell spectral stories from all over Thailand.

One of the most repeated tales has become an urban legend around the country's universities. "Two students are roommates, and one of them goes out at night to buy some food," shock-jock Pong told me. "He ends up getting cut in half by some psychopath, but his ghost feels guilty about not bringing back the food, so he goes back home. The ghost's roommate answers the door and sees his dead friend's upper torso floating there holding a bag of noodles for him."

Such tales, far-fetched as they seem, say a lot about the Thai sense of friendship, love of food and especially their faith in the spirit realm. As a matter of conjecture, Pong reckons that about 80 per cent of Thai people, particularly in rural areas, believe in the supernatural. One Thai friend, when asked about this, said many locals are unsure about the supernatural but, hedging their bets, are unwilling to say they are disbelievers.

The radio programme is also helping to keep the spirit of oral storytelling alive in Thailand. This is an age-old tradition that mostly relies on tales of the supernatural. In turn, this tradition has spawned countless comic books known as *phi saam baht* ('three-baht ghost stories', the Thai equivalent of the 'penny dreadful'), and a lot of music, from northeastern folk tunes to indie rock. Vasit Mukdavijitr, one of Thailand's most influential underground rockers, is a regular listener of Shock Radio. Some of his strange experiences on the island of Koh Chang inspired the creepy ballad 'Death Star' he wrote for Daytripper's second album, *Pop Music*.

"I was walking along this dark beach with my girlfriend when these ghostly hands appeared out of nowhere and, I don't remember this, but my girlfriend said I freaked out and tried to attack her. But I don't know for sure. I was kind of drunk that night."

Later in their bungalow, his girlfriend saw 'strange colourful shapes appear' just as the singer himself was spooked by a huge, seven-legged spider crawling up the wall. "My auntie told me that seven-legged spiders are signs of the Buddhist devil," said Vasit.

In addition to contributing a few classics to the growing genre of Asian horror—such as *Nang Nak* and the original version of *The Eye* (partly set and shot in Thailand by Hong Kong brothers Danny and Oxide Pang)—the Thai pantheon of the supernatural was also director

Apichatpong Weerasethakul's main muse. In 2010, he became the first Thai to ever win the world's most coveted film award: the Palme d'Or at the Cannes Film Festival. A profound meditation on science and reincarnation, cinema and mortality, and love and time travel, *Loong Boonmee Raluek Chat* (Uncle Boonmee Who Can Recall His Past Lives) is a witch's cauldron that boils over with surreal and supernatural elements such as scarlet-eyed monkey phantoms and a scene between a lonesome princess and a libidinous catfish whose whiskers tickle her fantasies. In his acceptance speech at Cannes, the director thanked the "all the ghosts and spirits of Thailand. They make it possible for me to be here." The Jury Director, Tim Burton, called the film "a beautiful strange dream that you don't see much of anymore".

Some of the stories aired on Shock FM are just as bizarre. The callers are anywhere from seven to 75 years old. But the majority are teenagers. For many college students, the show is a thrilling diversion from late-night studying. Anchana recalled how, in her student nursing days, the students in her faculty played pranks on each other based on stories they'd heard on Shock Radio.

"A friend and I switched off the lights in a lab where some of the students were studying, and where they had dead babies floating in jars. We put surgeons' masks over our faces, pulled our hair down over our eyes, and shuffled around the room like zombies, moaning, 'Give us our children back.' The other students started screaming. But after we switched the lights on, we saw that the babies were all floating upside down—completely the opposite of how they usually were. Playing jokes like that is bad luck."

Chulalongkorn University is Thailand's oldest and most venerable institution of higher learning. Consistently ranked in the top 20 of all Asian universities for its research facilities and international programmes, the institution has, over the course of a century, produced influential statesmen, award-winning scientists and great artists, authors and tycoons. In the Faculty of Science, however, freshman students are advised not to use the front stairway in the White Building (the faculty's oldest structure), because corpses once used for studying medicine used to be buried there. In the Faculty of Political Science, the main icon which students and staff pray to is the Black Tiger God. Freshmen students should not have their photos taken with the statue of the 'Serpent King' (*Phaya Nak*) from Buddhist lore in the Faculty of Art, for fear they may not graduate. Conversely, graduating students are urged to get their photos taken at this auspicious place.

These strange beliefs and superstitions are not secrets whispered among the students and faculty. No, they are all included in an official history book on the university that I edited for them in 2010.

Among the younger generation, old traditions may be dying a slow death, but their devotion to animism is very much alive. One of my former colleagues, Lek, a 25-year-old woman with a dyed-red bob, told me, "I'm not going to celebrate the Loy Krathong festival this year by putting a banana-leaf float in the water, but by floating my brain in alcohol." Then the smile faded and she said more seriously, "But I always pray to the 'Goddess of Water' before I go swimming or I might have an accident."

Such beliefs also have a more practical value. In *The Damage*

Done: Twelve Years Of Hell In A Bangkok Prison, Warren Fellows said that most of the Thai inmates did not crack the way the Westerners did. He attributed this to their ability to meditate and their faith in reincarnation and the spirit realm.

But the host of Shock Radio isn't that concerned about the serious side of the supernatural and whether the stories set off his bullshit detector. "The show is about entertainment," said Pong, who also co-hosts the weekly TV show *Chuamong Pitsawongse* ('The Hour of Supernatural Encounters') on Channel 7 every Tuesday night.

During the radio show's reign of terror, Pong and his crew have generated more volts of shock value by using a mix of theme songs from famous Thai horror movies, and sound effects of everything from villainous chuckles and bloodcurdling screams to excerpts from a CD titled *Demoniac Soundscapes*. But for the most part, the emphasis remains on the anecdotes shared by the callers, which seem anything but rehearsed. After six or seven of them have recited their spooky stories, Pong reads some of the emails and other tales sent in by listeners. Usually, they receive more than a 100 emails per week.

In 1999, Pong opened the Shock Pub near the Chatuchak Weekend Market. Five years later he closed that down and moved into a much bigger venue on Ramintra Road, near the expressway and the Tesco-Lotus on Ladphrao Road. Above the Shock Khao Tom Phi Restaurant and Pub (*khao tom phi* is a ghostly version of 'rice porridge') sits a bust of the horror-movie villain Freddy Krueger lit by a spotlight. On the menu are a variety of specialties like 'The Shock Khao Pat' (a thermonuclear version of fried rice); a snakehead fish that comes served in a tiny black coffin; and the 'Headless Ghost' (shrimp heads fried in garlic).

In the back of the restaurant is the 'Shock Gallery'. Bloodied with red light and air-conditioned to the freezing point of a morgue, the gallery has a boy's 'severed' head dangling from the roof and a Grim Reaper-esque figure hanging from steel bars. It also displays dozens of photos purported to be phantom sightings. Some are sketchy at best. The fog shrouding the spire of a Buddhist temple at night could be, well, fog, or an abortion from a film-processing lab. Other images give credence to the incredible. Take, for instance, the snapshot of a car wreck and what looks like a ghostly figure emerging from it.

Many of the images were shot when the crew from Shock Radio went out hunting for phantoms at haunted hospitals, hotels and houses in and around Bangkok. Usually, Pong said, they survey the place first before taking a group of listeners there and doing live reports via mobile phone.

One night, they visited a derelict house in the Rangsit district of Bangkok that is supposedly the haunt of two ghostly lovers. Urban legend has it that the couple moved in there against the wishes of their parents and later committed suicide together.

"A young Thai actress was with us, and she went crazy inside the house," said Pong. "We think the female ghost got inside her and made her jerk around and speak in this strange voice. It took seven of us to control her. When we finally got her out of the house and a few blocks down the street, she came out of this trance and said she couldn't remember a thing about what had happened."

Pong's researcher for both the radio and TV shows, Kohprew na Ratchaburi, who also works as a DJ at the pub and restaurant, said the ghost-hunting expeditions have caused the show lots of trouble. "Some of our listeners hear the reports and then they go and visit these places, too. Sometimes the teenagers get into fights with other gangs and we've heard reports that thieves have also showed up later on to rob people. That's why we've now been going to other nearby provinces and we also always take a policeman with us."

To celebrate the show's 13th anniversary, they released a DVD titled *The Reality Shock* in which 13 people agreed to spend 13 hours in 13 different spots allegedly infested with spirits. Some of the contestants, said Kohphrew, could not handle the experience and left early. It wasn't what they saw—Hollywood has given us an overblown version of the occult—so much as what they felt.

"It's very difficult to get the supernatural on videotape, but a lot of the time when we're out there, it's just the atmosphere, this horrible feeling of dread, that gets to me," he said.

The DVD cover proclaims that watching it will reveal '13 ways to meet ghosts', many of them based on ancient Siamese superstitions such as smearing your eyelids with the ash from a cremated corpse, or covering your face with a death shroud. Kohprew said the reality show was a precursor to a feature-length ghost story he and Pong are scripting, loosely based on the five CDs and anthologies of weird tales they've compiled from their radio show.

In all his years of hosting the radio and TV shows, and reporting from graveyards and abandoned hospitals, Pong said the creepiest experience was when they paid a midnight visit to the shrine for Thailand's most famous wraith, Mae Nak, at the Buddhist temple nicknamed after her on Sukhumvit Soi 77. They were there with director Nonzee Nimibutr, whose 1999 film, *Nang Nak*—about a woman who died in childbirth in 19th-century Bangkok—is still one of the highest-grossing Thai films of all time and a cult phenomenon in the genre of 'Asian horror'.

"The minute we lit some joss-sticks to pay respect to her, this big wind came up," said Pong. "It suddenly stopped when we planted them in the ground. Later on, I tried to play the theme music for the film on the show. But the tape didn't work, so I gave it to a technician, and he ended up taking it home with him. A few weeks later, he died in a motorcycle accident. At his funeral, I spoke with his widow. She told me that she'd had all sorts of nightmares about Nang Nak, who said she wanted to take him away to the spirit world."

Nang Nak:
The Ghost of Thailand's Past

The ghost of a woman who dies in childbirth—a *phi tai hong thong klom*—is regarded as the most fearsome of all phantoms in Thailand. In a scene from *Nang Nak*—the famous Thai horror movie based on the country's most enduring ghost story—a terrified widower and a group of Buddhist monks are sitting on the floor of a temple chanting mantras to protect themselves when drops of water begin falling on them. They all look up to see the man's dead wife standing upside down on the ceiling of the temple, glowering at them while dripping sweat.

At the 'Temple of Mother Nak' off Sukhumvit Road, where many believe her spirit still resides, a Thai man pointed out to me a strange indentation on the ceiling of the main shrine, declaring that this was the place where Nak once stood.

Long before the Siamese even had surnames, the real Nak was supposedly born here in the middle of the 19th century. The village of Phra Khanong, once a patchwork of rice paddies crisscrossed with canals—some of which have still not been paved over—later became a district of the capital. As the legend and the 1999 film go, her husband Mak went off to fight the Burmese, leaving his pregnant wife behind. When they were reunited, Nak showed him their newly born son. But Mak could not understand why she was so aloof and kept rejecting his overtures to make love.

A few scenes later, when the couple are making love on the floor, the scene is edited together with a flashback of Nak dying while giving birth in the old Siamese way—sitting on the floor, her arms tied above her head, as beads of blood drip through the floorboards onto the head of a water buffalo tethered below the house. Never mind the supernatural sex that left audiences around the world gasping and murmuring—"He's sleeping with a ghost and doesn't even know it!"—the scene was remarkable for the way it contained an entire revolution on the Buddhist Wheel of the Law: birth, death and rebirth.

The movie poster for Nonzee Nimibutr's version of *Nang Nak*. Produced by Tai Entertainment, and starring Sai Charoenpura, the film brought Thai cinema back from the dead by conjuring up the country's most legendary phantom.

Such deaths were common in Nak's day. In the film and the rural legend, Nak went on a killing spree to keep the other villagers from exposing her secret to her husband.

After watching her frightful and tender performance on-screen it was a shock to see that, in real life, the cinematic reincarnation of the country's most famous ghost was a teenaged college girl with spiky tendrils of frosted blonde hair. Only 19 at the time, Inthira 'Sai' Chareonepura radiated none of the menace she showed on-screen. Sitting in her school uniform of a black skirt and white blouse, beaming with smiles and politely answering questions, she could have been one of a million university students in the country.

Sai noted that Nak's story has been made into more than 20 different films, but the 1999 version was different because it focused more on the couple's relationship.

"The previous versions of *Nang Nak* are more about scary things and horror—not the love story. But the director [Nonzee Nimibutr] wanted to make this a love story about Nak's faithfulness to her husband as she waits for him [to return from the war]. Even after she dies, she's still worried about him and comes back to take care of him."

That's true. What made this version a cut above the usual slasher-and-horror fare is the full-bodied romance. The climax is especially heartrending when the couple is caught in the middle of a rainstorm while the Buddhist monk who moonlights as a ghost-hunter attempts to trap Nak's spirit forever.

Even the most oblique and subtle questions about the infamous sex scene turned Sai into a giggling and blushing schoolgirl. "Yes, giving birth in the old way... that wasn't me. They had a body double," she said, before breaking into a fit of laughter.

Since this was the most controversial part of the entire film, it certainly required an explanation. Further questions were answered by more giggles and denials. Tiring of this typically Thai coquettish routine, I asked her point-blank, "So was that really you rolling around on the floor of the house?"

You would've thought this was the funniest joke she had ever heard. Composing herself after another fit of hysterics, Sai managed to say, "Yes, that was me," before explaining that many previous productions of the film were plagued with problems thought to have occult causes. That's why cinemas once set up shrines to appease her spirit. One old movie house that did not follow this ritual was razed to the ground by a freak fire. As was, and still is the tradition, the whole cast and crew paid homage to her restless spirit before they shot the film, at the shrine behind the temple off Sukhumvit Soi 77 (officially known as Wat Mahabut).

The glass case in front of the statue of Nak holding her baby boy is laden with offerings such as cosmetics and jewellery. Off to the left is another cabinet full of toys and baby clothes for Nak's son. Hundreds of people (both male and female) come here every day to pray to her for wealth, love and other favours. As at any Buddhist altar, they light candles and incense before they kneel and bow, and stick gold leaves on the statue. Some of them also slip money into the hands of the icon. Outside the shrine, a number of people pour candle wax on a sacred *takian* (malabar) tree in an attempt to discern winning lottery numbers.

The older Thai man who gave me a tour of the temple (and who thought the movie was perfectly accurate) picked up a leaf from the sacred bodhi tree near the altar and handed it to me, saying it would bring me good luck.

Outside the shrine are dozens of little stalls in the business of divination: palm-readers, fortune tellers and tarot card experts. As a centre of spiritual power, blessed by Nak's presence, these oracles are legendary. Their customers are a cross-section of Thai society from every rung of the corporate and blue-collar ladder. Gay, a young businesswoman who had lived and studied in England for years, said, "I believe about 50 per cent of what they tell me. Sometimes they can be quite accurate. One fortune-teller told me I would get robbed in the next six months so I should be careful. A month or two later, I had my purse stolen by a guy riding by on a motorcycle."

Usually, she prefers consulting monks. The Buddha forbade such prophecies, but Thais follow the tradition of his student Mogellana. After the 'Awakened One' passed away, Mogellana put the teachings of his mentor and the mental power he had acquired from meditation to the task of divining the future.

"With the monks, I like to talk to a senior person with wisdom and experience whom I can trust. Thais don't like talking about their problems very much, and going to see psychiatrists is too much of a loss of face. So the monks and fortune-tellers serve many roles as consultants, psychiatrists and community leaders."

Many Westerners and Thais scorn these fortune-tellers and spirit-worshippers as superstitious throwbacks to the past. But the supernatural haunts so many different facets of Thai life, love and festivities, that exorcising those beliefs from the collective consciousness would purge the culture of its vitality and its history. Ghouls throng the streets of Dansai in Loei province during the *Phi Ta Khon* (Ghosts with Human Eyes) Festival, usually held in June, depending on what the local soothsayer deems an auspicious day. In weaving a hedonistic yarn around an ancient folktale about Prince Vessandara (the Buddha in his last reincarnation) returning to his hometown for a festival so jubilant that even the spirits could not help but join in, the Thai spin has young men wearing shamanistic masks and waving wooden phalluses as they cavort around the town impersonating spirits. Old men dressed as women offer shots of moonshine to all and sundry, while processions of beauty queens and traditional dancers wend their way through the crowds. It's about as surreal as religious festivals get; condensing a thousand years of Thai history into a few short and exhilarating days.

Until *Nang Nak* brought about a rebirth of Thai cinema, the local movie industry had languished in critical condition—filmmakers couldn't decide whether to emulate Hong Kong or Hollywood. But Nonzee Nimibutr's reliance on local folkloric colour—the entire cast and crew had to take a four-month course in Siamese history—proved that Thai exotica could enchant foreign audiences and inspire local moviemakers. Even the most horrific scene in the film, when monitor lizards savage the corpse

The spirits from a Buddhist folktale are reborn during the festival of *Phi Ta Khon* (Ghosts With Human Eyes).

Foreign women inspire ghoulish affections at this festival in Loei province.

of a villager Nak killed, has Thai teeth marks all over it. Without the influence of this ghost story, it's doubtful that local cinema would have enjoyed the global success it has in recent years and notched up the first Cannes Award for a Thai movie.

Some authors, like Tiziano Terzani in *A Fortune-Teller Told Me*, have speculated that these seers possess an 'ability' that has waned through the imagination-destroying influence of technology and consumerism, but still survived in remnants of Asia.

It's a point worth pondering. In the early months of 2003, Anchana had to wake up early to finish her last semester of university. Every morning, in the distance, she would see an old woman dressed in a traditional sarong sweeping the parking lot in front of our ground-floor apartment. When she asked the landlady who the woman was, Jazz asked her for a description. The landlady nodded. "That poor old lady was hit and killed by a motorcycle just outside our front gate a few weeks ago. I guess she doesn't realise she's dead yet, so she keeps on doing her duty."

This did not strike them as strange. In their belief system, these things happen all the time. As long as the old woman did not hurt anyone, they would practice the Thai-Buddhist doctrine of 'live and let live, *mai pen rai* (never mind)'. At some point, all of the Thai neighbours saw the 'ghost'. In spite of repeated reconnaissance missions, I never caught so much as a fleeting glimpse of her shadow. But I was trying to see her and they were not. I was out there as a spectator and a writer, a skeptic and debunker, and as someone from a Judeo-Christian background.

Does faith open doors that skepticism closes? Are Thais peering into a different realm by activating the 'third eye' of Indian lore?

The mystery of Thailand's most famous ghost story opens a pandora's box of far darker and much more ancient questions. First and foremost is: why are so many people worshipping a woman who, besides being a faithful wife and a good mother, was a multiple murderess?

Some of the answers to these questions may lie in the Hindu faith and Chinese beliefs, which inform much of Thai mysticism and culture. Hindu deities such as Shiva and his wife Parvati have vastly different incarnations that are at odds with each other. In Parvati's other guise as Kali—or Kalika, the goddess of death and time—her dress is fashioned from a tiger skin, her belt strung with severed heads, and her multiple arms clutch weapons such as a noose and sword.

Hindu legend has it that two demon overlords and their minions had ravaged the planet before launching an assault on the heavens, when Parvati, bathing in the Ganges River, heard the gods beseeching her for help. So she used her own body to create Kali, who in turn gave birth from a hole in her forehead, to a more savage incarnation known as the 'Dark Mother'. Engaging the demons in battle, she used her sword to maim and lacerate them, but every drop of blood that hit the ground spawned another fiend. Kali lashed out with her whip-length tongue to lick up the blood before it hit the ground. She then conjured up two assistants, giving them nooses to strangle the demons before their blood could spawn a new army.

To this day, Kali's bloodlust is appeased by animal sacrifices at the temple devoted to her in Kolkatta (a city named after the Dark Mother), India, particularly during the October festival held to pay homage to her. Hindu temples in Bangkok bear images of Kali and her incarnations, and the tributes to Pavarti are celebrated amidst much revelry each year.

Thais take their Indian idols very seriously. When a mentally ill man destroyed the beloved statue of Brahma at the Erawan Shrine in 2006, he was beaten to death by a couple of men who had witnessed the destruction. A monk who wrote in the *Bangkok Post* said that the dead man had received his karmic payback. His article drew a flurry of furious letters from foreign readers. The mystically inclined, however, saw the statue's destruction as a portent of disaster—they felt their beliefs had been vindicated when the government was ousted only a month later.

Guan Yin, the Taoist Goddess of Mercy, is also widely worshipped in Thailand. Illustrations of her, robed in white and standing on the nose of a dragon, are common currency for those who bank on the spirit world. Women pray at shrines devoted to Guan Yin in Thailand, leaving pearl necklaces in the hope she will make them pregnant. Stories of Guan Yin's powers of fertility are legendary. One Chinese fable states that the goddess fertilised rice paddies with her breast milk. But in other legends and statues she is a male Buddhist saint named Avalokitsvara (a Sanskrit word), who appears in different forms in Tibet, Burma and Indonesia.

Like Kali and Guan Yin, Nak is a figure shrouded in dualism. By turns loving and maternal, sinister and sexy, Nak's complex nature has made her attractive to a host of different filmmakers. In 2005, *The Ghost of Mae Nak*, the first movie version written and directed by a foreigner—Mark Duffield from England—was released to mixed reviews. According to Tom Waller, the producer of the film, they modernised the tale but remained faithful to its spirit. "The young couples' love awakens the spirit of Mother Nak, and it's told through the grandmother's eyes, so we can do some flashbacks to explain the legend. But mostly the film is set in contemporary Bangkok. We shot it at some creepy locations around Sukhumvit Soi 77 like the canal and the old market. Some of the Thai crew got a bit freaked out and would joke that Mae Nak was just around the corner."

Another strand of the story that continues to fascinate is the many different accounts of what happened to Nak's spirit. Was it ever laid to rest? Theories are rife, but evidence is scant. Tom, however, sides with folklorists who believe that after the monk took a bone out of the dead woman's forehead to contain her spirit, he wore it around his neck like an amulet.

"We've dramatised all this in the film, but nobody knows what happened to this 'bone broach' after the monk died. It just disappeared," Tom said. "We're hoping someone who sees the film will be able to tell us what happened to it."

Since then, there have not been any more films or TV series about Nak. Given the new breed of Asian horror with spectres crawling out of TV sets, using mobile phones, infesting penthouses and wreaking havoc in a phantasmagoria of special effects, the story of a rural woman from a 19th century farming community doesn't have a ghost of a chance at the box office these days.

That, however, has not stopped all the supplicants from coming to her shrine. Some are mystical mercenaries asking for wealth and looking for winning lottery numbers in the etchings on the trees outside the shrine, but many pray to her for love or seek to cure their maladies of the heart. As Gay said about locals consulting monks and fortune-tellers as psychiatrists, Nak is also something of a relationship counsellor. Before her shrine, the lovelorn can vent their bleeding hearts without losing 'face' in front of anyone.

In his non-fiction book *Heart Talk*, Christopher Moore reckons that Thais have more expressions about this muscle than any other culture. The outpouring of songs, films, soap operas and TV shows devoted to the ins and outs of love is a never-ending flood. In that genre of romantic tragedies, the tale of a woman who died in childbirth while her husband was on the battlefield and came back from the dead along with their child to take care of him, comes from a real and much more haunting place than any of these other make-believe stories about rampaging ghouls.

As every widower and lonely heart knows, all love sagas become ghost stories in the end.

Funeral Rites:
The Thai Way of Death

The wooden coffin had been placed inside a metal sarcophagus and covered with iridescent paper to seal in the stench of putrefaction. Bouquets of plastic flowers crowned and surrounded the coffin. On the left-hand side was a photograph of the deceased woman on a gilded stand strung with blinking fairy lights. After three days of mourning rites, the body would be burnt so her ghost would not loiter on this plane of existence.

As soon as a mourner entered the big wooden sala near the temple, in this village of 100 people close to the Cambodian border, they lit a stick of incense and knelt down in front of the altar, praying for Noobin to have a safe journey to heaven and a good rebirth. The nine monks who came to chant each morning and evening offered the same blessings.

Aside from the chanting, it was not a solemn occasion. More like an Irish wake, actually. Groups of family members and friends sat on the floor eating and chatting. Some of the men drank beer; others knocked back shots of rice liquor that tasted like pickled razor blades. Behind the scenes, the women cooked and served food.

At night, men knelt behind the curtain that separated the big room (with the coffin and Buddha images) from the kitchen, to put wagers on a simplified version of roulette, using a cardboard grid on the floor. Beside them, an older relative taught a gaggle of kids how to play the same game with one-baht coins he provided—and won back from them. Noopat, the dead woman's younger sister, told me that gambling is common at rural funerals; it helps to distract people from their grief and the fear of a possible haunting.

At some memorial services in the countryside, poor families auction off the gambling rights to local mobsters, who agree to pay for the funeral ceremony. A good send-off, which gives 'face' to the deceased's family, requires an investment of at least 20,000–30,000 baht. For many rural families, that's a crippling debt.

I'd never met the deceased, but she was the older sister of a friend's wife. Cameron Cooper (Noopat's husband, and the other co-founder of *Farang Untamed Travel* magazine) and I were the only two *farang* there. Stories of the dead woman's life leaked through the Thai-English language filter: she was a hard-worker who arose every morning at 4am to hitch a ride into the frontier town of Aranyaprathet to sell vegetables in the market. Afterward, she returned home to make fried bananas or sticky rice in bamboo tubes to sell in the village. When her mother died young, she weaned her baby sister, Noopat, and her own infant son at the same time, each child suckling a different breast. Noobin moved to the northeastern province of Loei where she and her husband tended cornfields, but came back to the village to nurse her father when he was dying. Years later, her own misdiagnosed case of angina, which could have been treated with the right medicine and enough money, led to a massive stroke that left her body and mind mostly intact, but her vocal cords could only transmit whimpers in place of words. Sometimes she'd get angry and cry when people couldn't understand her. Eventually, the untreated case of angina made her heart swell up to five times its normal size. Doctors gave her a year at most to live, but with incredible tenacity she hung on for three years. Liver failure turned her skin a yellowish-green tint and finally claimed her life. At the end, she suffered such fits of agony that death came as a tender mercy.

Sitting on the floor drinking and listening to all these stories, I kept stealing glances over at her husband of some 30 years. He'd been staring at the coffin and his wife's portrait for hours, sitting on a *dais* by the Buddha images, where the monks had chanted earlier. The husband, whose face had taken on the same scorched and barren look of the province's soil, must have been overwhelmed by the same memories everyone else was recollecting, except he had thousands more to sift through and sort out. We thought about walking over and offering him a drink and condolences, but bereavement is the most private of duties, and condolences are clichés that console no one.

* * *

In this village of Baan Pla Kaeng (named after a kind of fish found locally), 'Uncle Lom', as he's affectionately known, takes care of all the funeral rites, ordinations and the upkeep of the one-monk temple. Now in his 70s, he first moved here from Korat province in the late 1960s, when the government was offering free land to settlers to put up a human shield between Thailand and Cambodia, where the civil war was threatening to bleed over the border.

Uncle Lom grinned. "I was greedy for some land."

In those days, he recalled, all the roads were made of dirt. There were no cars or bicycles, and people got around by ox-carts. Most of the locals were so impoverished and uneducated that they did not know how to hold a proper Buddhist funeral. So when someone stepped on a land-mine or was blown apart by a mortar shell, their corpses were left to carrion birds and scavenging beasts.

In the 1970s and '80s, Noopat recalled how mortar shells exploded around the village every day. Families would flee into the jungle or hide in their own little bunkers. Tanks rumbled down the roads; bombers flew low overhead; tracer bullets pierced the night skies. Defeated but not disarmed, starving soldiers from the Khmer Rouge would come across the border looking for food and valuables, stealing into people's homes to slit their throats and rob them.

Old fears die hard. Even in Bangkok two decades later, come nightfall, Noopat still has an obsessive compulsion to check that the front door of her house is locked every few hours.

On the third afternoon, monks from a bigger village nearby came to spirit away Noobin's soul to heaven. As they solemnly intoned their baritone blessings in Pali, all of the mourners knelt before the *dais*, palms pressed together at chest level in a *wai*. A sacred white thread that the monks held was later used to wrap the deceased's coffin, which the pallbearers shouldered and carried towards the crematorium outside. Just in front of the plywood coffin, holding the white thread was Noobin's son, the one she had once weaned at the same time as her baby sister. He had ordained as a monk for this purpose, which is known as *buad naa fai* ('ordaining in front of the fire'). One of Noobin's daughters held her mother's photograph against her chest as the funeral procession circled the crematorium three times in a clockwise direction. Noobin's husband walked beside his daughter. In one hand he had a coconut, in the other a machete.

Each mourner picked up a little brown flower with a tiny candle and stick of incense tied to it. We walked up the steps of the crematorium to pay our final respects and left the flowers in a metal tray on top of the coffin. Unsure what to do next, Cameron and I lingered around the top of the stairs, when suddenly the husband lifted the lid of the coffin—*what?*—so we could see the dead woman, clad in a dress and with her eyes closed, her cheeks sunken and shadowed. From her bony hands, tied into a *wai* with white thread, bloomed a bouquet of white and purple orchids. As the putrid smell of decaying flesh trapped inside the coffin rushed out, I veered back.

But the sight and the smell were the least of our horrors, because the men cracked open the coconut with the machete and gave it to the newly ordained monk to anoint his mother's face and cover her body with the milk in an Indian purification ritual. The teenager then passed the coconut to his sister, who repeated the rite, and then—the real shocker—she passed it to me. Refusing would have been tantamount to disrespecting the dead, but it was difficult to look at the dead woman's face as I poured the milk onto it.

As we walked down the steps of the crematorium, they placed the coffin inside the brick oven. As is the custom at a Thai funeral, each of the guests received a small gift. Once, at a more upscale funeral in Bangkok, I got a leather key-holder. This time, I received a red plastic menthol inhaler. Under the circumstances, it was a very welcome gift.

The son-turned-monk anoints his mother's body with coconut milk at a rural funeral near the border with Cambodia.

The following morning, the relatives congregated to pick up Noobin's ashen remains, which had been collected on a sheet of corrugated tin inside the oven. The family members picked out the biggest bone fragments, washed them in a bucket of perfumed water, and placed them in a small vessel to inter in a concrete pagoda on the temple grounds. Using a hoe, another relative formed the remaining ashes into an outline of a human body. This is done to ensure that the deceased is reborn with all their limbs intact. Then her shaven-headed son, having disrobed as a monk and now wearing street clothes, upended the tin sheet into a hole in the ground and covered the remains with dirt.

For a vegetable vendor and farmer who'd scraped a living from the land for most of her life, it was a fitting grave.

* * *

Before the funeral in Isaan, the only time I'd ever made merit for the dead was after the bloated body of my friend and colleague, Teerapong Kansatawee, was fished out of Bangkok's Chao Phraya River in 1999. He was only 33.

An elfin guy with neatly trimmed hair, Teerapong had the biggest eyes I've ever seen. Perhaps that's why his parents nicknamed him Gop, or 'Frog'. Over his shoulder, he always carried a homespun bag of cotton embroidered with Isaan or hilltribe motifs. The bag was laden with novels, heavyweight tomes on history, politics and economics, as well as cassettes of Thai folk music. He wore ordinary jeans (never torn, always clean) and button-down shirts. He had none of the derogatory qualities I sometimes associate with Thai men—the juvenile, non-sense of humour and the lust for lechery. Which made him an alien in his own country and an outcast at *Hyper*, the Thai alternative magazine where we both contributed freelance stories.

On weekends, most of the magazine crew buzzed around the nucleus of Bangkok nightlife—Silom Soi 4—which resembled a smaller-scale Mardi Gras. Among all the preening and flamboyant drag queens, pill-gobbling expat ravers and whore-mongering gay and straight 'sex pistols', under the constant bombardment of blasting dance music, Gop could usually be found outside a bar by himself, sipping a Thai (never foreign) beer while reading a book and listening to local folk music on his Walkman. Occasionally, he'd order a tequila shot and say, "I want to fly high," before launching into another diatribe with a grin, "Western culture same as AIDS in Thailand. We have no immune." Then he'd smile, laugh and return to his reading and protest songs. His earnestness and social autism made him the death of the party for most of the gang, who tended to avoid him.

The stories Gop contributed to magazines like *Hyper* and Thai dailies like *Matichon* crystallised his interests in rural hardships, injustice and crime. The one I remember the most vividly was about the famous Buddhist temple in Saraburi province named Wat Phra Baht Num Phru, where drug addicts are virtually incarcerated and forced to swallow massive doses of water and herbal medicine every day. On the temple grounds, they vomit up all the toxins in their systems. The monks hold them while they writhe, retch and groan. Echoing that guttural chorus line, Gop entitled his story 'The Junkie Philharmonic Orchestra'. We had a good laugh over the title in the office. The feature was around 20 pages long. He told Mam, the female editor, that was no way he could cut it down.

Shaking her head with disbelief, she said, "But nobody runs stories this long anymore."

Gop did not believe in compromising his features and his stubbornness did not endear him to many editors. Still, he didn't raise his voice or lose his temper. He didn't wear his CV on his sleeve, or brag about how difficult it was to do the story. In short, he didn't behave (and never did) like so many of the prima-diva writers and photographers out there.

Wearing his smile like a shield, Gop cheerfully insisted,

again—and again—and again—that the story had to run as it was. In the end, he eroded her resistance. When the article, with his original title in English, appeared in *Hyper* magazine, it ran 16 pages long: the kind of indepth feature that was the byproduct of what is now a bygone era in print media.

The magazine's editor, Veeraporn 'Mam' Nitiprapha, and I talked about his famous article the night she called to tell me that he'd died. Mam thought that Gop had probably jumped off a bridge and drowned. But his family, who came from the south, would never admit that, she said. If a Thai overdosed on drugs, the family would say that he'd suffered a heart attack in order to salvage some 'face'. Everyone would know what really happened, but nobody had to lose face.

Nevertheless, a few other rumours were making the rounds. Somebody else said he'd been HIV-positive—unlikely, I thought, given his flaccid interest in womanising. Another journalist thought that maybe he'd written a story condemning some corrupt official or gangster, and that their goons had given him a push-start into the river—which seemed more likely.

But I didn't think that he'd even been writing much lately. The last few times I'd seen him, he'd been so depressed and drunk that he already looked like a suicide-in-progress. He would rant about how his old job as a full-time reporter only paid 7,000 baht per month and now, as a freelancer, he was lucky to earn half that much. *Hyper* had closed down. And the only literary magazine in Thailand where he could publish his short stories had also drowned in red ink.

Like a lot of heavy drinkers, he'd become erratic (lashing out at people one minute and getting maudlin the next, so I never felt comfortable around him anymore) and would repeat the same sob stories, "I have no money. Nobody respect me. Thai people only like cartoon. Why you never help me publish stories in English?"

Mam said that when the morgue attendants were looking for identification in his wallet, the only money they found was a single 100 baht note.

That was sad enough, but what really choked me up was when she added, before hanging up, "I just wanted to tell you because you're the only person from the magazine who ever asked about him or tried to keep in contact with him."

So I felt obligated to pay my final respects, but his bones had already been kindling for the crematorium. Since he'd died in a violent way, his body had been burnt within three days so the ghost would not linger or try to get back inside the corpse. Excessive displays of bereavement are also frowned upon at Thai funerals because it's believed these will cause the dead person's spirit to loiter.

After a bit of soul-searching, I remembered one of the most moving passages in the Dalai Lama's autobiography *Freedom in Exile*, when he recounts the death of his mother. After reciting Buddhist prayers for her to have a good rebirth, he went to a place of worship to make merit for her.

So I went to my local temple on Sukhumvit Road, near Soi Ekkamai. Along the way, I stopped at the supermarket to buy an orange bucket filled with necessities for monks: toothpaste, soap, Chinese tea, canned sardines and a saffron robe. The various offerings for monks, spirit houses and temples were tucked away in the furthest back corner of the supermarket, between the shelves for children's toys and pet food. The juxtaposition seemed like sacrilege. But it was the same at the magazine rack: all the publications devoted to Buddhism and amulets had been sidelined to the bottommost rack, next to magazines about firearms and tropical fish.

I hadn't even made it to the temple yet and I was already losing what little faith I had. As I walked along Sukhumvit Road, carrying the orange bucket, I felt like a fool. I didn't know the etiquette for presenting it to the monks. I didn't know any of the prayers. I didn't even understand any of the most basic fundamentals of making merit for the deceased.

I arrived at the temple in time for the late afternoon prayers and chanting in the main chapel. Kneeling on a *dais*, the monks droned like bees, turning the chapel into a hive of spirituality. The abbot sat in the front, reading Pali prayers from a rectangular, palm-leaf manuscript. Aside from me, there were only three older Thai men praying. All of them were sympathetic to my plight. One of them brought me a glass of hot Chinese tea. Another gave me an amulet from the temple, which came in a little plastic case, replete with an image of the Buddha covering his eyes.

He introduced me to the abbot and I bowed slightly as I handed him the orange bucket. Unlike many of the monks I've met, he was robust and handsome with massive forearms. Out of humility, perhaps, he wore cheap glasses with black plastic frames. Even though he was middle-aged, his white skin showed few lines except for a few rows of parentheses around his mouth when he grinned. As the abbot bantered with the three laymen, he kept them in stitches. One of them said to me, "He always funny."

Between the abbot's fractured English and my then-infantile Thai, I managed to explain that a friend had died and I'd come to *tam boon* ('make merit') for him. He nodded solemnly and pursed his lips. The abbot told one of the men to bring over two glasses, one empty, the other filled with holy water. The abbot motioned for me to kneel before him as he sat on the *dais*. Following his instructions, I slowly poured the water from one glass into the other while he chanted in Pali. After intoning a few more prayers in one of the deepest and most melodious voices I've ever heard, the abbot told me to go outside and pour the holy water on a tree.

When I came back, he smiled and said in English, "See you again." The smile offset the irony of his words.

The whole ritual took no more than three or four minutes to complete. This must be part of the reason why Buddhism has become the world's fastest growing religion: the etiquette is easy; the ceremonies, like anointing the tree, are both practical and poetic; and while I was there, no one tried to convert me to the faith.

Alone in the chapel, I sat before the shrine and a jumble of statues, lotus blossoms and smoldering joss sticks of sandalwood. As twilight bruised and later blackened the sky, the shadows in the corner of the prayer hall lengthened, the room became smaller and the candles brighter. But the only prayer I could think of was a Buddhist-sounding stanza from a poem by Walt Whitman, the great grandfather of the 'beat poets' (Kerouac, Ginsberg, Corso, et al.), "He who walks a mile without compassion walks to his own grave wearing his shroud." Gop would've liked that poem.

I went home and called Mam to explain how I'd made merit for him. She was impressed, but told me that since his death, someone else had come forward to say they'd seen him, the night before his body was found, slurring, staggering drunk, and threatening to end his life before he left some bar.

"I'm sorry to say, but in Thai belief, you can't make merit for someone who commits suicide," Mam said. "They're too far down in hell to receive your merit or offerings. Thai Buddhists believe that suicide is worse than murder."

That was strange. I'd never heard of that belief. So much for the merit-making plan. What to do now? At the time, I had a monthly column in *The Nation* about crime and the supernatural titled 'Heaven Forbid'. So I figured I'd turn my next effort into an obituary for Gop while delving into the topic of Thai funeral rites.

At least that that was the plan, but the copy-editor—whom I had once dubbed the 'Jack the Ripper of Journalism'—vivisected it. As Anais Nin wrote, "The role of a writer is not to say what we can say, but what we are unable to say." It was the sort of grave irony which had killed Gop's interest in print media and become a catalyst for his suicide.

In early 2010, the abbot's ironic farewell, "See you again," proved to be prophetic when another friend and writer, Torgeir Norling, died much too young.

On the third night of his funeral at the Khlong Toey Temple in Bangkok, nobody had anything to offer except the usual 'rest in peace' condolences, but it was comforting enough to see old friends, and colleagues from as far afield as Hong Kong and Liverpool had a chance to reunite and pay homage to his memory. Another friend of his lit a constant string of cigarettes that he left smoldering in an ashtray, beside a glass of beer behind the Norwegian's portrait to appease Tor's hard-drinking, serial-smoking spirit.

As a journalist for many years, Tor would have been touched by all the colleagues who had left messages on his Facebook page, retelling encounters they'd had with him, and recounting stories he'd written, from all over the world. For a requiem, I uploaded a video of Nick Cave and the Bad Seeds, a group we'd often discussed in the same reverential tones, singing '*I Had a Dream, Joe*', except I wrote out some of the more poignant lines and changed the name of the narrator's dead friend to 'Tor'.

Of all the messages from friends and family members on his page, the one that struck me most came from his mother who had changed the lyrics of a Bob Dylan song into an elegy for her son. I got in touch with her through Facebook to share a few personal recollections that she appreciated.

Tor's ability to empathise with the wounded and the downtrodden shone through his best stories about the uprising led by Buddhist monks in Burma, the genocide in East Timor and the civil war in Sri Lanka. It was ironic, everyone said, that a journalist who had survived so many danger zones would get hit and killed by a bus while crossing a street near the Erawan Shrine, one of Bangkok's enclaves of spiritual power.

On the last night of the funeral rites, I was standing outside the hall talking to the photographer Dan White, after the monks had finished chanting and the mourners were pairing off in conversations and making plans to have a wake at a bar and restaurant. Watching these events unfold, Dan hit the coffin nail on the head when he commented, "Funerals are not for the dead. They're for the living."

Of all the supernatural rites at these final farewells in Thailand, one of the strangest is seeing the bereaved gather to watch the smoke rise from the crematorium's chimney as the body is cremated and the deceased gives up the ghost. Whether it's a human or a monkey does not matter; they wish them a safe trip to heaven and a good rebirth.

The Buddha always claimed that Buddhism is a science and not a religion. So it isn't necessary to impart any mystical importance to this last rite. It's all quite natural. The smoke rises into the clouds where it forms condensation and rains back down on the earth to nourish the crops and fields that yield the food and fruits on our tables.

Gop, Tor, Tiziano Terzani and Anais Nin are not really dead. They're ghosts too. Through the lines of their stories, and between the covers of their books, where their spirits are very much alive, they inspire other wordsmiths to join the frontlines of the profession.

In Buddhist reincarnation on the Wheel of the Law—circles within circles that are forever spinning—from death springs life anew and art eternal.

DIRECTORY OF
THE BIZARRE

CRIME SCENES

Bang Kwang Central Prison: The prison has tightened up in recent years. If you want to visit a foreign inmate, it's best to dress up a little and pretend you're a friend or a relative. Some embassies have lists of their nationals imprisoned in Thailand.

The maximum-security jail is located near the last stop on the river taxi line at Nonthaburi, just north of Bangkok. Take the first left and the prison is on your right. From the pier it's a 10-minute walk. To fill in the form you must go to the Visitor Information Centre across the street from the prison.

For the morning sessions from 9.30–11.30am, you need to register by 9am. The afternoon visits run from 1.30–2.30pm. Once again, you have to register half an hour before the start time. Bring a photocopy of your passport and know the name and building number of the prisoner. Visiting days are subject to change and cancelled on national holidays.

One of the best sources of information about prison visits is a website run by an Englishman sentenced to 30 years in jail for possessing 250 speed pills: http://scottsbangkwangtime.net/25.html. He has now been sent back to England to finish his sentence but his website lists other nationals to visit.

The Corrections Museum is on Mahachai Road, on the ground of the Rommaninart Park, down the street from the Golden Mount, heading towards Chinatown. The guard towers and some of the cells from the old prison where author Warren Fellows was once interred are still there. Inside the museum are displays of ancient torture instruments replete with life-size mannequins, as well as old photos, homemade syringes and the original machine-gun from Bang Kwang. This penal hall of Kafka-esque horrors raises gooseflesh from Mon–Fri, 8.30am–4.30pm.

Museum of the Macabre: The Siriraj Medical Museum 6 is located on the west bank of the Chao Phraya River, across from Thammasat University, at 2 Phra Nok Road, on the grounds of Siriraj Hospital. Take the river taxi or cross-river ferry. From the pier near the hospital it's easy to get directions to the building housing all six museums. Admission is 40 baht. Visiting hours are Mon–Sat from 9am–4pm.

MISADVENTURE TRAVELS

A Bizarre Expat Odyssey: The Museum of Siam is located on Sanam Chai Road, not far from Wat Pho. Featuring interactive exhibits on everything from the foreign populace of ancient Ayuthaya to rock 'n' roll culture in Bangkok of the '50s, this is one of the country's most high-tech museums. It's open from 10am–6pm, Tues–Sun. Admission is 300 baht.

Military Tourism: Of all the military bases open for tourists, the most accessible is the Chulachomklao Royal Military Academy in Nakhon Nayok province. Equipped with a shooting range, golf course and other programmes, the academy has produced many generals. Thai speakers can call 037-393-3634-9.

One of the oddest military attractions in the country, not mentioned in the story, is 'Friendship Village No. 1', some 15 kilometres outside Betong, near the border with Malaysia. This former encampment of Malay communist soldiers, who laid down their weapons in 1989, has a 1.6-km tunnel dug by hand, battle photos and redder-than-Mao souvenirs. Some of the old guerrillas are on hand to recount their experiences and share their secrets for waging jungle warfare.

Siamese Twins: The sporadically open and sometimes shut museum for the twins' old photos and sideshow posters is situated in the Lat Yai subdistrict of Samut Songkhram city, which is about four kilometres from the City Hall. Outside the museum is a life-size replica of their floating home and a statue of the twins with engravings depicting highlights from their conjoined lives and a plaster cast of their autopsy.

The province, only 90 minutes from Bangkok, is famous for its ancient canals, home-stays, floating markets and nocturnal boat journeys to see fireflies mating.

Cowboy Ranch: Pensuk Great Western is about 230 kilometres northeast of Bangkok in Nakhon Ratchasima province. It's located at 111 Moo 2 Nong Takai in Amphur Soungnoen. Many hotel sites handle online bookings. The best time to get your duds and spurs on is Saturday when they have the big cowboys and Indians show and a barbecue at night.

THE SEX FILES

Empower: The head office is located at 57/60 Tivanond Road in Nonthaburi province, just outside Bangkok. Call 02-526-8311 for details in English about the Patpong office in Bangkok, the Can Do Bar in Chiang Mai, and their other centres and projects. Email them at: badgirls@empowerfoundation.org.

The Third Gender: All of the major tourist destinations like Bangkok, Pattaya, Phuket and Koh Samui have nightly ladyboy cabarets. Now in its 13th year, the Miss Tiffany Universe Competition is held at Tiffany's Theatre in Pattaya over the course of four days every May.

Fertility Shrine: The shrine is located behind the Swissotel Nai Lert Park Hotel at 2 Wireless Road. To get there you have to walk through the hotel and into the garden and pool area in the back. The shrine is off to the north, close to the canal.

STRANGE CELEBRITIES

Bizarre Architecture: Sumet Jumsai's most monumental creations are in Bangkok. The Robot Building is the main office of the United Overseas Bank at 191 South Sathorn Road. On the outskirts of Bangkok, right beside the boundary line for Samut Prakan province, on Bang-na Trat Kilometre 4, are the Nation buildings. In the city's mid-section is the ship-shaped Delta Grand Pacific Hotel on the corner of Sukhumvit Soi 19.

The Scorpion Queen: Kanchana and her husband, the Centipede King, still perform their capers with creepy-crawlies twice daily at 11am and 2pm at the Samui Snake Farm on the island of Koh Samui. The website can be found at: www.samuisnakefarm.com

The Angel and She-Devil of Bang Kwang: Susan's website is http://onelifesusan.homestead.com/onelife.html. Email her or subscribe to her regular e-newsletters at: onelifesusan@hotmail.com

CREATURE FEATURES

Monkey Hospital: The world's first and only such facility is located on the grounds of the Lop Buri Zoo in the provincial capital, around three hours north of Bangkok, served by regular buses and trains. The zoo is behind the Army Theatre near the Sa Kaew Circle and the hospital is open every day from 9am–4pm. To catch the high-wire shenanigans in the simian street circus, head for the Khmer-style shrines in the city's historic downtown core. Every November, the city holds a special buffet and free-for-all food fight for the town's mascots and miscreants at the main shrine.

Buffalo Bonanza: Wat Hua Krabeu (The Buffalo Head Temple) is on the fringes of Bangkok near Samut Sakhon province on Bangkhuntien-Chai Taley Road, Soi Tientalay 19. On weekends they sometimes have a flea market and an exhibition of vintage cars.

The Buffalo Villages is outside the capital of Suphanburi province, about 2.5 hours from Bangkok. During the week they have buffalo shows in Thai at 11am and 3pm. Over the weekend there are shows at 11am, 2.30pm and 4pm. The show, admission to the grounds and a buffalo cart ride costs 300 baht for foreigners.

The Buffalo Racing Festival is held annually in the capital of Chon Buri province near the City Hall. Along with the races there are processions and—feminists take note—beauty contests for both buffalo and local women.

Reptilian Threesome: From the centre of Khon Kaen, it's a 50-kilometre slither to the Cobra Village of Ban Khok Sa-nga. Take Highway 2 and hang right at Kilometre 33 to Highway 2039. At the temple of Wat Sri Thamma is where they stage the daily snake shows and python dances.

From there it's only a short ride to the Turtle Village (Mu Bahn Tao). The hamlet is two kilometres from Amphoe Mancha Khiri, accessed by the same turn in the road as the village of Ban Khok Sa-nga. Opposite the temple of Wat Sri Samang, it's easy to spot the two models of giant tortoises beside the entrance to the village.

The Phu Wiang Dinosaur Museum is a bag of primordial bones in the national park of the same name. It's open from 9am–5pm daily.

In the capital of Khon Kaen province, the Tourism Authority of Thailand's office at 15/5 Prachasamosorn Rd (043-236-634) has free maps and brochures on all the province's attractions. If you leave the capital by mid-morning, you can see all of the reptilian sights in a day. The city of Khon Kaen is an eight-hour drive north of Bangkok. Near the city, the province's airport has daily flights from Bangkok.

THE SUPERNATURAL

Vegetarian Festival: In Phuket, Taoist Lent is celebrated with grisly abandon over the course of nine days every October. The piercing rituals, bloodletting and main processions of 'spirit warriors' only take place on the last three days.

Shock Airwaves and Restaurant: Shock FM 102 broadcasts (in Thai) every Saturday and Sunday night from midnight to 3am. The Shock Khao Tom Phi Restaurant and Pub is not easy to find in the north of Bangkok, off Lad Phrao Road. Even their Thai-only website lists the restaurant as being 'two bus stops past the Tesco-Lotus beside the Ramintra Expressway'. The menus are in Thai. In the back of the restaurant and pub is the Shock Gallery decked with ghostly images sent in by their listeners and horror memorabilia. Ask a Thai friend to take you there.

Nang Nak: The shrine for the mother of all Thai phantoms is on the grounds of Wat Mahabut (sometimes referred to as Wat Mae Nak) on Soi 7 off Sukhumvit Soi 77. It's open daily from early morning until 6pm.

About the Author

Jim Algie has been chronicling the dark and sexy side of Thailand for the past 17 years in publications including *Bizarre* magazine, the *International Herald Tribune* and the *Japan Times*. His short fiction has picked up several awards, including as a co-recipient of the Bram Stoker award. He was a co-founder, chief editor and senior writer of Southeast Asia's most gonzo publication, *Farang Untamed Travel* magazine. His most recent books include the travel guides *Spotlight on Bangkok* and *Spotlight on Athens* (AA Publishing, London, 2008), as well as *Off the Beaten Track in Thailand* (Bosphorus Publishing, Bangkok, 2009).

During the '80s, he toured and recorded with seminal Canadian bands including pop-punksters the Asexuals and alt country rockers Jerry Jerry and the Sons of Rhythm Orchestra. *Now*, Toronto's entertainment weekly, referred to his musical doppelganger Blake Cheetah as 'the musician who has reinvented dangerous rock 'n' roll maneuvers onstage in the 1980s'.

Jim's virtual lair is at www.jimalgie.com. More of his stories can also be found at www.bizarrethailand.com.